RhetoricalRefusals

DEFYING AUDIENCES' EXPECTATIONS

John Schilb

Southern Illinois University Press
Carbondale

10 09 08 07   4 3 2 1

Library of Congress Cataloging-in-Publication Data
Schilb, John, 1952–
Rhetorical refusals : defying audiences' expectations /
John Schilb.
    p. cm.
Includes bibliographical references and index.
ISBN-13: 978-0-8093-2789-8 (pbk. : alk. paper)
ISBN-10: 0-8093-2789-9 (pbk. : alk. paper)
  1. English language—Rhetoric. 2. English language—
Style. 3. Audiences—Psychological aspects. I. Title.

PE1404.S35 2007
808'.042—DC22   2007006617

Printed on recycled paper. ♺
The paper used in this publication meets the minimum
requirements of American National Standard for Information Sciences—Permanence of Paper for Printed
Library Materials, ANSI Z39.48-1992. ∞

In memory of my parents

CONTENTS

Acknowledgments ix

Introduction 1

PART ONE. TOWARD A METHOD OF ANALYSIS AND EVALUATION

1. Studying Rhetorical Refusals: Basic Principles 27
2. Evaluating Rhetorical Refusals: Categories and Criteria 43
3. Croce's Refusal as a Test Case for Evaluation 61

PART TWO. RHETORICAL REFUSALS AND AMERICAN TRADITIONS

4. Agents, "Truth," and Salience 77
5. When a Refusal's Context Changes 114
6. The Embedding of a Rhetorical Refusal 141
7. A Literary Rhetorical Refusal 158

Conclusion 177

Notes 183
Works Cited 187
Index 199

ACKNOWLEDGMENTS

Although the word *refusal* figures a great deal in this volume, as I worked on it I was delighted to accept the help of several people, to whom I express my deep gratitude now. Karl Kageff, editor-in-chief of Southern Illinois University Press, has consistently supported this project for several years. Krista Ratcliffe, who read the book for the Press, made valuable suggestions, as did another reviewer. My colleague Christine Farris read the manuscript and contributed her usual keen insights. I am especially indebted to her for aiding my thinking about the novel I discuss in chapter 7, Tim O'Brien's *In the Lake of the Woods*, which we taught together in spring 2003. Another colleague, Alvin Rosenfeld, incisively reviewed chapter 4, which benefited as well from talks I had with its main subject, Deborah Lipstadt, when she visited my campus in 2005. My discussion of the Shoah in that chapter has been influenced, too, by the students in my undergraduate course Popular Representations of the Holocaust, which I have taught in Indiana University's Intensive Freshman Seminars Program for the last four summers. More generally, many of my ideas about rhetorical refusals have emerged through conversations I have had with Dana Anderson, John Clifford, Paul John Eakin, Patricia Harkin, Matthew Johnson, and David Levine. I received extremely useful feedback from audiences at the University of Missouri–Columbia and the University of North Carolina–Wilmington (in particular, Elizabeth Ervin) when I orally presented sections on those campuses. I learned much from my own university's Life Writing Studies group when I gave presentations at three of its meetings. The following pages draw a lot on the work on Chaim Perelman, and I appreciate Jeanne Fahnestock's alerting me to how much he has to teach us.

I dedicate this book to the memory of my parents, David and Florence Schilb, who did not live to see it but who will always be for me an inspirational force. Wendy Elliot vividly remains the love of my life; her constant support is the main reason this book exists at all.

RhetoricalRefusals

In its year-end issue for 1994, the *New Yorker* featured a polemic that proved immediately controversial. Within the world of the arts, it became one of the most talked-about arguments of the decade. Entitled "Discussing the Undiscussable," it was written by the magazine's celebrated dance critic Arlene Croce. Her article focuses on Bill T. Jones's dance piece *Still/Here*, which he had recently staged in Brooklyn. Jones's piece is based on workshops he conducted around the country. Like Jones himself, who is HIV-positive, the participants were struggling with mortal illness. *Still/Here* adapts movements they used to express their plight. It also includes videotaped footage of their gestures and testimonies. Early in her critique, Croce makes plain that she hates *Still/Here*. She scorns not only the work itself but also the trend she links it with, which she dubs "victim art" (55, 60). Maybe her diatribe would have sparked debate no matter what its mode. After all, an esteemed white critic was attacking a respected black choreographer. But her article became notorious because she hadn't even watched his production. In her very first sentence, Croce announces that "I have not seen Bill T. Jones's *Still/Here* and have no plans to review it" (54).

In the subsequent controversy, which dance critic Marcia Siegel called "Croce-gate" (qtd. in Salisbury), Croce's calculated non-attendance was cited by friends and foes alike. Sympathizer Hilton Kramer labeled her stance a "bombshell" (11), while Homi Bhabha mockingly called it a "*succés de scandale*" ("Dance" 43). Though admiring Croce's views, Robert Brustein felt that "to build an aesthetic theory on a work she hadn't seen . . . is tactically unsound." Certainly the tactic failed with Deborah Jowitt, who wondered, "Am I naive in thinking that a critic's main tool remains the ability to *see* what a work is and is not, and to criticize it accordingly?" (67). With outright sarcasm, Roger Copeland remarked that Croce had put forth "a daring new critical credo: Don't even waste a minute looking at works you fear you'll dislike. But feel free to write about them anyway" (35). Meanwhile, bell hooks declared that "to write so contemptuously about work one has not seen is an awesome flaunting of privilege" (10), and Richard Goldstein proclaimed that "to condemn a work of art without even seeing it has a Helmsian, not to say Stalinist, stench." Whatever the observer's particular opinion, Croce's ploy gained notice. *Time*'s Martha Duffy pointed out that "if she had not made the provocative gesture of writing about a work she refused to see, her piece would have lost some of its eclat" (68). Terry Teachout suggested that Croce performed this move knowing it would create "the maximum possible amount of journalistic noise" (60).

"Journalistic noise" seems as good a term as any for the brouhaha that Croce caused. Her article even inspired a 1998 collection, *The Crisis of Criticism* (Berger), where it serves as the lead essay. Years after its first publication, "Discussing the Undiscussable" continues to be discussed, especially by theorists concerned with art's depiction of suffering.[1] Interest in Croce's argument was stimulated anew with the 2000 publication of *Writing in the Dark, Dancing in* The New Yorker, a book of her essays that includes her attack on Jones. Most reviews of her book paid particular attention to "Discussing," and in her introduction, she herself pronounces it her "most notorious piece" (8).

Her refusal to see *Still/Here* has long interested me as a scholar of composition and rhetoric. What a rhetorical move! Evidently, Croce assumed her critique might prove cogent even if she never beheld her target. Actually, she seems to have thought this avoidance would make her attack *more* persuasive. In the aftermath, many readers balked at this policy. But probably Croce remains content with it, for at least it made people take notice. Certainly she seems complacent about "Discussing" in her book's introduction. There she states that, for the most part, she would not "have written it differently." Indeed, she would have amplified the article's argument with "a sentence or two about the pornography of atrocity, which often goes hand in hand with victim art and by which we are insidiously seduced in such prestigious ventures as the movie *Schindler's List*" (9). Presumably Croce has seen *Schindler's List*. Presumably she has yet to see *Still/Here*.

Whether pro or con, commentators on Croce's spurning of *Still/Here* see her move as unique. Is it, though? Have other critics judged works they haven't seen? Does her text belong to a larger rhetorical corpus? If so, what are the implications for rhetorical theory? In this book, I contend that Croce's move *is* part of a larger group of acts, which have been unfortunately neglected by specialists in rhetoric, composition, and communication studies. I call these acts *rhetorical refusals*.

Defining the Term

Much of this book will involve my defining rhetorical refusals as a term, especially by presenting numerous examples. But let me attempt brief definition at the outset. Although the term seems close to *rhetorical questions*, I mean by it something quite different. I use rhetorical refusal to denote an act of writing or speaking in which the rhetor pointedly refuses to do what the audience considers rhetorically normal. By rejecting a procedure that the audience expects, the rhetor seeks the audience's assent to another principle, cast as a higher priority. Readers turning to Croce's article in the *New Yorker* surely assumed that, as a professional critic, she would critique only works she had seen. Yet she violated this protocol, so that her audience would learn "victim art" isn't art at all.

Sometimes a rhetorical refusal includes quite explicit and sustained acknowledgment that audience expectations are being challenged. Such was the case, for example, with a speech that the Ukrainian novelist Yuri Andrukhovych gave in Germany upon receiving the 2006 Leipzig Book Prize for European Understanding. An occasion like this usually calls for expressions of thanks. Yet, while Andrukhovych said he appreciated the honor, he mainly used his platform to vent. The specific target of his wrath was the European Union. He criticized the obstacles it posed to Ukrainians hoping to visit its countries, and, more generally, he lashed out at the Union's reluctance to deem Ukraine truly "European." In his speech, he told those assembled that he would probably seem to them "impolite"—as "spouting things that are quite offensive." He even admitted that "you are not the audience that deserves this, and this is not the right place to focus your attention on this particular drama." Nevertheless, Andrukhovych proceeded with his complaints, which did encompass at least some people present. "Not a single writer, philosopher, or scholar," he charged, "[had] questioned the representation of Ukrainian society as a bunch of criminals and prostitutes."

Admittedly, sometimes rhetorical refusals can be hard to distinguish from other discourse. For one thing, the people performing them don't always describe themselves as refusing. Again, Croce simply announces that "I have not seen Bill T. Jones's *Still/Here* and have no plans to review it." And right away I confess that I'm not passionately invested in *refusal* as a label for the behavior I analyze. It has the virtue, though, of recognizing the conscious repudiation these acts involve, whatever their particular language.

Their wording may, in fact, be brief. Consider two rejoinders by Joan Didion to letters criticizing reviews she'd written. The first letter, from Alfred Kazin, appeared in a 1977 issue of the *New York Times Book Review*. Kazin protests remarks that Didion made about him in reviewing John Cheever's novel *Falconer*. More specifically, he fulminates at length against Didion's charge that he insufficiently appreciates Cheever and other Protestant writers. He even climaxes his five-paragraph tirade by proclaiming that one of Didion's statements about him "is worse than outrageous—it is stupid." On the other hand, Didion's reply to him is wearily succinct: "Oh, come off it, Alfred."

Two years later, Didion was similarly terse in the *New York Review of Books* when responding to Columbia professor John Romano. His letter takes exception to her review of Woody Allen's film *Manhattan*. Especially upset by Didion's charge that Allen is narcissistic and pretentious, Romano situates him in the context of Western cultural history. At the end of his letter, he defends *Manhattan*'s allusion to Gustave Flaubert's *Sentimental Education* by proclaiming the two works akin: "In Frederic Moreau as in the character Woody is endlessly playing, strength of feeling isn't a source of action but an enfeeblement. By reminding us of the barely sympathetic, weak Frederic, Woody Allen is reinforcing not the central character but those others in the film (or in the audience) who doubt his strength, his maturity, his authenticity." Again, the whole complaint against Didion is lengthy, but again, her response is short: "Oh, wow."

These two responses are alike enough to suggest that Didion had hit upon a particular rhetorical strategy, which she thought usable more than once. For me, the strategy amounts to a rhetorical refusal, for it meets three criteria I associate with the term. First, with both replies to her critics, Didion challenges audience expectations. Most readers of the *New York Times Book Review* and the *New York Review of Books* assume that responses to letters will be longer and more engaged with the letters' content—especially when the letters themselves are substantial and their authors widely respected. Second, Didion's break with protocol is clearly deliberate. She even adopts the strategy twice. Third, though her retorts are curt, she suggests that a higher principle trumps common rhetorical decorum. The statements "Oh, come off it, Alfred" and "Oh, wow" imply that the letter writer is pompous, a trait that Didion evidently feels deserves scorn.

By repeating this particular mode of rebuff, Didion shows that it needn't be a once-only occurrence. Granted, her two uses of this strategy differ in form: "Oh, come off it, Alfred" is a direct rebuke, while "Oh, wow" is a mock expression of amazement. But these statements are alike in resisting debate. As I will show, many rhetorical refusals have precedents and counterparts. If, by definition, rhetorical refusals disconcert audiences, these moves have recurred over time, enough to be categorizable. Throughout the book, I will identify types of them. For instance, Croce is hardly alone in writing about a work she hasn't seen. In part 1 of this book, I analyze and evaluate her critique as part of a whole class of acts that might be called one's refusing to see what one criticizes.

I thereby take issue with critic-novelist Ishmael Reed, who regards Croce's behavior as a peculiarly recent phenomenon. Linking her to Bob Dole, who as a presidential candidate attacked movies he hadn't seen, Reed opined in 1995 that "public officials commenting on art they haven't witnessed is the inevitable result of a German- and French-influenced trend in criticism that holds that the critic's interpretation of a work is more artful than the actual work. It was only a matter of time before critics decided that it wasn't even necessary to investigate the work in question." It's doubtful that Dole's briefing papers included *Of Grammatology*. Nor has Croce ever been all that postmodern in her tastes. Rather, she prefers the modernist formalism of choreographers such as George Balanchine. Of course, one can fault Reed's historical assumptions and yet share his dismay over Dole's and Croce's conduct. But I will compare their refusals to several similar cases that have nothing to do with sinister forces from the Continent.

Most rhetorical acts, I suppose, can be deemed refusals of sorts. Or so I imagine Kenneth Burke would argue. Burke considered the Negative basic to human linguistic activity.[2] For example, the opening sentence of my introduction can be seen as a refusal to begin some other way. When I began by noting the Croce controversy, in effect I rejected the idea of starting with a disquisition on Aristotle. Whether or not the Negative is ubiquitous, however, the kinds of acts I have in mind tend to strike their audiences as blatantly and deliberately breaking protocol. Imagine my beginning this book by pointedly refusing to tell you anything about it because the freedom to discover your own path through it is vital. Moves like this are worth analyzing as special.

In many respects, the work that these refusals perform is comparable to what sociologist Erving Goffman calls *breaking frame*. In his book *Frame Analysis: An Essay on the Organization of Experience*, Goffman seeks to identify not only the perceptual schemas by which we organize our everyday experience but also ways in which particular situations disrupt these schemas, forcing us to redraw them. As he puts it, "My aim is to try to isolate some of the basic frameworks of understanding available in our society for making sense out of events and to analyze the special vulnerabilities to which these frames of reference are subject" (10). Through what I am calling rhetorical refusals, writers and speakers deliberately challenge the frame that their audience brings to the occasion. In Goffman's words, the audience suddenly finds itself wondering anew, "What is it that it is going on here?" (8). The person addressing this audience has an answer: he or she is proposing another frame through which to comprehend the rhetorical event.

Audiences and Their Expectations

An audience's sense of the *typical* frame may stem from several factors, whose individual importance may vary from case to case. "In the world of phainomena in which rhetoric must dwell," Thomas Farrell points out, "norms for speakers, messages, and constituencies are evoked which are provisional and situation-specific" (288). Nevertheless, often we can identify an audience's expectations, even if the audience didn't grow fully aware of them until a rhetorical refusal occurred.

Some of these refusals deserve to be called such because the rhetor is, in fact, declining a gift, award, or invitation that most others would accept. A famous example occurred during the 1972 Academy Awards ceremony. Best Actor Marlon Brando refused his Oscar in protest against Hollywood's treatment of Native Americans. He even skipped the affair, having Sacheen Littlefeather reject the prize in his stead. The result was several boos during her speech as well as much criticism of Brando afterward. A more recent case was Adrienne Rich's 1997 refusal of the National Medal for the Arts. Her rejection of this honor took the form of a letter to National Endowment for the Arts chair Jane Alexander. Subsequently, Rich explained her decision in an article for the *Los Angeles Times*, which now appears along with the letter in Rich's book *Arts of the Possible: Essays and Conversations*. As with the Oscar, most people would accept gladly the honor conferred upon Rich. But she spurned it, telling Alexander that "the very meaning of art, as I understand it, is incompatible with the cynical politics of this administration" (98). In Rich's view, art strives to end oppression, and the Clinton regime had neglected this task. Thus, like Brando, she invoked higher principle, hoping her refusal would prod the federal government to share her priorities.

A rhetor's audience may also expect him or her to follow a previously announced agenda, so that a rhetorical refusal seems evident when this person shifts course. A case in point is offered by philosopher Linda Alcoff in an account of a presentation given at her school:

> [A] prestigious theorist was invited to lecture on the political problems of postmodernism. The audience, which includes many white women and people of oppressed nationalities and races, waits in eager anticipation for his contribution to this important discussion. To the audience's disappointment, he introduces his lecture by explaining that he cannot cover the assigned topic because as a white male he does not feel that he can speak for the feminist and postcolonial perspectives that have launched the critical interrogation of postmodernism's politics. Instead he lectures on architecture. (97)

Going by Alcoff's report, I would say that the speaker engaged in a type of rhetorical refusal that may be called refusing to address the announced topic. Apparently, speaker and audience saw different political implications in his act. He seems to have believed that, by changing topic, he was showing respect for marginalized groups, conceding they were greater experts on his assigned subject. In contrast, Alcoff and people sitting around her found him woefully oblivious to their interests: "[H]e offered no contribution to an important issue and his audience lost an opportunity to discuss and explore it" (114). To their great dismay, he deliberately failed to provide what they had expected: a talk on his previously advertised subject.

Sometimes an audience's expectations are shaped by institutional setting. In chapter 5, for instance, I will discuss Bill Clinton's less-than-revealing grand jury testimony about his relationship with Monica Lewinsky. Refusing to describe his affair in detail, he exasperated his questioners, who in this hearing had the legal right to more. For another example, consider reporter Jonathan Chait's frustration with Ari Fleischer, who was then the White House press secretary. Chait's expectations were influenced by Fleischer's particular position, the institutional responsibilities he associated with Fleischer's job. Of course, Chait wasn't naive. He knew that people in Fleischer's role have often been less than candid. But, as a regular audience for Fleischer's remarks, Chait found him unusually determined to stonewall:

> After the non-sequitur, the other kind of non-answer [characteristic of Fleischer] is more straightforward: the open refusal to reply. This is tricky business. A press secretary, after all, is supposed to provide information to the press, not deny it. The straight rebuff, then, must be couched in terms of some broader principle. And it is here that Fleischer's particular genius is on clearest display. As press secretary, Fleischer has developed a complex, arbitrary, and constantly shifting set of rules governing what questions he can answer. If a reporter's question can be answered simply by reciting talking points about process, Fleischer will comply. If he can't, he will find a way to rule it out of order. (22)

While Fleischer and Chait participate in political discourse, we who have academic jobs identify with *disciplinary* discourses. For us, rhetorical refusals may challenge the fields that form our institutional lives. In chapter 5, I discuss a famous example in literary theory, Jane Tompkins's 1987 essay "Me and My Shadow." Her aggressively personal prose was, at that time, rare in literary studies. Quite consciously, she was renouncing her discipline's predominant writing style, even inviting her peers to follow suit.

Another influence on audience expectations is, often, genre. Tompkins had been asked by the journal *New Literary History* to comment on another writer's essay, but she swerved from the typical academic response, disconcerting her first readers with her confessional mode. Of course, even journals outside of academe feature certain patterns; usually exchanges they publish include more elaborate retorts than Didion's "Oh, come off it, Alfred" and "Oh, wow." Genres of oratory, too, lead audiences to anticipate certain kinds of performance, which rhetorical refusals may reject. In chapter 6, I discuss how Frederick Douglass broke with conventions of epideictic when he criticized Abraham Lincoln in a memorial speech.

In a sense, tampering with genre involves violating a contract felt to be in place. Indeed, perhaps all rhetorical refusals can be said to shatter an implicit or explicit agreement. Still, there are times when such violation seems more evident. David Kaufer and Brian Butler provide an example as they discuss a rhetorical tactic they call the *face threat*. "To threaten the opponent's face," they explain, "the speaker must first have had some implicit agreement to share a platform, an arena, with the opponent. The face threat is the sudden, unexpected suspension of this agreement during the course of rhetoric" (213). Specifically, they cite Stephen Douglas's belittling of Abraham Lincoln during their famous exchanges. Although both Douglas and Lincoln had agreed to the debates, more than once Douglas resorted to "ridiculing Lincoln's qualifications to appear on the same platform with him" (213). To me, Douglas's behavior constitutes a rhetorical refusal. By debating Lincoln in the first place, he appeared to grant him legitimacy but then sought to deprive him of it during their jousts.

The factors I've mentioned as shaping audience expectations may operate singly or jointly. In the following pages, I try to determine which are most relevant for the specific cases I examine. Throughout, I assume that various elements can affect what audiences anticipate as well as how they interpret what they subsequently perceive. Admittedly, I haven't polled these audiences to determine their sense of the normal. Nor, in each case, have I scientifically verified that they find the normal defied. With some of the rhetorical refusals I analyze, audiences have indeed claimed a break with protocol. One such case is Croce-gate. Another, which I discuss in chapter 4, is historian Deborah Lipstadt's much-noted refusal to debate Holocaust deniers. With most of my cases, though, I start off from my own belief that audience expectations have been deliberately flouted, even if the audience may have been hazy about these expectations before.

I realize that the term *audience* itself risks being problematic. A vast, and growing, body of scholarship has shown how the word can oversimplify what happens when a text is produced, received, and circulated. These processes can certainly prove complex, involving a number of variables. Many of the texts that I will discuss have been read or heard by several groups concurrently and then have traveled to others. As Jenny Edbauer argues, we need to study "the amalgamations and transformations—the spread—of a given rhetoric within its wider ecology" (20). Still, *audience* seems an indispensable term for any analysis of rhetorical refusals, though one obviously needs to make clear what one means by it in a given instance. When I refer in this book to *the* audience for a rhetorical refusal, I'm thinking of its main constituency. They're the people whom the rhetor likely had foremost in mind. I do try to be as specific as possible in characterizing them, not taking their demographics for granted. Furthermore, in several instances I discuss other groups to whom the text has traveled, noting changes in effect and meaning it has undergone. Such journeys to multiple audiences are the focus of chapter 5. In addition, I recognize that sometimes we need to distinguish different *types* of audiences. This issue can loom especially with literary texts, a subject I address in chapter 7.

This Book's Scope

I can imagine readers who believe that some of my cases deserve less than others to be called rhetorical refusals. They may feel, too, that I've omitted whole categories of discourse meriting this label. But I'm not so much concerned with pigeonholing as with calling attention to such acts' existence and examining their implications. Whatever disagreements there may be with me about what is and isn't a true rhetorical refusal, I hope the book prompts more thought about practices I point to with this term.

In the following pages, I do limit the term's scope. Above all, I distinguish rhetorical refusals from many other acts of defiance. To me, such refusals involve more than just spitting in an interlocutor's eye. They also involve more than Bartleby's verbalized "I would prefer not to" as well as other mere expressions of 'tude. By calling them rhetorical, I conceive these refusals to be actively aimed at persuading their audience of something. Yes, these acts break with the audience's norms. This is why I call them refusals. Still, they are not indifferent to the audience. Rather, they are efforts to shape its thinking, however unusual the means.

My operative notion of rhetoric may itself look quaint. Although many a theorist now gives the term an epistemic spin—associating it with our basic ways of constructing our identities and worldviews—I work here with the classical notion of rhetoric as persuasion. I do so because I want to ponder quite a bit the impact of certain texts, their effect on the human beings who encounter them. Perhaps I will seem old-fashioned, too, in sticking with spoken and written texts. Much research is now being done, for example, on pictorial modes of persuasion. In fact, I've contributed to this scholarship.[3] What might rhetorical refusals look like when they take imagistic forms? In the future, I hope to confront this question. Meanwhile, I dwell on refusals expressed in words. In part, I do so because these utterances are enough for one book. But I also focus on them because they have been insufficiently studied, despite their use of rhetoric's traditional medium. By "words," I hasten to add that I don't mean just writing. I take examples from oral performances as well, striving to integrate rhetorical concerns pursued by English and communication departments.

Although I use the term rhetorical refusals for the various acts I study here, I don't claim they have a great many properties in common. It's fruitless to aim for an essentialist concept of them. As always with rhetoric, the specific circumstances and dynamics of each case matter. It seems better for us to follow Ludwig Wittgenstein and tease out loose family resemblances among them. In part, this effort entails identifying various categories of refusals, each of which has some distinctive features. Again, Croce's act can be classified as a refusal to see what one is criticizing, while Didion's rebuffs seem refusals to debate.

Refusing to Debate in Composition

To define rhetorical refusals right here in more detail, let me turn now to a particular set of events that I would put in the same category as Didion's. This time, though, the examples come from my own main field, composition studies. Later, I will draw cases from other disciplines and professions, but for the moment I'll focus on some closer to home.

If Didion's curtness toward her critics is unusual for New York's leading book review journals, in the academy it would stand out even more. A prime value in academic scholarship is openness to questioning and criticism—or, at least, apparent openness. Rarely, then, do scholars declare that certain interlocutors, real or potential, aren't worth addressing. In chapter 5, I look at Deborah Lipstadt's taking of this position. Here, however, I turn to the fact that in the last twenty years of composition studies' main journal, *College Composition and Communication*, I find only three appearances of this stand.

The first is a December 1984 exchange between Thomas Blom and the author of an article previously published in *CCC*. The article, "The Winds of Change: Thomas Kuhn and the Revolution in the Teaching of Writing," applies Kuhn's theory of paradigm changes to composition studies. Enthusiastically it notes that more and more teachers of composition view writing as a process rather than as merely a product. This trend, the article argues, constitutes a revolution in Kuhn's sense of the term. In a letter criticizing the article, however, Blom argues at length that Kuhn's theory fits only the sciences. Also, he spends much time deploring the article's contempt for writing teachers wary of the professional shift it welcomes. But, in reply to him, the article's author announces that "I will not attempt to refute Professor Blom's accusations about my view of the profession. Obviously he and I see a different reality" ("Reply" [1984], 493). Most likely Blom, as well as much of the larger *CCC* audience, saw these words as a non-response to his letter. The author hardly tries to work though his charges. While she does point out that others like her article, and goes on to note that others appropriate Kuhn's ideas, her comments scarcely grapple with Blom's criticisms. When she submits that she and he "see a different reality," she even intimates that the two of them occupy separate paradigms. This is a Kuhnian rationale for shrugging him off.

Nevertheless, I hesitate to call this rejoinder a rhetorical refusal, for it eschews appeal to higher principle. Basically, the author just seems indifferent to Blom's complaints. A better example appears in "Breaking Our Bonds and Reaffirming Our Connections," published in the October 1985 issue of *CCC*. This article was actually the chair's address at the previous spring's national meeting of the Conference on College Composition and Communication. The speech quickly became memorable for its sustained attack on literature faculty. The chair saw them as hopelessly indifferent, or hostile, to their composition colleagues. She went so far as to recommend that her field secede from English departments and form alliances with speech communication and journalism (281). A rhetorical refusal occurs, I maintain, in the following section of her argument. It's pessimistic about getting literature faculty to discuss writing instructors' concerns:

> First, I think we need to realize that at the present time we are wasting our time trying to establish a dialogue. In addressing the mandarins, we are not in a rhetorical situation. You'll remember Lloyd Bitzer says that in order to have a rhetorical situation there has to be an *exigence* that can be modified by discourse, and there has to be an *audience* of persons who are capable of being influenced by that discourse. . . . Chaim Perelman also reminds us that the specific requisite for argumentation is this: "the speaker can choose as his points of departure only those theses accepted by those he addresses." . . . In most of our departments right now, I don't think we have either of those conditions. (277)

The CCCC meeting has long served as a venue for English department–bashing. Many of the convention-goers who heard the chair's speech, as well as many of its subsequent readers, would be prone to share her ire. Yet, as someone present at her talk, I can attest that she startled many of us when she called for utter suspension of dialogue. In part, she justifies this suspension by noting the desirability of not wasting time. But she broaches, too, what is for her an even higher principle. To survive as a field, she suggests, composition must defy an academic ideal: willingness to converse with one's possible critics.

Reinforcing her speech's distinctiveness is the chair's allusion to Bitzer and Perelman. Admittedly, warrant for her stance does appear in their theories of rhetoric. Her Perelman quotation, which she takes from his short book *The Realm of Rhetoric* (21), can in fact be bolstered by other words of his. Earlier in *Realm*, he observes that "even the most fervent partisan of dialogue is not disposed to engage in a discussion with anyone on any subject whatsoever" (11). And in his magnum opus, *The New Rhetoric: A Treatise on Argumentation*, he and coauthor Lucie Olbrechts-Tyteca explain at greater length why argument may sometimes be worth avoiding. "[As] has been said many times," they remark, "it is not always commendable to wish to persuade someone; the conditions under which contact between minds takes place may, indeed, appear to be rather dishonorable" (16). Still, the CCCC chair wasn't just shunning potential conversation partners. In her speech, she announces the shunning to another audience and encourages it to share her contempt—a more dramatic act. Besides, however fair her citation of Perelman and Bitzer, the field of composition isn't used to them being invoked this way. Usually they figure in proposals for courting potential audiences. Rarely do they loom in calls for breaking with one.

In my third case, again an author reacts to criticism of her previously published piece: an article entitled "Diversity, Ideology, and Teaching Writing" that appeared in the May 1992 issue of *CCC*. There, she argued that writing instruction is now horribly politicized by left-wing members of her field who see teaching as a chance to indoctrinate. Needless to say, the article generated a host of mail, including several dissents from the wing of composition studies it scolded. In fact, *CCC*'s editor, Richard Gebhardt, received a record number of letters about the piece. Faced with these responses, he announced that a future issue would feature several of them as well as a counter-response by the article's author (295).

The exchange occurred in the May 1993 *CCC*. Following a number of letters, most of them critical, the article's author replies by developing in her second and third paragraphs what I would call a rhetorical refusal:

> I see little point in trying to rebut the criticisms of those who disagree with me so sharply because I am not in a rhetorical situation with them. We differ so radically about basic premises—about teaching, about our society, about the purpose of education—that we have little foundation on which to base a useful discussion that is likely to change any of our minds.
>
> . . . I hope I've convinced some people with my arguments. Now, however, I'm out of the classroom, and ready to exit the conversation. At this point in my life I find it more rewarding to focus my energy in my own community, particularly on projects that directly help disadvantaged women and children. ("Reply" [1993], 255)

The author does go on to discuss some things, including intrigues at her own institution, the University of Texas at Austin, where she succeeded in stopping a required first-year writing course she deemed propagandistic.[4] But, as the words I've quoted indicate, her *CCC* response to her critics is basically a refusal to debate.

Again, this resistance is unusual in an academic setting. It's especially striking in the present case, given the controversy surrounding the original article. Numerous letters were confronting the author, enough to make the journal's editor announce he would hold a special forum on her piece. He even advertised this forum on the cover of the issue supposedly containing it. Yet, as far as the author was concerned, there would be no forum at all. Just as the author of "Breaking Our Bonds and Reaffirming Our Connections" declares that "in addressing the mandarins, we are not in a rhetorical situation," so the author of "Diversity, Ideology, and Teaching Writing" declares that she and her critics are "not in a rhetorical situation." Also, as with the chair's address, one higher principle invoked is efficiency: the author of "Diversity" suggests that substantial exchange will be not be "useful." Furthermore, just as the chair ultimately recommends secession from English departments, so the author of "Diversity" reports that she is now leaving the profession. In fact, her description of her departure conveys yet another principle evidently more vital than waging debate. The author is off to "help disadvantaged women and children," an action she implies is more socially beneficial and concretely political than the pedagogy of her critics. While they impose mind control in the classroom, she'll be a Lone Star Mother Teresa.

Let me recap my discussion of these three *CCC* authors. The author of "The Winds of Change" resists debating a critic but doesn't really cite a higher motive. The author of "Breaking Our Bonds and Reaffirming Our Connections" rejects talk with literature faculty, valuing more her own field's integrity. The author of "Diversity, Ideology, and Teaching Writing" rejects engagement with her critics by claiming that exchange would be fruitless and by suggesting she's off to a life better than theirs. All three authors defy convention in spurning debate. Indeed, in the second and third cases, this defiance seems quite pointed. While the first author notes unbridgeable differences, the other two declare that they and their interlocutors aren't even in a rhetorical situation.

If you're familiar with composition scholarship, you already know that these three authors are the same person, the late Maxine Hairston. As with Didion, I've been examining one person's refusals to debate. Hairston's reply to Blom seems a first stab at a strategy she used more vigorously and skillfully on the two later occasions. By then, she evidently realized that she had found a potentially strong rhetorical move.

Why Study Rhetorical Refusals?

That a leading composition scholar has repeatedly choked off debate is one reason for her field to join others in studying rhetorical refusals. Yet specialists in composition and rhetoric have paid little attention to these acts as a set of available moves, and the field of communication studies has slighted them, too. I would argue that they do deserve more scrutiny, for several reasons.

Whether or not we like particular instances of these acts, they alert us to rhetorical norms that we shouldn't just take for granted. Again, sometimes an audience isn't even aware of its expectations until these have been defied. Through breach rather than observance, then, a rhetorical refusal can help us identify our assumptions as readers or listeners. But, in addition to reminding us that these norms exist, rhetorical refusals prod us to critically reexamine such orthodoxies, an inquiry surely valuable in itself. Take, for example, Hairston's CCCC address and her reply to critics of her "Diversity" article. Recall that in the first, she declares flatly that "we are not in a rhetorical situation" with literary studies, and that in the second she professes herself to be "not in a rhetorical situation" with her critics. In both instances, she invokes a famous 1968 article by Lloyd Bitzer entitled "The Rhetorical Situation." Furthermore, evidently she agrees with Bitzer that key elements of a writer's or speaker's context can be objectively identified. Since his article was published, a great many theorists have disagreed with him. They argue that specifying exigence, as well as other components of "the rhetorical situation," entails interpretation rather than mere acknowledgment of fact. Indeed, Hairston's repeated use of Bitzer's concept is suspicious. If the concept can be for her a reusable device, good in particular for avoiding debate, then rhetorical situations do seem analytical constructs instead of transparent realities. Nevertheless, however we may finally feel about her conduct on these occasions, I would argue that it has a heuristic benefit. She reminds us that when writers and speakers *do* identify something as a "rhetorical situation"—seeing it as a circumstance to address—they may be accepting power relations they should probe and perhaps resist. Similarly, as I will discuss in chapter 5, a refusal to debate Holocaust deniers has at least this virtue: it encourages review of premises behind the more frequent calls for "tolerance."

Another reason for studying rhetorical refusals is that they help us consider issues in postmodern thought. As I noted earlier, people don't necessarily commit these acts out of loyalty to European intellectual fashion. Yet often these refusals appear consistent with postmodern theory's emphasis on the difficulty of mediating conflict through discourse. On the one hand, postmodern thinkers such as Jean-Francois Lyotard have given new life to rhetoric by questioning supposedly objective truth and by stressing that knowledge stems from acts of persuasion. On the other hand, many of these theorists also stress the incommensurability of language games, as if common ground is rarely achieved. Lyotard refers to the experiences of Holocaust survivors testifying in war crimes trials and investigations. Often, he contends, they face insuperable gulfs between their narrative discourse and the official language of law. [5] Thus, for all his recognition of rhetoric, Lyotard casts doubt on its ability to overcome human divisions. Yet, while rhetorical refusals admit human differences, they presume more than Lyotard does that rhetoric *can* deal with conflict. Though we may criticize particular instances of these acts, together they at least acknowledge human agency.

Much recent scholarship in the humanities is concerned with concep-
tualizing and rescuing agency, especially because for decades the world of
theory has stressed constraint. Of course, as a discipline, rhetoric has always
explored and taught strategies for verbal action. Hence, its theorists have
tried earnestly to keep some notion of agency in the postmodern age. This
interest was evident at the 2003 conference of the newly formed Alliance
of Rhetoric Societies, which devoted a major part of the meeting to the
question "How ought we to understand the concept of rhetorical agency?"
It's a query that rhetorical refusals can help answer. After all, they rely on
individual craft as well as custom, since the writers and speakers doing the
refusing depart from patterns their audiences expect. Whether or not we
appreciate each of these acts, collectively they demonstrate Farrell's point
that "rhetorical practice itself may be inventional" (273).

That Farrell feels he must make this point is a sign that rhetorical practice can, in fact, be conventional to a fault. Speaking of classical rhetoric,
Sharon Crowley observes that "the very weightiness of this tradition invites
reification, and this tendency is exacerbated by an equally long history of
reduction and simplification of its major terms for us in elementary instruction" (46). More bluntly, Maurice Charland finds the field of rhetorical
studies to be "rather staid," too wedded to "the 'mainstream,'" marked
by an "ideological commitment that tends to inhibit a reflection upon
its own presuppositions" (469, 471). Of course, as each of these theorists
would probably grant, several scholars of rhetoric have challenged premises
and practices long dear to the field. Especially in recent years, numerous
recommendations for teaching experimental discourses have appeared,
and a number of the specific moves they propose can be called rhetorical
refusals. For example, Elizabeth Ervin has argued that the "principle of
inappropriateness" (320) central to the 1960s-era movement known as the
Situationist International can serve contemporary writing classes; among
other things, she reports engaging in the SI practice of "misappropriation"
(320) by having her students circulate their own parodic Barbie valentines.
Still, especially in writing instruction and in courses on public speaking,
there's always a chance that traditional maneuvers will be taught as necessary formulae. Thus, Farrell is wise to stress that while rhetoric "always
relies on what *appears*, as inflected by received opinions and convention, it
may also recombine and reindividuate these so as to *interrupt* the quotid-
ian of ordinary policy and practice" (273, emphasis in original). Rhetori-

cal refusals, I would argue, are such interruptions and worth our notice precisely because they are.

To be sure, we should examine social influences on their performers. Conspicuous as their personal agency may be, these rhetors aren't autonomous, aloof from all ideologies and worldly conditions. Just as important to note is that they're not refusing rhetoric itself, however much they break with normal procedure. Even Hairston's refusals to debate are expressed to audiences, people whom she does aim to engage. Also important to bear in mind is that consciously or not, the audience for a rhetorical refusal sees it in relation to other discourses. These include not only discourses that the refusal renounces but also any that the refusal affirms, as well as any to which the audience may subsequently link it. In the spirit of Kenneth Burke and Mikhail Bakhtin, then, we should attend to how rhetorical refusals fit within larger conversations. This rule of thumb applies even to a text such as Hairston's CCCC address. Though she rejects further talk with literature faculty, her refusal is still in dialogue with them, insofar as it constitutes her response to their typical modes of speech.

Hairston is right, as are Perelman and Bitzer, to intimate that rhetoric can't heal every rift. And, though we may dispute her view of English department politics, she is right to suggest limits to dialogue. It may not bridge conflicts between groups, especially if the parties differ in status. Indeed, rhetorical theories informed by feminism, Marxism, multiculturalism, and other such perspectives have been much concerned with asymmetries of power, especially with how they shape or thwart discourse. Again, even as they demonstrate agency, rhetorical refusals can also serve to illuminate dynamics of power. Consciously or unconsciously, often the refusers contest hierarchies that would otherwise govern their utterances.

Once we become more familiar with these bolder moves, we who teach rhetoric, composition, and/or oral communication can share them with our classes. That is, another benefit of learning about rhetorical refusals is that they can ultimately expand our students' repertoires. The idea wouldn't be to turn students into habitual refusers. "Reifying" these moves, to use Crowley's term, would seem quite at odds with their original daring. Besides, regularly applying them might simply earn students a reputation for crankiness! The point in sponsoring experiments with these acts is that students would acquire strategies they could then occasionally use for particular ends. At the same time, I'd want them to see rhetorical refusals as more than just a grab bag of new "tricks." Even first-year undergraduates can gain *theoretical* insights by studying cases like the ones in this book.

Politics

I have suggested that the insights might include elements of *political* theory, and I want to say more about this subject here. Recall the anecdote that Alcoff tells about the speaker who vexed her and others by refusing his assigned topic. To her, he came across as insensitive to the oppressed. But someone else's refusal of topic might have a different effect. Basically, each type of rhetorical refusal is politically ambidextrous, capable of serving various partisan ends. Furthermore, in a given case, rhetor and audience may agree or disagree about which ends are served most. In Alcoff's anecdote, the two parties differed. On the other hand, note what happened at a lecture that novelist Douglas Adams gave on my own campus. According to our college newspaper,

> Adams diverged from the planned lecture topic "Living in a Virtual World" because it is one he usually gives to technology companies, and he said it wasn't as appropriate for the audience.
>
> "There's no use giving a technology speech to students because they know much more about technology than technology companies," he said. (Miskell 1)

Instead, Adams preferred to tell amusing personal stories. Far from being chagrined, though, his audience responded with "regular surges of laughter" (Miskell 1). Both Alcoff's speaker and Adams attribute authority to their audience. The first speaker suggests that his listeners know more about his assigned subject than he does, while the second declares his listeners' knowledge of technology greater than the corporate world's. Yet, evidently the first speaker's audience found him retrograde, whereas Adams's audience adored him for epitomizing anti-capitalist cool. We needn't share these audiences' perspectives. We might argue that Adams was simply charming students through flattery—a venerable form of manipulation that perhaps hid his true political stripes. The larger point I want to make here, though, is that no type of rhetorical refusal serves one faction for all time. If a rhetorical refusal circulates to various audiences, it may wind up serving any number of political views. Even at its first appearance, its ideological character may be variously interpreted.

I stress this point because the word *refusal* may automatically evoke the Left. For the last several years, many cultural theorists have looked for resistance and subversion, and they've associated these acts with populist progressivism. But the politics of a rhetorical refusal can't be just assumed. A person who engages in one may seek a classless society; then again, that person may revere Adam Smith. Furthermore, authors may not be the best diagnosticians of their own biases. As always with rhetorical analysis, when it comes to politics, we may have to distinguish between affiliations that the refuser claims and those that the refusal actually serves. Above all, we need to examine specific details of each case.

Still, I suspect that rhetorical refusals are most likely to be performed by people at polar extremes: that is, those who already enjoy high prestige (thus having little to risk) and those who feel quite abused by dominant powers. On the other hand, these acts are not apt to be practiced by, say, middle managers. Of course, people of high status might *claim* to be beset and use their established authority to advance this argument. When Croce refused to see Jones's production, she depicted herself as oppressed by his sort of art, but her stature as the *New Yorker*'s dance critic meant she could get away with snubbing him. Though the refusal was denounced, her livelihood remained. It's also true that even people with more credible reasons to feel disenfranchised must, when they make a rhetorical refusal, have *some* standing if *any* audience is to hear them. Hairston's stand against talking with literature faculty was based, I'd argue, on a legitimate belief that many look down on writing instructors, but as CCCC chair she had a big forum to assert this view. Even in studying rhetorical refusals by the severely alienated, then, we ought to remember that other people still struggle for a public voice.

But issues of politics also arise when rhetorical refusals put in question key aspects of societies' governing frames. That these acts may shed critical light on core elements of a political order is yet another reason for studying them. Indeed, I would argue that it's one of the most important reasons of all. Hence, I devote much of part 2 to examining how rhetorical refusals have challenged or complicated terms, concepts, and practices central to present American civic culture.

The Structure of This Book

In the following pages, I perform several case studies, using them to develop an overall method for analyzing and evaluating rhetorical refusals. Methodology is very much the focus of part 1. Throughout its three chapters, I work with the category of refusing to see what one criticizes, using Croce's article "Discussing the Undiscussable" as a central example. In chapter 1, I argue that helpful principles for studying rhetorical refusals can be found in Perelman and Olbrechts-Tyteca's 1958 book *The New Rhetoric*. More precisely, I show the applicability of two particular notions they put forth: the concept of "dissociations" and the idea that "audiences pass judgment on one another" (35). In chapter 2, I propose that examining—and judging—a rhetorical refusal means considering its precise discursive features; its differences from other conceivable members of its category; the position it explicitly or implicitly takes on various philosophical issues; its role in advancing the interests of larger groups; and its relations to matters of both politics and ethics. The emphasis of chapter 3 is squarely on evaluation, as I apply the ideas I have developed so far to the assessment of Croce's act. You will see that my view of it is far from wholly favorable; still, my bigger aim is to stress considerations applicable to rhetorical refusals besides hers. As part of this chapter, I argue for comparing a refusal like Croce's to less provocative verbal performances and for understanding how, especially in America, the world may value renegade polemic merely as commercial entertainment.

The chapters in part 2 continue elaborating methodology. But as I've already noted, they also show how rhetorical refusals can expose shakiness in civic foundations—here, the vulnerability of American traditions. Focusing on Lipstadt's unwillingness to debate Holocaust deniers, especially as she registers this in her book *Denying the Holocaust: The Growing Assault on Truth and Memory*, chapter 4 proposes investigating which elements of Burke's famous "pentad" are emphasized by a particular rhetorical refusal. In Lipstadt's case, I argue, her stress falls on the "agent," for she condemns deniers as sinister kinds of beings. I also show through the Lipstadt example how a rhetorical refusal can entail a certain theory of "truth" and raise issues of salience. The chapter's political topic is the American belief (voiced, if not always enacted) in free, open exchanges of speech, a value endorsed on most college campuses. In refusing to converse with deniers, Lipstadt destabilizes this ideal, pushing her readers to reconsider its assumptions.

Chapter 5 calls for looking at shifts in impact that rhetorical refusals can undergo when they circulate or "travel" into new forums. I examine in particular (1) an interview with Michel Foucault in which he insisted on remaining anonymous; (2) a brazenly personal essay that Jane Tompkins wrote for an academic venue; and (3) Bill Clinton's refusal to tell the grand jury much about his affair with Monica Lewinsky. For each of these acts, I trace the long-term effects. With respect to politics, I deal with a classic desire undergirding American democracy: the aim of establishing clear, permanent distinctions between "private" and "public." These three refusals, I argue, expose the sheer utopianism of such hope.

The next chapter raises the possibility that even when a rhetorical refusal appears in a text, its other sections may prove more conventional. My example is Douglass's speech about Lincoln, which includes acerbic remarks about the slain president but ends by exalting him. More precisely, the middle of Douglass's address dwells on how Lincoln had frustrated African Americans, whereas the conclusion honors him as their Great Emancipator. A "mixed" text like this, I observe, leaves its immediate and subsequent audiences having to decide which parts of it are ultimately most significant. All the same, I argue for tracing the history of the text's actual reception, the perspectives on it advanced by various commentators. I contend as well that the text's heterogeneity may alert us to nuances of its genre—in Douglass's case, epideictic discourse—that we haven't fully appreciated before. On the political level, I argue for using Douglass's speech as a lens for analyzing and evaluating current American memorial practices: that is, the nation's efforts to consolidate itself *as* a nation through the ways in which it mourns tragic events. By bringing up racial inequality, Douglass complicated a ceremony devoted to commemorating Lincoln's saving of the Union. I argue that in remembering 9/11, the country should acknowledge racial barriers revealed by Hurricane Katrina, even if such memory spoils the fantasy of a united people.

Chapter 7 recognizes that rhetorical refusals can occur in works of fiction. Clearly, this prospect might cheer people who study and teach fictional texts. But I call for a particular approach to the rhetorical refusals of imaginative literature. It's one that, in the name of rhetoric, not only considers audience but also the larger world, relating these refusals to real events and "nonfictional" discourse. I demonstrate this approach by applying it to Tim O'Brien's *In the Lake of the Woods*, a 1994 novel about a Vietnam veteran who conceals his role in the My Lai massacre. To a great extent, the book is a mystery, for the protagonist's wife vanishes. Yet O'Brien frustrates conventional expectation by leaving the mystery unsolved, and thus, I argue, the term rhetorical refusal suits this fictional work. I then relate O'Brien's novel to a recent memoir, former U.S. senator Bob Kerrey's *When I Was a Young Man*, which deals heavily with Kerrey's military service in Vietnam. I explain how *In the Lake of the Woods* alerts us to ways that Kerrey obscures his role in a massacre. Overall, this chapter extends the political topic of national memory by showing how a rhetorical refusal—even one in a novel—can promote a more searching conversation about America's wars.

In my conclusion, I briefly explore the idea that rhetorical refusals can be innovative responses to opportunities for political discourse. Again, we should bear in mind that even so-called democracies have their limitations; they don't beckon all their citizens to join forums. Still, the political discussion that does exist is now all too predictable, and rhetorical refusals can help us think about how to make it less so. Stressing this possibility, I look at refusals performed by three people—Sharon Olds, Stephen Colbert, and Cindy Sheehan—each of whom had been invited to hobnob with Washington's elite. As with all the cases I treat, these three should be judged on their individual merits. Nor am I suggesting that the strategies at work in them should be made routine. Rather, I bring them up at the end to encourage greater rhetorical adventurousness in the discourses of civic life.

Although I maintain that each category of rhetorical refusal constitutes a tradition, this book isn't a history. True, many of the types I explore span centuries. Yet, for better or worse, most of my examples are present-day, culled from contemporary publications and Web sites. I have chosen this focus because I want to stress that relevant cases are, in fact, always emerging. They're increasingly available for our inspection—if we choose to look for them.

PART ONE

Toward a Method of Analysis and Evaluation

Basic Principles

In part 1, I introduce principles for analyzing and evaluating rhetorical refusals. Mostly, I focus on instances of people's refusing to see what they criticize, taking Arlene Croce's refusal to see *Still/Here* as my main case. To fathom what's going on with acts like hers, let's begin by considering this excerpt from an interview with actress Natasha Lyonne:

> A waifish looking woman with wide eyes, she takes a dim view of today's filmmaking.
>
> "It's all really pandering. Like, *You've Got Mail* . . . is not a normal movie. That is, like, just a dumb movie . . ."
>
> Then she pauses to rethink her position.
>
> "OK, that's a bad example," she admits, "because I haven't seen *You've Got Mail*. But you can just sometimes tell what things are . . ." (Kennedy)

Even a waif may provide revelations. Here, she brings out important aspects of Croce's sort of act. When Lyonne initially blasts *You've Got Mail*, she shows that occasionally people do judge things sight unseen. Nevertheless, she admits her case against the film seems weak. Most readers, she implies, will expect her to have seen it. Indeed, few critics of a work blatantly avoid it, if they hope to make others find their judgment sound. Avoidance is striking when it occurs precisely because it defies rhetorical norms. This is why, in refusing to see *Still/Here*, Croce caused a stir. Acts such as hers are numerous enough to constitute a type yet so uncommon that they merit notice.

Their distinctiveness grows even clearer when we compare the following two passages. The first is from rhetorical theorist Arabella Lyon's book *Intentions: Negotiated, Contested, and Ignored*. Lyon faults philosopher of hermeneutics Hans-George Gadamer for defining literary criticism as a conversation between reader and writer. According to Lyon, Gadamer fails to recognize that some texts should be rejected rather than taken as opportunities for dialogue. Furthermore, she suggests that some texts should be shunned in the first place:

> For example, though it is a historically interesting text for me to understand, should I want to risk my prejudices by listening to Rush Limbaugh (or for that matter Hitler)? . . . Obviously the refusal to enter a dialogue is a dangerous strategy, one that can benefit the status quo. Even so, if an audience's purposes are important (part of a life-world), then that audience might well refuse to risk prejudices due to misgivings about being entangled in the traditions of an other. . . . If I try to engage, let alone present, Limbaugh's perspective, I give up the discursive space of my biases and my claims on aspects of the world. (66)

Lyon's position is itself debatable. Plenty of rhetoricians have read works by Limbaugh and Hitler. Although usually they denounce these texts, they back up their condemnation with the texts' actual words. One of the finest pieces of modern rhetorical criticism is Kenneth Burke's "The Rhetoric of Hitler's 'Battle,'" which delineates at length the sinister strategies of *Mein Kampf.* Yet Lyon seems to recognize that her stance may be controversial. Moreover, she admits that avoiding a text can be hazardous. Besides, her Limbaugh and Hitler examples are just hypothetical. She indicates that she *might* condemn these authors without reading them but refrains from declaring that she *will.* The passage I have cited is still unusual; seldom do academics even raise the prospect of ignoring texts. Lyon would be more unusual, though, were she to scorn Limbaugh's or Hitler's prose while plainly refusing to read it.

Now consider the following remarks about Limbaugh's book *The Way Things Ought to Be.* They appear in the Web zine *h2so4* under the title "Thinly veiled philosophical tracts masquerading as: Reviews of Books I Haven't Read and Why I Haven't Read Them." Here, Gridley Minima goes a step further than Lyon, complacently declaring that Limbaugh is "a man who will not read this, whom I have never met, nor wanted to, whose voice I have never heard, and (needless to say) whose book I have not read." Even so, Minima permits himself to meditate upon Limbaugh, saying among other things that Limbaugh is for him

[a] symbol of an absolute limit to my optimism, embodiment of that hatred and fear of the unknown that masquerades as "realism" even among my most intimate enemies, even, perhaps, in me. . . . He is, in sum, the face of everything I turn my back on every morning . . . [and] the razor-toothed teddy bear I hug to my chest at night. For I love him, of course, like a brother, like myself—and he is, in the end, nothing more or less than the ridiculous yet pervasive idea that "I" was ever anything other than a temporary, amateurish, uncertain arrangement between a few handfuls of cells; something provisional, doomed to failure.

Minima's remarks hardly amount to Gadamerian conversation with Limbaugh's book. Clearly he prefers another sort of discourse. Specifically, ignoring Limbaugh's real words allows him to explore what Limbaugh stands for as a cultural figure. This agenda, Minima suggests, is more worthwhile than a book review's. Of course, Minima's own readers may not share his vision of Limbaugh as superego. But his freewheeling rumination encourages them to ponder what Limbaugh means to them.

For certain of his readers, the impact of Minima's act may be minimal. I can imagine people less startled by this actual rejection of Limbaugh than by Lyon's hypothetical spurning of him. Perhaps you put high demands on printed academic scholarship, expecting it to examine books it cites. When Lyon verges on avoiding some texts, you may think this stance provocative in itself. Meanwhile, you might dismiss Minima's writing as sophomoric stream-of-consciousness, an all-too-familiar phenomenon on the Web. Whatever our reactions to these two theorists, we should place rhetorical acts in context. Hypothesizing a rhetorical refusal may prove as dramatic as engaging in one.

Still, we need to distinguish between Lyon's hedging and Minima's bluntness. It matters, if in ways to be determined, that Minima clearly forgoes reading Limbaugh while Lyon just supposes this move. In the rest of part 1, I examine cases more like Minima's than Lyon's, developing a method of studying them. Because I will be attending so much to Croce's famous (or notorious) article, first I will summarize the argument it makes. Then I will explain briefly how Burke's observations on "entitling" can help us understand her rhetorical refusal and others. The remainder of this chapter, though, argues chiefly for applying to rhetorical refusals two ideas from Chaim Perelman and Lucie Olbrechts-Tyteca's *The New Rhetoric*. One is their theory of "dissociations." To explain it and to begin demonstrating its usefulness, I return to Maxine Hairston's CCCC chair's address, noting various dissociations at work in her call for spurning literature faculty. I proceed, however, to Croce, tracing how her refusal involves similar dynamics. Her article remains my key reference as I turn to another plank of *The New Rhetoric*: the proposition that "audiences pass judgment on one another" (35). This idea, too, is valuable for the study of rhetorical refusals, as I show by relating it to Croce's act. To be sure, plenty of writers and speakers besides her have judged works they've refused to experience. In a coda to the chapter, I call attention to this fact, through looking at two refusals by legendary cultural critic James Agee.

Croce's Argument

Recall that Croce's article gained attention because she criticizes a dance piece, Bill T. Jones's *Still/Here*, while refusing to see it. Croce justifies her truancy by citing a key element of Jones's production: videotaped testimonies by people with AIDS and other potentially fatal diseases. For her, these testimonies demand sympathy, not assessment, so they prevent her from doing her usual job. "By working dying people into his act," she asserts, "Jones is putting himself beyond the reach of criticism" (54). At the same time, Croce regards *Still/Here* as more than an isolated phenomenon. To her, Jones is simply "the most extreme case among the many now representing themselves to the public not as artists but as victims and martyrs" (54).

Elaborating her claim that Jones exemplifies a trend, Croce proceeds to make a historical argument. In part, she chronicles developments on the dance scene since the 1960s. Increasingly, she contends, choreographers and their patrons have abandoned her cherished ideal, "disinterested art" (56). Instead they exalt dances that emphasize multiculturalism and political usefulness. For example, Jones has repeatedly turned to the subject of AIDS after candidly announcing his own HIV-positive status. Croce is just as disturbed that many contemporary choreographers mock their audiences. In particular, she laments, they target professional critics like her, demanding "No back talk!" (58). To her, Jones conveys this message when *Still/Here* parades testimonies of the seriously ill.

Not that Croce finds such moves confined to the world of dance. Rather, she thinks "victimhood" pervades our culture (53). Therefore, while focusing on Jones's piece, she sneers at the photography of Robert Mapplethorpe, the NAMES quilt, the play *Angels in America*, and "grisly high-minded movies like *Schindler's List*" (60). She does admit that the arts have long expressed suffering. Even so, she argues, pained artists such as John Keats and Frédéric Chopin differed from the current priests of victimhood by achieving a "transcendence" that showed that "the grandeur of the individual spirit is more worth celebrating than the political clout of the group" (59).

As you can probably tell from my summary, Croce's article is polemical. Even if she had seen *Still/Here*, her scorn for the work and for others like it might still have provoked much talk. Because she did refuse to see the piece, controversy was certain. In chapter 3, I will fully join the debate over how to evaluate her stance. Right now, I want to trace more precisely what's involved in her refusal.

Burke: Naming the Situation

Croce's rhetorical refusal, as well as many others, exemplifies one of Burke's perpetual interests: "the nature of language as a means of entitling" (*Language* 378). More precisely, Burke was concerned with the art of deliberate, purposeful, and selective labeling. Of Burke's several statements on this subject, quite useful is the second paragraph of his essay "The Philosophy of Literary Form." There, taking *poetry* to mean "any work of critical or imaginative cast," Burke further defines it "as the adopting of various strategies for the encompassing of situations." He adds that "these strategies size up the situations, name their structure and outstanding ingredients, and name them in a way that contains an attitude towards them" (1). Burke held that innumerable texts can be profitably analyzed from this perspective. It seems especially relevant, though, to rhetorical refusals. In several of these, the rhetor seeks to justify his or her defiance of protocol by conspicuously naming the circumstances at hand in a particular way. Moreover, often this labeling amounts to a *renaming* of the situation, for the audience has had other terms for it in mind. For instance, by applying the neologism *victim art* to Jones's production, Croce tries to shift her readers away from their premise that it's purely *art* so that they'll accept her absence from it. As I noted in my introduction, Burke was also preoccupied with the role of the Negative in human thought, and a rhetorical refusal's act of renaming can involve declaring what the circumstances are *not*. Repeatedly, we've seen, Hairston has excused her refusal to debate by claiming that her situation isn't Bitzer's "rhetorical" one. Her circumstances, she maintains, don't deserve to be so entitled. Consequently, in the honorific sense of "entitlement," literature faculty aren't entitled to composition faculty's attention, and critics of her "Diversity, Ideology, and Teaching Writing" article aren't entitled to a response.

In analyzing human beings' strategic uses of nomenclature, Burke observes that "basically, there are two kinds of terms: terms that put things together, and terms that take things apart" (*Language* 49). This point reflects another of his continual interests: the various ways that rhetoric involves identification and division. Most rhetorical refusals, I suspect, use terms primarily to make the audience separate things it might otherwise unite. That is, these refusals resort heavily to what Perelman and Olbrechts-Tyteca call *dissociations*. Let me turn, then, to *The New Rhetoric* for help in explaining Croce's refusal and similar acts.

Dissociations in Hairston's Chair's Address

Like Burke, the authors of *The New Rhetoric* are interested in processes of merger and separation, finding that rhetoric often entails both. One important concept for Perelman and Olbrechts-Tyteca is association, which they define as "schemes which bring separate elements together and allow us to establish a unity among them." By contrast, dissociation consists of "techniques of separation which have the purpose of dissociating, separating, disuniting elements which are regarded as forming a whole or at least a unified group within some system of thought" (190). Both processes may be said to occur in any rhetorical refusal. Focusing on dissociations, however, is an especially good means of analyzing the acts I study in this book. Of the two processes, Perelman and Olbrechts-Tyteca themselves seem more interested in dissociation. In particular, they see it as playing a crucial role in many efforts to reform existing philosophies.

With dissociation, the rhetor argues that conceptual unity in the case at hand is illusory. Till now, the audience has glimpsed only one concept, but this conceals two or more. *The New Rhetoric* finds that many dissociations even involve an appearance/reality split. In effect, the latter distinction serves as prototype. Furthermore, this split and its variants are usually value-laden, for rhetors and their audiences tend to prefer the real to the fake. In general, as Alan Gross points out in elaborating Perelman and Olbrechts-Tyteca's ideas, "Dissociation is a way of taking the argumentative high ground" (320). Through it, rhetors contend that a concept held by their audience obscures something truer *and* better.

To sense how arguments rely on dissociation, let's turn from Croce's article for a spell and recall the title of Hairston's 1985 chair's address: "Breaking Our Bonds and Reaffirming Our Connections." The phrase "breaking our bonds" implies that Hairston will resort to dissociation. She does proceed to challenge the concept of "English" as a genuinely unified discipline. To her, this concept is a misguided hope, for reality is quite different: literature specialists refuse to treat compositionists as kin. Eventually, Hairston's conceptual dissociation leads her to recommend an institutional dissociation: the exodus of composition from English departments. Hairston recognizes that much of her audience will dislike this idea or think it unenforceable. At the very least, she declares, composition specialists must dissociate *psychologically* from English's literature-oriented elite:

> [W]e must pay attention to what our inner selves tell us, find our own values and listen to our own voices—values and voices that are not *against* someone else, but for ourselves. We must no longer try to be "good" by trying to live up to someone else's visions for us by saying, "Tell me what you want me to be and I'll be it. I want to please you." If we do that, when we win, we lose. (278)

Throughout her speech, Hairston works with an appearance/reality distinction by denouncing English as merely a pretense of communal bliss. The passage above does a classic variation on the appearance/reality split, distinguishing between outside and inside. We compositionists, Hairston argues, have been "trying to live up to someone else's visions." Now, we must detach ourselves from these externally imposed ideals, returning to "our inner selves" and "our own voices." In other words, the outside is artificial, the inside genuine.

Like any dissociation, this one by Hairston can be criticized. Many a deconstructionist has questioned attempts to split outside from inside and to privilege the latter. The phrase "our own voices" would have infuriated Ludwig Wittgenstein, for he denied the possibility of a private language. Mikhail Bakhtin, too, found our speech marked by others'.[1] Actually, theorists of various stripes would say our psyches are social products, so that Hairston's phrasing misleads. I suspect Perelman and Olbrechts-Tyteca would stress, however, that Hairston is engaged in rhetoric. Mainly, she aims to get her specific audience to accept and act on her dissociations, whether or not these pass muster in an epistemology seminar. It's still the case that any of her dissociations may be evaluated, and by anyone. But their pragmatic dimension is important to note.

Rarely does the rhetor get to determine everything. Quite rightly, Perelman and Olbrechts-Tyteca think the audience crucial in all sorts of ways. Whatever the rhetor's strategies, they suggest, the audience has ample power to decide whether a dissociation is being made in the first place. An alternative view is that the rhetor is just separating things loosely piled. Take an audience member who's thought "English" a haphazard mélange of pursuits. To this person, Hairston may just be disentangling elements that have never cohered. On the other hand, take a believer in the current or potential coherence of "English." To this person, Hairston may epitomize dissociation, insofar as she explodes an ideal.

Certainly both types of respondents can be found in composition studies at large. Certainly both were in Hairston's audience when she spoke to the CCCC and when her speech then appeared in composition's leading journal. Yet, on either occasion, probably the audience included relatively few hard-core advocates of secession from English. For the most part, Hairston would have been addressing writing instructors who habitually think English their institutional home, however much it abuses them. Even today, the number of composition programs outside English remains small. Thus, Hairston's main listeners and readers were apt to regard her as dissociating terms when she wedged composition and literature apart. Hairston herself, it seems, expected to strike them as utterly redefining their field. Her title calls for major change, and she proceeds to defend this call at length.

The second half of her title, "restoring our connections," implies that Hairston will use association as well. Together, her title's two phrases suggest she will even give dissociation and association the same weight. Indeed, *The New Rhetoric* observes, "The two techniques are complementary and are always at work at the same time" (190). Consistent with this point, Hairston refers to "breaking our bonds" and "restoring our connections" as interdependent processes. According to her, composition specialists will detach from English only when they reconnect with their souls. Yet, when Hairston declares that "we must no longer try to be 'good' by trying to live up to someone else's visions for us," she clearly stresses dissociation. Again, this emphasis accords with what seems Perelman and Olbrechts-Tyteca's own larger concern.

Hairston also stresses dissociation when she prods writing teachers to stop talking with the literati. As I've said, this move of hers constitutes a rhetorical refusal. And, when Hairston performs this move, she dissociates in more than one way. She not only divides English into multiple competitive fields but also challenges her audience's likely notion of an academic address. In effect, she says to her audience, "I know you assume that the CCCC chair's speech will, if anything, exalt debate, but my speech is going to be different." This dissociation can be seen as a change in genre. Or, it can be taken to indicate that a certain genre has more forms than its audiences realize (a possibility I'll explore with another case, Frederick Douglass's speech, in chapter 6).

Thus, as with many other dissociations, Hairston here distinguishes between appearance and reality. She implies that her audience has entertained an illusion: namely, that there's only one model of the chair's speech, a model that holds dialogue sacred. In reality, she suggests, multiple conceptions of the speech are possible. She herself uses the occasion to defy academe's supposed welcoming of debate, proposing instead that literature faculty be snubbed. Hairston invokes reality, too, when she justifies her stance by announcing as fact that "we are not in a rhetorical situation" with them.

Remember that appeals to reality tend to reflect a hierarchy of values, too. After all, it seems wiser to confront the real than to languish in illusion. As Gross says in commenting on *The New Rhetoric*, dissociations take "the argumentative high ground." Throughout her speech, Hairston claims this territory. In general, she defends her departure from protocol by finding the academy's commitment to debate incompatible with a greater agenda. She insists that it's better for her audience to focus on composition teachers' welfare, which literature specialists inevitably slight.

As I observed in my introduction, rhetorical refusals also seize "the argumentative high ground." Often they do so through dissociations, and as Hairston's speech demonstrates, they may engage in several of these. Still, what distinguishes rhetorical refusals in the first place is a particular dissociation: that between a procedure their audience expects them to follow and a presumably better course.

Croce's Dissociations

This dissociation of procedure is one that Croce makes. Surely she's aware that her readers will expect her to have attended *Still/Here*. Thus, she knows she will pique interest when she claims the only sensible move in this case is "to write about what one has not seen" (54). Interestingly, Croce also claims she has been more or less forced into this position, for Jones's emphasis on victimhood renders his production "unintelligible as theatre" (54). Why, then, does she write about *Still/Here*, especially if she thinks it alienating? One answer is that her article provides her a platform for denouncing Jones and his ilk. Moreover, as I'll elaborate in chapter 3, discussing his dance sight unseen ensures publicity for her attack.

Croce supports her dissociation of procedure with two other dissociations. Both concern genre. The first pertains to classification of her own article. During her many years of service to the *New Yorker*, she specialized in dance reviews. It's the type of writing she is identified with most. At the outset of "Discussing the Undiscussable," however, she distinguishes her article from this genre. In her first sentence, she announces that she has "no plans to review" *Still/Here* (54). In the same paragraph, she reiterates that she is "not reviewing" it (54). Later, referring to Jones's inclusion of the seriously ill, she declares that "I can't review someone I feel sorry for or hopeless about" (55). In fact, her article appeared in the *New Yorker* outside the section devoted to reviews. Treating it as a full-fledged essay in its own right, editor Tina Brown placed it nearer to the magazine's front (a move that strengthened readers' chances of noticing it). By dissociating this article from her usual genre, Croce tries to justify her avoidance of *Still/Here*. Were she reviewing the piece, she implies, she would have been obligated to see it. Since she's *not* reviewing it, staying home is fine.

Croce's second dissociation is related to genre in the way she classifies Jones's piece. To justify shunning it, she does more than claim that her article isn't a review; she also suggests her readers are wrong if they think *Still/Here* qualifies as art. True, she does refer to it repeatedly as "victim art" (55, 60), thereby indicating that it's still art of a sort. But much of the time, she consigns it to lesser categories. Explicitly resisting the idea that Jones's production is "a new art form," she characterizes it instead as a "messianic travelling medicine show" (54). To her, Jones "has crossed the line between theatre and reality," thereby extending the tradition of "anti-art" (56). He and Mapplethorpe are "not so much above art as beyond it" (58), a comment that Croce hardly intends as praise. Significantly, the heading below Croce's title poses the following question: "When players in a production aren't just acting out death but are really dying—as in Bill

T. Jones's 'Still/Here'—is it really art?" (54). The heading may not have been written by Croce, but its definitional question seems hers, and her answer is evidently "No!" Although widely regarded as an aesthetic work, *Still/Here* is an inferior species. Its indulgence in victimhood removes it from the purview of professional critics. This kind of thing, they shouldn't be made to see.

When Croce distinguishes Jones's piece from "art," she challenges her audience's possible understanding of this word. Presumably, many of her readers think "art" a neutral term, denoting a category whose members belong together even if they range in quality. Croce, though, proceeds to make an appearance/reality distinction: some works, such as Jones's, may appear to be art, but they really aren't. And, as with many dissociations, real is better than ersatz. Some works *deserve* to be called art, while others, such as Jones's, fall short. Thus, Croce turns "art" into an evaluative term.

Her maneuver exemplifies what *The New Rhetoric* calls a definitional dissociation. Often such dissociations divide appearance from reality and favor the latter. Moreover, often they take an ostensibly neutral word and load it with value by distinguishing good forms of it from the bad or mundane. An example I use in classes is the play-by-play announcer who observes a great tackle, catch, or touchdown and yells, "Now *that's* football!" With this remark, "football" is no longer a matter-of-fact designation of a sport. Now it points to a reality that merits esteem. Some plays are only *apparently* football, for although they're technically part of the game, their clumsiness disappoints. Other plays are *real* football, for their splendor shows the sport at its best. Of course, Croce and the announcer move in different directions when they convert a bland term into passionate judgment. "Now *that's* football!" elevates a certain feat, deeming it better than ordinary gridiron activity. Croce's definition of "art" excludes *Still/Here*, thus lowering its status. Her dissociation is like that of the parents who, when their child plays a heavy metal CD, yell, "My God! You call *that* music?"

Others besides Croce have performed dissociations with the term "art." Recall, for example, Adrienne Rich's letter refusing the National Medal for the Arts. Again, she declared that "the very meaning of art, as I understand it, is incompatible with the cynical politics of this administration" (98). She thereby distinguishes her own definition of art from the definition that she thinks the award implies. The latter notion of art, she proceeds to claim, treats it as something that "simply decorates the dinner table of power that holds it hostage." In contrast, she sees art "as breaker of official silences, as voice for those whose voices are disregarded, and as a human birthright" (99). Rich's handling of the term "art" is a classic definitional dissociation. Indeed, when she elaborates it by using the word "incompatible," she confirms a key comment that *The New Rhetoric* makes about dissociations: namely, that they are "prompted by the desire to remove an incompatibility arising out of a confrontation of one proposition with others, whether one is dealing with norms, facts, or truths" (413). Probably Croce would object to Rich's concept of art, finding it too concerned with victims. Nevertheless, both these writers are troubled by seemingly incompatible meanings of the term, and both address the problem through dissociation.

Audiences Judging Audiences

Besides dissociations, *The New Rhetoric* offers another valuable concept. It, too, helps us analyze Croce's text as well as other rhetorical refusals. The idea is this: "audiences pass judgment on one another."

Perelman and Olbrechts-Tyteca declare this principle as they explain how audience is a key subject for them. In general, they hold that *"all argumentation aims at gaining the adherence of minds, and, by this very fact, assumes the existence of an intellectual contact"* (14, emphasis in original). Of course, most rhetorical theories deal with audience. By and large, they see it as a force that would-be persuaders must heed. But *The New Rhetoric's* treatment of this subject is special, for the book makes audience utterly central. Note again that it explicitly refers to "the adherence of minds" as argument's ultimate goal.

Nevertheless, Perelman and Olbrechts-Tyteca don't assume that the audience for a given argument is its best evaluator. They're well aware that people may be seduced by demagoguery. As a veteran of World War II's Belgian resistance, Perelman was especially familiar with the insidious power of Nazi propaganda. Thus, he and his co-author venture to say that "an audience can be praised or blamed depending on the kind of speech to which it will listen, the kind of speakers it likes to hear, and the kind of reasoning which meets with its approval" (321). That is, any assessment that an audience makes can be criticized by others. Furthermore, the critics may include other audiences. This is the possibility that Perelman and Olbrechts-Tyteca have in mind when they state that "audiences pass judgment on one another." It's a prospect that rhetorical refusals exploit.

I've said that such refusals exhibit a dissociation of procedure. They reject a move their audience expects for one supposedly more virtuous. Now, I can rephrase this point. In effect, rhetorical refusals evoke two different audiences. One consists of people who count on protocol's being followed. They think normal procedures will hold sway, and they value these. The other audience consists of people who accept the refuser's break with custom. The refuser begins by assuming that his or her actual audience is the first group. The refuser then tries to show that this group's reasoning is limited. More generally, the refuser works at converting the actual audience into the second group. Indeed, as Steven Mailloux shrewdly observes, "Rhetoric involves the transformation of one audience into another" (*Reception* 4). The refuser hopes that only the second audience will exist at the end. These people will see the first group as their former, less enlightened selves. In essence, the new audience "passes judgment on" the audience it used to be, and the judgment is negative.

With her CCCC address, Hairston pushes her audience to stop being people open to debate. Become a different audience, she exhorts. Turn into people who fault those who seek dialogue with literature faculty. "Discussing the Undiscussable" is a comparable case. There, Croce prods her readers to stop being the sort who would require her to have seen *Still/Here*. She strives to make them people who accept her snub of it. If she succeeds, they might turn to scolding those who demand she view it.

Thus, even if she's never come across *The New Rhetoric*, Croce's discourse reflects the principle that "audiences pass judgment on one another." It's a principle she encourages her own audience to share. In part, she does so through disparaging remarks about Jones's audience. Basically, she calls for her own audience to condemn his. To use a term from sociologist Herbert Gans, she identifies Jones's fans as a particular "taste public," and she prods her own audience to join another.

Gans defines a "taste public" as a group whose members share certain aesthetic values. To be sure, people within such a group may not realize their commonality. These collectives, Gans admits, are "analytic aggregates"—categories formulated by researchers (4). They may not be pure fiction, but neither are they universally recognized as fact. Thus, Croce may be seen as *creating* separate taste publics rather than simply acknowledging them. Certainly her differentiation of them is a rhetorical strategy, aimed at making her readers distrust Jones's fans.

She promotes this distrust with her observation that "when a victim artist finds his or her public, a perfect, mutually manipulative union is formed which no critic may put asunder" (55). Then, she depicts Jones's audience as comprised of sheer dupes, claiming that his works resurrect "the defiant anti-conventionalism of the sixties, when you were manipulated into accepting what you saw as art" (58). Her most sustained denunciation of his audience, though, comes at the end of her article:

> People for whom art is too fine, too high, too educational, too complicated may find themselves turning with relief to the new tribe of victim artists parading their wounds. They don't care whether it's an art form. They find something to respond to in the litany of pain, and they make their own connection to what the victim is saying. Of course, they are all co-religionists in the cult of Self. Only the narcissism of the nineties could put Self in place of Spirit and come up with a church service that sells out the Brooklyn Academy. (60)

Croce's final sentence refers to the commercial success of *Still/Here*'s Brooklyn run. Many people did go to see the production. Moreover, probably its audience included several readers of her article. These readers may identify with the "they" of Croce's last paragraph, seeing her as actually attacking "us." Even so, she might change their minds about Jones's piece. If she does convert them, they will believe that avoiding *Still/Here* makes sense. At the same time, they will be detaching themselves from an audience they once joined. In effect, they will be denigrating their former taste public as they shift to another.

At any rate, consistently Croce tries to turn her audience against a pair of alternative audiences: people who want her to have seen *Still/Here*, and people who saw it themselves. Actually, her two-pronged effort is characteristic of people's refusals to see what they're criticizing. Like other rhetorical refusals, this type defies fans of certain rhetorical norms. Often, though, this kind of rhetorical refusal goes further, discrediting people who *do* see the work at hand.

James Agee's Refusals to See

Though part 1 takes Croce's act as a recurring example, hers is just one rhetorical refusal, albeit one that has spawned a lot of talk and has rich theoretical implications. Even within the category of refusals to see, hers has had plenty of precedents. Let me close this chapter by noting two, both of them by major cultural commentator James Agee. Both can be found in *Agee on Film*, an esteemed collection of his writings. Agee is much admired for his discerning attention to particular details of films. Thus, it's ironic that occasionally he refused to see what he judged.

One such occasion was his article "Pseudo-Folk." In this 1944 piece for *Partisan Review*, Agee denounces Broadway productions and jazz performances that for him are degraded simulacra of folk culture. His specific targets include the musical *Oklahoma!*, which he labels "a white disease" and "whose accents, premises, and success" he finds "questionable" (434). Another object of his scorn is the all-black musical *Carmen Jones*, which he calls a "traduction and zoo-exhibition of their race" (433). Similarly, he lambastes Margaret Webster's staging of *Othello*, which featured iconic African American singer-actor Paul Robeson in the title role. To Agee, both the production itself and its "record-breaking success" are "painfully dubious phenomena" (433). Yet, halfway through his article, Agee makes a startling admission: "(Postscript: I should explain that I have not seen *Othello*, *Carmen Jones* or *Oklahoma!* because I felt sure they would be bad. People who spoke well of the shows have reinforced me in this feeling and helped give it detail. People who spoke ill of them, I regarded as even more trustworthy)" (435). At this point, Agee performs a rhetorical refusal. Never, he indicates, will he see the works he has condemned. Simultaneously, he presses his readers to break with the sort who demand he attend these productions. Like Croce, in other words, he invites his audience to pass judgment on another audience. Moreover, like Croce, he pushes his readers to scorn an additional audience: fans of these shows who actually attended them. "People who spoke ill of" these productions are, in his view, "more trustworthy" than those who enjoyed them. Elsewhere in his piece, Agee scoffs specifically at professional critics who liked *Othello* and at black theatergoers who liked *Carmen Jones*. Ultimately, he sneers at "the great corrupted audience" for all these works while grudgingly noting it "might be teachable" (437).

The following year, Agee made similar gestures in another piece. In his May 19, 1945, film column for the *Nation*, he condemns newsreels that exposed the brutality of Nazi camps, believing that these movies served merely to provoke vindictiveness toward all Germans. Once again, though, he levels his charge without having seen his target. Watching the newsreels, he asserts, is not "necessary" (150) in order for him to opine about them. Although Agee expresses mildly his refusal to see the films, it's a refusal nonetheless. Moreover, he would have his readers not be the kind that requires him to watch such footage. At the same time, he encourages them to condemn anyone who does view it. Consumers of the newsreels, he suggests, are caught up in "a passion for vengeance" that is "fatally degrading and destructive" (150). He goes so far as to declare that this wrath makes Americans "worse, in some respects, than the Nazis," for "[t]here can be no bestiality so discouraging to contemplate as that of the man of good-will when he is misusing his heart and mind" (151).[2]

I don't know the reaction to Agee's column, but I suspect it disturbed many. In 1945, with the war just concluded, the newsreels gripped Americans. Previously ignorant or complacent about the camps' slaughter, they were now determined to confront it. Yet Agee not only scolded them for watching the newsreels but also compared them unfavorably with the enemy! This move was bound to alienate them further.

Looking back, I too shiver at Agee's argument. Prior to victory, he watched numerous films promoting the Allies. Though they often left him ambivalent, he did see them. So why single out the Holocaust newsreels for contempt and avoidance? After all, they introduced many Americans to the Nazis' mass exterminations. Unfortunately, Agee's column approaches the rhetoric of Holocaust deniers, some of whom I will discuss in chapter 4. True, he himself accepted the existence of the Holocaust. Yet his shunning of the newsreels as just hateful propaganda would please the David Irvings of today.

Obviously I'm turning from analysis to evaluation. Indeed, many rhetorical refusals are hard to discuss neutrally. Still, evaluating them may be a complex process, taking a number of things into account. The next chapter stresses this point, as it begins to consider how to assess Croce's article and other acts whereby people refuse to see what they criticize.

Categories and Criteria

A s I move more into a method of evaluating rhetorical refusals, I want to stress that none are utterly unique. They fall into types. Indeed, we can better evaluate an act like this if we compare it to other conceivable members of its specific category. Here, then, I proceed to suggest criteria for judging Arlene Croce's act by examining other instances when a writer or speaker resisted encountering an artwork but opined about it anyway. More precisely, I will first identify standards of evaluation we might apply to humorous refusals and to what I will call semi-blind ones. Then I will point out how various cases of critics' refusing to see what they criticize, including Croce's, compel us to take positions on recurring issues in philosophy: specifically, questions of epistemology and ontology. Next I will explain the special considerations that can arise for us when these refusals to see, as well as other rhetorical refusals, are evidently connected to larger causes, even bans and boycotts. I close the chapter by exploring a particular risk that rhetors court when they judge a work sight unseen: the danger of making false claims about its specific details. Throughout the chapter, I note that assessing rhetorical refusals often involves judging the rhetor's style, ethos, previous history, and negotiation of genre—factors that have long been important in rhetorical studies.

Humorous Refusals

So far, I've referred to rhetorical refusals as if they're basically serious in aim, meaning, and tone. Yet some of these refusals are obviously humorous, and others can be interpreted as such. Of course, humor can take any number of forms, from subtle flippancy to outrageous buffoonery. Whatever the case, how we judge a rhetorical refusal may depend on whether we deem it serious or playful. We're likelier to tolerate a ludic refusal and more apt to scrutinize one made in earnest.

Clearly playful is a text by Timothy Church, written for the on-line edition of *McSweeney's*. Both the print and Web versions of this magazine favor sophisticated wit. Church declares his intent to be humorous with his very title: "Actual Reviews Posted On Amazon.Com By Me, In Utter Slack-Jawed Ignorance Of The Books Involved, And With Grammatical Errors Intact." What follows are four book reviews that Church has, in fact, sent to Amazon. For example, he says of Scott Turow's *Personal Injuries* that this novel "is like going to Law School; it's in Chicago and it sucks." Church doesn't explicitly *refuse* to read the books he critiques, but he willfully resists perusing them, even though book reviews are supposed to be based on knowledge of the text. Therefore, his piece seems a rhetorical refusal—more specifically, a refusal to see what he criticizes.

As with other rhetorical refusals, Church's involves an appearance/reality dissociation related to procedure. In effect, he tells his *McSweeney's* readers that while they expect book reviews to be knowledgeable, the truth may be different; indeed, his own reviews are uninformed. Yet, Church's wit distinguishes his act from many others of this kind. Unlike Croce, he seeks laughs, a fact that may lead us to give him more latitude than we'd give her.

At the same time, comic needn't mean *merely* comic. Even from jocular rhetoric, people may draw implications for their lives. So, we might ask whether Church goes beyond sheer humor. Does he take the "argumentative high ground," Alan Gross's phrase for the work that dissociations perform? He doesn't seem morally superior to those who respect traditional reviewing practice. Perhaps he does achieve elevation, though, by alerting his readers to certain things. Through parody, he points out that crisp pro-or-con reviews pervade Amazon, and he encourages his audience to distrust such extremism. His satire also encourages doubt about Amazon reviewers' veracity, for they may be just as guilty of the "slack-jawed ignorance" he admits.

The pedagogical function of Church's humor can be described in other terms. As Chaim Perelman and Lucie Olbrechts-Tyteca might say, he prods his audience to judge other audiences. Obviously, to appreciate his piece, readers must find it funny, thereby separating themselves from anyone whom his ignorance chills. Simultaneously, Church invites his readers to distance themselves from a second group: those who rely on Amazon reviews. Significantly, Church's four reviews have won praise from visitors to Amazon's

Web site. Last time I checked, thirty-six out of thirty-eight had declared his account of Turow's book "helpful." Only readers of *McSweeney's*, we should note, have seen Church's confession. Unlike visitors to Amazon, they're in on the joke. By letting them know his ignorance, he coaches them to be doubters, skeptics toward Amazon reviews that seem well-informed.

Readers may disagree about what is funny and what is instructive. Some might be troubled that Church get laughs by deceiving visitors to Amazon. They might complain, too, that his reviews there mess with the reputations of authors. (Actually, he pans only Turow and Emily Brontë, both of whom still sell plenty of books). Whatever the qualms, the *McSweeney's* piece reminds us that when we assess rhetorical refusals, humor may be important to note. And humor that educates may win bonus points.

If humor appears in Croce's piece, it takes the form of scattershot sarcasm. Interestingly, she first designed her article for "Shouts & Murmurs," a page of the *New Yorker* geared to sly comedy. Subsequently, her argument grew more serious, and it wound up elsewhere in the magazine. Had "Discussing the Undiscussable" been thoroughly droll, would the response have been different? Even if we think this question unanswerable, we need to bear humor's impact in mind.

Semi-blindness

Both Church and Croce refrain from encountering the artworks they discuss. Other critics have written reviews that are willfully semi-blind. More precisely, they've blasted shows they left early. Indeed, they've told their readers about their premature exit, unashamed and maybe proud of it. In some ways, inevitably, their rhetoric of partial attendance differs from reviews based on sheer avoidance. Yet, by studying this semi-blind writing, we can develop ways of evaluating absolute refusals such as Croce's.

Consider a review by the late Dwight Macdonald, who in the 1960s wrote about films for *Esquire*. In his July 1965 column on the biblical epic *The Greatest Story Ever Told*, he candidly reports that he departed at intermission:

> For the finale of Part One, Handel's *Hallelujah Chorus* was belted out with such deafening *brio* that, what with Lazarus rising from the dead and the extras running around like grand-opera peasants telling each other, needlessly since we and they had seen it happen, "Lazarus has risen! He's *alive!*" and Ed Wynn recovering his sight (*I think*, but there was so much confusion) and tottering up to Herod's palace to shout

triumphantly up to the guards on the high Babylonian ramparts that Lazarus has risen . . . is *alive*, etc. I then decided I had spent a reasonable amount of time, two hours, on *The Greatest Story* and that after this the Crucifixion could only be an anticlimax. So I left. (435)

Macdonald uses several techniques to make his departure acceptable. Like Church, he resorts to humor. I still laugh when he follows "*alive*" with "etc." and when he fears that the Crucifixion would be anticlimactic. Also, to head off a charge of arrogance, he admits being hazy about the events on screen. Indeed, he strongly conveys his "confusion" with a sentence that is long, intricate, and breathless. It evokes a chaos that would repel other moviegoers besides himself. His brief sentence "So I left" then comes across as an understatement, diplomatically hinting at the consternation he felt.

Strategic use of ethos is, apparent, too, in Pauline Kael's 1983 *New Yorker* review of the film *Betrayal*. "I couldn't sit through it," she reports. "My body wouldn't let me." She explains that her physical distress began with the movie's onset, as a married couple bickered in their "hideously proper upper-middle-class house." She asserts, however, that she "stayed long enough to learn that the three characters are engaged in semi-parasitic cultural work . . . [s]o we know what [writer Harold] Pinter thinks of them right off the bat." Though admitting that "I deserted my post," Kael suggests she is writing the review only because regular readers of hers were wondering why it had yet to appear. Otherwise, her early exit from *Betrayal* would have kept her mute. In any case, she chiefly defends her leave-taking by portraying it as somatic revolt. To use the subtitle that the *New Yorker* gave Croce's piece, Kael depicts herself as "a critic at bay," though unlike Croce she has briefly subjected herself to the work she discusses. In fact, this wasn't the first time that Kael justified an early departure by announcing her frailty. She does the same thing in her 1977 *New Yorker* review of *Fellini's Casanova*. There, she reports that although she entered the theater "all primed for" Fellini's movie, "after an hour I staggered out."

As rhetors, Macdonald and Kael make arguments rather than just declare truths. Moreover, their claims are disputable. Others may think better of the works they dismiss. Evidently, the "quiet, attentive audience" surrounding Kael at *Betrayal* found it seductively enigmatic. Conscious of their enthrallment, Kael encourages her readers to disapprove of them. As with other rhetorical refusals, she invites her own audience to criticize this other. When Kael panned a film, often she mocked people at the screening who were more enthusiastic. In this case, probably she hoped that her readers would avoid *Betrayal* completely. Certainly she aimed to persuade them that she was right to abandon it. In an interview with Susan Goodman, however, Kael admitted that not everyone endorsed her leaving films partway through: "Damned if people didn't say I should go back and see the rest, as if it were a duty to be bored" (Goodman).

To claim that one is threatened by boredom is to ask for sympathy. Essentially, Kael makes this request within her two semi-blind reviews, when she remarks that the films were torment. In aiming for pathos, though, refusers like Kael actually have to navigate between two extremes. On the one hand, they need to avoid seeming consumed with self-pity. On the other hand, they need to avoid seeming arrogant, privileged enough to slough off duties that lesser mortals must face. Refusing to see what you criticize, then, also requires quite skillful management of ethos, a point that I'll return to in the next chapter when I discuss the image that Croce projects.

Whether a semi-blind review is accepted depends, in part, on the critic's power to harm. Often this power is a matter of venue. The *New York Times*'s film critics have influenced many a movie's commercial fate; hence, they're closely observed by media watchdogs. When Renata Adler left a screening of *The Sound of Music* before Maria's final climb, she received much flak, especially because her published review was negative. (Adler claimed she had left due to illness and said she wrote her review only after seeing the whole movie.) Most publications, though, lack the impact of the *Times*. Since *Esquire*'s influence is much less, Macdonald's treatment of *The Greatest Story* provoked no outcry. On the other hand, the *New Yorker* has long helped to shape high culture, with Kael affecting the reception of many art films. Therefore, it's not surprising that some readers balked at her Pinter and Fellini critiques.

Much depends, too, on the critic's track record. Reviewers known for their endurance may remain respected when they do leave productions now and then. As far as I know, only with his *Greatest Story* review did Macdonald ask readers to let him escape. The same goes for Kael, who seems to have deserted just *Betrayal* and *Casanova*. Hence, I'm inclined to take their exits as a legitimate form of commentary. Of course, other factors may lead me to criticize Macdonald's and Kael's departures. But I think better of semi-blind reviews that are rare.

There do exist critics who habitually leave theaters early. When I presented an earlier version of this chapter as a talk, an audience member told me, "You've got to deal with John Simon! He leaves plays early all the time!" She was exaggerating, but only some. In several of his drama reviews for *New York* magazine, Simon admits bolting before the evening's end. In his column of May 17, 1999, he reported leaving *two* contemporary plays. And that same year, he confessed to abandoning two different productions of Molière's *Tartuffe*. Of course, critics like him risk being called irresponsible, their often-early exits seen as habitual nastiness rather than principled judgment.

To summarize: Evaluating semi-blind writing means considering the critic's style, ethos, impact, history, and negotiation of genre. These features remain pertinent as we move from partial attendance to complete avoidance. But semi-blind reviews have another key element in common with stances such as Croce's. Both types of rhetorical refusals require their audiences to take stands on issues of epistemology (how we know) and ontology (the nature of what exists).

How We Know

Having seen part of the work under review, semi-blind critics presume they can judge the whole. Still, they may seek to demonstrate this ability, especially by predicting how the work turns out. When he reports leaving before the Crucifixion, Macdonald shows he knows *The Greatest Story*'s climax. Notwithstanding her limited exposure to *Betrayal*, Kael foretells how it ends. Because she "stayed long enough to learn" the main characters' jobs, and because she is familiar with Pinter's writing in general, she can guess what these people will do and how Pinter will view them.

Of course, readers may dispute these forecasts. They may find that Kael and Macdonald fail to anticipate key developments in the films they left. Still, critics who discuss works they have utterly shunned are in a tougher position. Not having seen the target of their scorn, they must show that they still know enough about it. They face a hard epistemic test.

Often, these critics try to pass it by claiming or implying they have good sources. In fact, some complain of being inundated with information. Croce submits that she is well-acquainted with *Still/Here* because "the publicity has been deafening" (54). The same argument is made by one of her supporters, Terry Teachout. Though he, too, avoided Jones's production, he feels able to join Croce in denouncing it because "its subject matter had been so heavily publicized in advance of the New York premiere as to make it a largely known quantity" (60). To be sure, such confidence may or may not be earned. As I will discuss in the next chapter, Croce's knowledge of *Still/Here* seems inadequate. She can be accused of ignorantly distorting the piece.

Nevertheless, in referring to publicity, Croce and Teachout point to a real phenomenon. Many works of culture today *are* relentlessly hyped, both through official advertising and infotainment reports. Hence, potential consumers of a work may easily feel they know it without really experiencing it. Probably all of us have endured so many previews of a certain film and so many interviews with its stars that we think we're experts on it without having seen it. My local newspaper's film critic, Eric Pfeffinger, wryly points out that because "we're living in an age of such pervasive infotainment, I'm not sure anyone actually needs to attend a movie anymore." He adds that "I've seen enough credit card and soft-drink tie-in commercials and post office ads that I'm convinced I actually saw *The Cat in the Hat*." He further spoofs this media overkill by proceeding to judge *The Last Samurai* without having watched it, relying on flackery about it circulated by such outlets as *Entertainment Weekly*. In addition, we may think we have learned enough about a work from reviews, especially when they're written more seriously than Pfeffinger's *Samurai* notice. And nowadays, reviews abound. In particular, the Web teems with professional and amateur criticism of films. Even if you're interested in *The Da Vinci Code*, why bother watching it when the Internet Movie Database provides many accounts of it? Needless to say, arguments for actually viewing the film can be made. But our media environment does encourage us to believe that we can judge some works of art with secondhand knowledge.

This belief seems to operate, for example, in a 1997 letter to the editor of the *San Francisco Chronicle*. The writer, Caroline Grannan, protests Anthony Minghella's film version of *The English Patient*, faulting it for departing from the novel. At the same time, she makes clear that she hasn't seen the film, nor does she intend to, "because I'm so troubled by what the reviews describe as the elevation of Laszlo de Almasy into a dashing sexual superman who happens to be a Nazi." Without having seen Minghella's film, Grannan feels able to declare its key moves. After all, she's read reviews. Moreover, they abounded, for this was a Hollywood epic based on a much-praised book.

Yet, when they describe a work they have avoided, writers risk charges of misrepresentation. Viewers of the work might note details at odds with the writer's account. For instance, in a subsequent letter to the *Chronicle*, Rob Blackwelder points out that the film's Almasy is not, as Grannan suggests, a Nazi, and that the character turns to the Germans in a last desperate effort to rescue his lover. As another viewer of the film, I find Blackwelder right. Nor does the film make Almasy into a "sexual superman." It depicts him as a manic, frustrated suitor doomed to a torturous death. In these respects, Grannan's shunning of the film leads her to distort it.

Furthermore, she seems naive about cinematic practice when she wants Almasy's affair rendered through monologue. In filming novels, most directors aim to visualize, if only to justify adapting the book for the screen. But, going further, we might argue that Grannan is inevitably unfair to Minghella's film because she hasn't experienced it as cinema. "Images are dense, iconic, visual symbols," observes W. J. T. Mitchell. "[T]hey convey nondiscursive, nonverbal information that is often quite ambiguous with regard to any statement" (127–28). Since Grannan refuses to confront the film's images—and, for that matter, its sounds–isn't she bound to reduce it to one or two messages supposedly conveyed by its plot? So we might claim. Film critic Roger Ebert might even accuse her of violating one of "Ebert's laws": "A movie is not what it is about, but about how it is about it" (*Ebert's* 59). To be sure, this argument leaves Grannan no chance to pass the epistemic test. If knowledge of a work depends on observing its distinctive form, then someone who avoids that work can never really "know" it.

Ontological Questions

In other words, the epistemic test may spark debate about a medium's very "nature" or "being." The domain of such disputes is traditionally referred to as *ontology*. I touched on the latter in chapter 1 when I mentioned definitional dissociations. Recall that this technique distinguishes between "real" and "apparent" forms of things. Though many people regard *Still/Here* as art, Croce denies it this status. She thereby makes an ontological claim, for she declares two orders of being and assigns Jones's piece to the lesser. A roughly similar claim gets made when critics of Grannan argue that reading reviews never substitutes for seeing the film itself. Grannan might respond that cinema isn't a fixed, pure medium; rather, it blends the arts in all sorts of ways. Or, granting it an essence, she might claim that reviews still capture most films' key traits. Other rebuttals by her are possible. So are other challenges to her stand. Here, I am not out to settle the conceivable controversy. I simply note its ontological frame.

Issues of ontology arise as well in the essay by Mitchell I have quoted. Mitchell criticizes New York mayor Rudolph Giuliani's effort to stop the Brooklyn Museum's 1999 show Sensation. When Giuliani announced his crusade at a press conference, he hadn't yet attended the show. In fact, it had yet to open. By demanding it be canceled, Giuliani made clear his wish to avoid it forever. In effect, he performed a rhetorical refusal. Recognizing this posture, Mitchell faults Giuliani for judging something the mayor refused to see. Specifically, Mitchell focuses on Giuliani's outrage at a certain entry in Sensation: Chris Ofili's collage The Holy Virgin Mary. The mayor was furious that Ofili's Mary is a black Madonna who is surrounded by magazine cutouts of vaginas and who sports real elephant dung on one breast. For Giuliani, Ofili's collage was blasphemy. In particular, he thought it mocked Catholicism. Mitchell, however, finds Giuliani irresponsible in at least two respects. First, the mayor ignored Ofili's declared intent. According to the artist, his use of dung honors Mary, for in Africa it traditionally symbolizes fertility and respect for Mother Earth. Second, Mitchell would have interpreters of the collage view the actual work. Again, he submits that images "convey nondiscursive, nonverbal information that is often quite ambiguous with regard to any statement." To Mitchell, the mayor violated this principle when he resisted seeing Ofili's creation. By blinding himself to Virgin, Giuliani disregarded its richness, thus permitting himself to call it an offensive speech act.

But is Mitchell correct that Giuliani "never saw" the piece (129)? An odd question, perhaps, but worth pursuing. Evidently, Giuliani's fury was sparked by the show's catalogue, where he would have seen Virgin reproduced. Probably Mitchell would think this encounter not the same as visiting the collage itself. Do works of art, in fact, have a nature that reproductions of them lack? Philosopher Noel Carroll observes that "if the Mona Lisa in the Louvre were shredded, we would lose da Vinci's masterpiece, despite the continued existence of all those museum postcards" (194). Even if Ofili is no Leonardo da Vinci, presumably Carroll would also distinguish his original Virgin from duplications of it. Indeed, philosopher Nelson Goodman calls paintings autographic, meaning that they're thought to be qualitatively different from copies made of them.[1]

New technology, however, adds a twist to this issue. In a famous essay, Walter Benjamin referred to "the age of mechanical reproduction," but it's become an age of electronic reproduction as well. Nowadays, we can easily make and circulate copies of artworks. The result is a growing flood of simulacra, which can easily lead people to condemn or praise art they have never directly beheld. For Giuliani, apparently, the catalogue's version of *Virgin* told him all he needed to know. True, had he visited Ofili's piece, he might still have found it profane. Nevertheless, Mitchell and others would argue the need for that visit. They might add that, because reproductions abound, we must attend more than ever to features of the real thing.

Larger Causes

So far, in discussing rhetorical refusals, I have focused more or less on the individuals performing them. But evaluation of such an act may go beyond the rhetor. It may involve judgment of a larger cause the person is deemed to represent.

Macdonald and Kael hardly ever reported and tried to justify early departures. Hence, we might assume their semi-blind commentaries reveal no pattern at all. Yet, if only in hindsight, these reviews do appear typical of their authors. Throughout their careers as film critics, Macdonald and Kael took particular approaches to culture. Both were known for criticizing middle-class philistinism. Well before his tenure at *Esquire*, Macdonald wrote a famous diatribe against what he called "midcult." It was a manifesto in his constant campaign against bourgeois love of uplifting platitudes. With his *Greatest Story* review, probably several readers saw him as continuing this struggle. Macdonald did use his *Esquire* column to champion various European art films, valuing their philosophical and technical complexity. On the other hand, Kael could bristle at cinematic versions of high art. Besides middle-brow films, she loathed allegedly sophisticated ones that struck her as pretentious.[2] Most likely much of her audience took her Pinter and Fellini reviews as salvos in her war against affectation. Admittedly, I'm conjecturing about first responses. Because many years have passed since Macdonald and Kael wrote these reviews, and because both critics have died, we may be more prone to situate these pieces in historical and biographical context. In any case, present judges of these reviews may easily wind up judging cultural stances they served to promote.

As I've already noted, such broader evaluation occurred with Croce's article. Many loved or hated it because they linked it to wider factionalism. Specifically, they saw it helping conservatives in the 1990s "culture wars." Of course, while the latter term is recent, struggles over culture are nothing new. Macdonald's and Kael's refusals indicate as much. In fact, many refusals to see what you criticize take a position on an entire movement, fashion, or discourse. The target is less the individual work than a trend it supposedly represents. Recall Agee's attack on *Oklahoma!*, *Othello*, and *Carmen Jones*. When he vilified these shows, he was engaged in a larger tirade against the decay of folk art. Furthermore, as Richard Porton notes, his rant grew out of his burgeoning skepticism toward the culture of the Popular Front (5).

Consider, too, the opening paragraph of a more recent article, one by Sam Tanenhaus that appeared in the *New York Press*:

> I've made what for me is a momentous decision, though it won't cause a tremor in the greater world. I've decided not to read David Laskin's new book, *Partisans: Marriage, Politics and Betrayal among the New York Intellectuals*. I will spare myself the latest gossip about Mary McCarthy's sex life, Diana Trilling's creative frustrations and what Sidney Hook may or may not have said to William Phillips at the time of the Moscow trials.

This opening implies that *Partisans* says nothing new about its subject. Thus, Tanenhaus can be seen as criticizing the book. Yet, already he indicates that his main target isn't Laskin's text. Rather, he targets the New York intellectuals themselves. Significantly, Tanenhaus's title is "The NY Intellectuals' Shabby Legacy." And, as he proceeds, he thoroughly denounces this group. To him, they "abhorred the common touch," "were hopelessly provincial," and launched "absurdly wrongheaded polemics." He sees them as contributing just the concept of "cultural politics," which for him amounts to "spouting half-baked opinions from the safety of endowed chairs and magazine editorships."

Given his contempt for these figures, Tanenhaus also scorns their apparent descendants. He climaxes his piece by mocking the New York intellectuals' "shabby heirs, the pundits, those facile scenarists whose ideas are mercifully detached from consequences." Moreover, he rebukes scholars who still write accounts of the group: "[H]aven't we heard enough by now?" Again, in this sense, Tanenhaus does indict Laskin. He will skip reading *Partisans* because he feels that it swells a "bibliography . . . [already] stupefyingly long."

Objections to this refusal might focus on Laskin's book, arguing that it offers more information or insights than Tanenhaus imagines. But critics of Tanenhaus are more apt to challenge his view of the New York intellectuals. Recall that Agee's article appeared in *Partisan Review*, the house organ of this group. Were he alive today, I suspect he would object to Tanenhaus's portrait of them. Similarly, Tanenhaus's supporters probably admire him most for attacking this coterie. Quite possibly, several responses to Tanenhaus would even ignore his slighting of Laskin, taking his judgment of Mary McCarthy and company to be the main issue at hand.

An analogous, if briefer, text is a letter to the editor that appeared in a 1995 issue of *Newsday*. The letter's writer, Zena Morris, was responding to an editorial prompted in part by the box office success of *Apollo 13*. Observing that the film had revived interest in human space flight, the editorial had called for a lean NASA budget, arguing that funds were better spent on earth-bound woes. Morris agrees with this position. But, as if to stress her disgust with NASA, she declares that she will avoid the film: "I refuse to see this Hollywood 'Apollo.'" With this rhetorical refusal, evidently she blames the movie for reinforcing a cultural enthusiasm she deplores.

As with Tanenhaus, objections to this refusal might entail defending the film. Ironically, the original editorial doesn't criticize *Apollo 13*. Rather, it identifies with the film's audience and honors the film's plot through a shrewd bit of allegorizing: "[T]he urge to reach for the stars that so many of us felt as we left the theater should be seen as a metaphor—and as a motivator—to get hold of the problems on Earth" ("At What Price?"). Conceivably, others would try to rebut Morris's implication that the film is propaganda for the space program, arguing that its portrait of NASA is more complex. Clearly, though, Morris is more disturbed by the film's subject than by the film itself. Like the editorial, her letter basically calls for diversion of NASA's funds. Both texts focus on an issue of social policy, notwithstanding the merits or faults of *Apollo 13*.

Bans and Boycotts

The larger cause that a rhetorical refusal promotes may actually amount to a ban or boycott, in which case an evaluator of the act faces an additional set of issues. Recall, for example, that Giuliani did more than object to Ofili's collage. He tried to stop the Brooklyn Museum from opening the show. He went so far as to threaten the museum, saying he would deny it the city's annual financial support if it mounted Sensation. This cut would have been roughly seven million dollars, or one-third of the museum's funds. When the museum resisted him, Giuliani even tried evicting it from its premises. Eventually, then, the central issue became constitutional. People debated whether Giuliani was violating the museum's First Amendment rights. Ultimately, a court found that he was, and the show survived. Whatever the outcome, Giuliani's criticism of *Virgin* was part of a legal war.

When rhetors refuse to see a work they criticize, usually they want others to avoid it as well. But many of these rhetors go further. Like Giuliani, they seek a ban or boycott. Blatantly they try to get the work plucked from the public. Of course, practically speaking, attempts at censorship may backfire. There are risks in seeking to eliminate a work that people might otherwise ignore. By making it salient, its would-be censors may spark curiosity about it. As art critic Dave Hickey observes:

> The raw investment of attention, positive or negative, qualifies certain works of art as "players" in the discourse. So, even though it may appear to you that nearly everyone hates Jeff Koons's work, the critical point is that people take the time and effort to hate it, publicly and at length, and this investment of attention effectively endows Koons's work with more importance than the work of those artists whose work we like, but not enough to get excited about. (111)

The logic that Hickey traces was borne out by Sensation's commercial success. Because New York's mayor invested much attention in the show, record numbers attended it. I'll return to this kind of effect in the next chapter. There, I consider that Croce's attack on *Still/Here* boosted its public importance, thereby ensuring packed houses for its later engagements.

Practicality aside, censorious refusals may involve deciding whether it is right for the target of their scorn to vanish. This issue may arise even when the refuser is hardly in a position to eradicate the work. Take a 1999 complaint against the posthumously released American version of Stanley Kubrick's film *Eyes Wide Shut*. Hollywood editors had altered Kubrick's print, using digital imagery to conceal a tableau of nude sex. Many film critics protested the tampering. In a phone message to the *Seattle Times* "Rant & Rave" column, an anonymous person called for a boycott (Jann). This proposal even frames criticism of the film: the complainer starts by seeking "a grassroots movement" and ends by asking "Who's with me?" Of course, the latter question is every rhetor's *cri de coeur*. Clearly, though, this person wants readers to *do* something, and together. Specifically, they're to shun the revision of Kubrick's film en masse. Thus, we would be denying the drift of this missive if we judged only its doctrine. It pushes us to evaluate, too, its call for collective avoidance.

Granted, the stakes with this "rant" aren't as high as they were with Giuliani's. The author of this message was unlikely to wreck the revised film's box office career. On the other hand, the mayor stood a good chance of getting Sensation shut down. Though eventually he was thwarted, he commanded plenty of resources, forcing the museum to deal with his threats. Meanwhile, these threats led a broader public to debate the merits of censorship, not just the merits of Giuliani's taste.

A refusal like his may serve various phases of a censorship movement. Not always does it function as an initial catalyst. Sometimes it sustains a campaign already underway. When it does, probably members of the public have already judged the larger movement. Hence, they're not likely to weigh the refusal in itself. To them, it has value insofar as it helps or hurts the bigger cause.

Rosa Eberly provides an example in her book *Citizen Critics: Literary Public Spheres* when she discusses the 1960s squabbles in Chicago over *Tropic of Cancer*. All sorts of civic forces strived to get Henry Miller's novel banned. They, too, finally lost in the courts, but until then—and even after—they waged mass protest against the book. Much of it took the form of letters to the city's newspapers. Eberly reprints one that I would call a refusal to see what you criticize. The writers are four students: one named Marie Chrupka and three others who refer to themselves as "The Class Presidents, Jones Commercial High School." In their letter, they bemoan the fact that Miller's novel circulates. More precisely, they criticize "the adult citizens of Chicago" for "making it available and accessible to youth," an act that reflects "complete disdain and contempt for the healthy minds for which they are directly responsible." They want the book's marketing to be regulated just as adults "regulate the sale of dope, intoxicating liquors and other poisons." As Eberly points out, the students dissociate themselves from censorship, saying "we must be extremely careful" about it (qtd. in Eberly 92). All the same, despite their anxiety about the word, censorship is what they essentially seek. Furthermore, their quest seems not to be based on actual inspection of the novel. As Eberly notes, they claim it is a book they must "be protected from" (92).

The students received varying responses to their letter's specific thrust. Even those who also wanted *Tropic of Cancer* banned didn't necessarily stress its harm to youth. Still, the students' writing was a foray within a larger war, and its readers saw it as such. Their attitude toward the letter reflected whatever feelings they themselves had toward the censorship campaign as a whole. Even now, though we can study the letter as a discrete text, it's notable chiefly as a contribution to a series of polemics against Miller's book. Furthermore, Eberly reports, "It is clear that the vast majority of those who wrote about the book had never read it—and had absolutely no intention of doing so" (99). Thus, we should go beyond the letter writers and evaluate the overall movement's refusal to see the novel it criticized.

Risks of Specificity

Large-scale attempts to eradicate pornography, blasphemy, violent images, or other alleged decadence have surfaced again and again. Moreover, usually the crusaders haven't pored over each artifact they would erase. In fact, many of these movements have been general in their targets, driven in the abstract to expunge rot. In 1994, for example, columnist Joan Beck tried to launch a boycott by exhorting her audience to "[r]efuse to watch violence on TV or pay for violence as entertainment in the movies or in music." However passionate her call, she didn't indict specific depictions of carnage. Often, opponents of would-be censors have been just as general. True, some might remind Beck of the violence in *Hamlet* or the gore in another masterpiece. Commonly, though, they appeal to broad principles, such as freedom of speech.

But the campaign in Chicago to ban Henry Miller's novel targeted a particular text. Indeed, plenty of censorship campaigns and boycotts have specified their quarries. In such cases, criticizing a work without thoroughly examining it is riskier. After all, other citizens may want to discuss certain features of it. And, when people seeking to ban the work are willfully ignorant about it, they may stumble when faced with counterarguments based on detailed knowledge of it.

Such dynamics were evident in the presidential campaign of Bob Dole. Repeatedly he denounced the movie industry for trying to "profit from the debasing of America" (qtd. in Claiborne). This phrase comes from his most-discussed speech on the subject, given May 31, 1995. In his address, Dole did more than scold Hollywood in general. He lambasted particular films, *Natural Born Killers* and *True Romance*, for wallowing in bloodshed. Interestingly, the speech received much criticism in the press. Several noted that a film Dole had praised, *True Lies*, was extremely violent, and that probably he touted this Arnold Schwarzenegger opus because its star was a GOP bigwig. But most of the criticism focused on Dole's not having seen the movies he scorned.

In my introduction, I quoted Ishmael Reed's outrage at this negligence. Film critic Roger Ebert was similarly exercised by it. Recall the "Ebert's law" I cited: "A movie is not what it is about but about how it is about it." During a presentation with his partner Gene Siskel at the National Press Club, Ebert brought up this principle to charge Dole with violating it. In particular, he was incensed at Dole's dismissal of *Natural Born Killers*, which Ebert claimed "actually attacks the glorification of violence in the media" (qtd. in Roger Simon). Dole's unfamiliarity with this movie was clearly on Ebert's mind when, in his regular newspaper column, he proclaimed that the candidate "will not get far . . . unless he sees the works he attacks. . . . To criticize a work of art on the basis of its subject matter, without considering style, treatment, purpose, or message, would get him failing marks in any freshman film class" ("Senator"). Perhaps Ebert and others would have disliked Dole's speech even if it had remained general. Yet I suspect their ire would have been less severe. At any rate, especially galling for them was his specification of targets, based as it was on hearsay.

I wouldn't call Dole's speech a rhetorical refusal. Yes, he condemned certain films sight unseen, and he implicitly encouraged his audience to shun them. But he didn't present himself as deliberately evading them. Nevertheless, the negative reaction he got holds a lesson for culture warriors bent on avoidance. Even more than Dole, they might be criticized if they ignore specific works named on their hit list.

Some rhetorical resources are available for justifying this stance. Throughout Dole's campaign, his press secretary resorted to a couple. Nelson Warfield argued that even though Dole hadn't seen the films he condemned, he'd consulted reviews of them. As I noted before, this sort of claim is epistemological and ontological. But Warfield went farther, asserting that "you don't have to look in every trash can to know there is garbage inside" (qtd. in Harden). This statement, too, raises the issue of how we know and define reality. It does so, though, by affirming a method of classifying. Because everyone agrees that *Natural Born Killers* is violent, clearly it's just a "trash can," and Dole needn't excavate its specific debris.

Of course, retorts to both of Warfield's arguments are possible. Earlier I referred to the claim that reviews provide only limited information and that reading them isn't the same as directly encountering their subjects. Similarly, the "trash can"/"garbage" assertion is debatable. In effect, Ebert challenges it by dissociating inside from outside. Considered from afar, his argument runs, the subject matter of *Natural Born Killers* makes it seem a mere "trash can." But if we really study its contents—exactly *how* it represents violence—we will find it filled with art, not "garbage." As Ebert would admit, many who did see the film liked it less than he. Yet they might still prefer his stand to Dole's. More precisely, they might take Ebert as inviting them to inspect the film themselves, whereas Dole assumes such probing is pointless. In other words, they might link Ebert with free inquiry, which is often invoked in protests against censorship. Indeed, several observers thought Dole a foe of independent thought. Though he didn't openly call for a ban, they took him to be inciting one.

Say Dole did want to prohibit some work he refused to see. At least two additional arguments would be available to him. Conceivably, they can also be used by more modest refusers—snubbers of the work who would let it exist. The first argument holds that exposure to the work is defiling. Merely to look at it harms the psyche. In one form, this argument is religious. Millions think Salman Rushdie's *The Satanic Verses* is satanic itself; they shun it because it pollutes the soul. In other circumstances, the argument is quasi-religious. Of Chicagoans who refused to read Miller's book, only some found it devilish. Most thought it human profanity while still declaring it taboo.

The second argument relates to a Western archetype: the false puritan. This figure may be fictional (for example, Shakespeare's Angelo) or real (for example, Jimmy Swaggart). Whatever the case, he or she is a hypocrite—outwardly pious, secretly impure. Had the enemies of Miller's novel pored through it, they might have been slapped with this image. Thus, the second argument. It holds that avoiding the work prevents charges of prurient interest. Recall, after all, the fate of Clinton prosecutor Kenneth Starr. For many, he undercut his puritan image when he stuffed his report with sexual testimonies. In the 1980s, the same thing befell the Meese Commission on Pornography when it wallowed in texts it called obscene. So, refusing to look at a work may be prudent. On occasion, it may seem the best stance to take.

How to Evaluate

Still, the specifics of the occasion should matter—not just to the rhetors involved but also to judges of their refusals. In this chapter, I've discussed several cases of people refusing to see what they criticize. How might we evaluate such rhetoric? With my examples, I have suggested that various factors may prove relevant, and to varying degrees. Obviously pertinent are features of the text, such as the ethos it evokes and the genre it seems to fit. In many cases, the rhetor's past conduct is also germane. So, too, perhaps, is his or her social leverage. Over whom does the rhetor have power, and to what effect? In addition, we may grapple with issues of epistemology and ontology. We may find ourselves assessing as well an entire social movement—some crusade that the rhetor promotes or rejects.

Of course, we'll consider audience. Useful to know, if possible, is the refusal's impact on its main readers or listeners. Yet, even if we discern their response, we needn't think as they. Whatever their view, we are free to decide the refusal's suitability for us. What constitutes suitability? Let's go beyond measuring skill. Even when a refusal is technically adroit, let's ponder its logic and ethics. Of course, such reflection might be hard, for it requires testing our standards and perhaps revising them.

This assessment is hardly aloof. It does attend to the refusal's worldly effects. Besides tracing them, it broods about them, seeking to determine whether and how they show the refusal's worth. In the next chapter, I demonstrate this process. There, I return to Arlene Croce, evaluating her refusal to see what she criticizes.

Now that I've identified various criteria for evaluating rhetorical refusals—especially refusals to see what one criticizes—I want to apply
these standards to a test case. Here, then, I focus very much on Arlene
Croce's willful avoidance of Bill Jones's *Still/Here*. In particular, I consider
this act's logic, ethics, and effects, features related to such discursive moves
as Croce's negotiation of genre and her projection of ethos. I will also show,
however, that to judge refusals like hers, we might compare them with other
acts—especially those advancing similar views while *not* defying audiences'
expectations. Furthermore, I will argue that assessing refusals like Croce's
involves evaluating motives and habits of their sponsoring institutions. In
this case, the vehicle was a magazine, the *New Yorker*, which was strongly
steered by its then-editor, Tina Brown.

But I must confess at the start of this chapter that, like Croce, I haven't
seen *Still/Here*. To be sure, I'm not thoroughly ignorant of what Jones's
piece looks like. I've viewed excerpts from it on videotape. Publicly available,
the tape is a 1997 PBS documentary entitled *Bill T. Jones—Still/Here with
Bill Moyers*. Although mostly the documentary shows scenes from Jones's
workshops with ill people, it also shows parts of his eventual production.
Even so, I haven't managed to view *Still/Here* as a whole. Jones has staged
it only in certain cities, each far from my home. In fact, many of Croce's
original readers had to judge her article without having seen the production yet, for it had just started to tour. And, now that Jones has "retired"
his piece, nobody can see it live. In addition, there's no complete public
record of it on film or videotape.

In the last chapter, I referred to an epistemic test. When people refuse
to see a work they criticize, usually they must still seem familiar with it.

Otherwise, their judgment may be doubted, and they may even be accused of distorting the work by those who have in fact seen it. Recall Caroline Grannan's attack on the film *The English Patient*. Without having watched it, she declares it makes Almasy "a dashing sexual superman" and "a Nazi." As a viewer of the film, I contend she gets it wrong. Her terms don't fit the Almasy I saw. To support her charge, she reports that she's read reviews. But in her case, they prove inadequate guides.

To weigh a refusal like Grannan's, must *we* have seen the work? More to the present point, must *we* have viewed *Still/Here* if we're to appraise Croce's stance toward it? Surely direct acquaintance helps. If we intimately know the refuser's object of scorn, we gauge better how fairly the refuser describes it. Still, we may be able to get by with less, especially if we're just seeking some evidence that the refuser doesn't know the work well. Like Grannan, we can consult reviews of the work, though respecting their limits. If we can see excerpts from the work, these may also help. In any case, we can appraise the refusal as rhetoric. As an attempt to persuade, it uses various strategies and makes various points, many of which we can judge. Such is my premise as I evaluate "Discussing the Undiscussable."

Evaluating "Discussing the Undiscussable"

Croce's article is interesting. Otherwise, I wouldn't ponder it so much in this book. Yet, the more I reflect on it, the more it disturbs me. I think Croce fails to justify her shunning of *Still/Here*. And, by avoiding it, she hurts her case against it. Simultaneously, she compromises her complaint against "victim art," the trend that *Still/Here* epitomizes for her. Overall, her article doesn't persuade me. Especially questionable are the ways she addresses matters of genre and ethos.

As I noted in the introduction, often we perceive a rhetorical refusal as violating a particular genre's norms. Hence, in evaluating the refusal, we decide the worth of this breach. Croce's handling of genre is especially provocative. In chapter 1, I pointed out that immediately she distinguishes "Discussing the Undiscussable" from dance reviews, the genre that has been her forte. She declares right away that she has "no plans to review" *Still/Here* (54), and a few sentences later, she emphasizes that she is "not reviewing" it. This dissociation, I noted, functions for her as an escape clause. It suggests that she needn't see Jones's piece. While reviews demand attendance, her article is supposedly another kind of prose.

Croce's ploy is, however, shaky. For many of us, her choice of genre doesn't matter. To write extensively about a work requires seeing it, whether or not the result is a review. For those of us with looser standards, Croce still undercuts her credibility because she is vague about the genre she *has* chosen. If her article isn't a review, then what is it? On this issue, she is suspiciously reticent. Her title isn't informative: what does a "discussion" entail? The body of her text also lacks clues. Croce does say that "I enter a plea for the critic" (55), yet "plea" seems at odds with her text's hostility. She's more on the offensive than the word suggests; rather than beseech, she attacks.

In *Writing in the Dark*, the later collection of her writings, Croce identifies her article differently. In her preface to the volume, she calls "Discussing the Undiscussable" a "screed" (8). This term was applied by one of her critics, Deborah Jowitt, when the article first appeared (67). Indeed, often this word isn't meant as a compliment. By the time the book appeared, however, Croce evidently thought "screed" a fair label. Yet her shift in terms suggests that the issue of her article's genre has continually vexed even her. At any rate, because the original article leaves its genre hazy—and because it includes the misleading word "plea"—Croce's dissociation from reviewing is suspect. As reader, I stick with my default premise. I'm inclined to regard her article as a review, which normally entails encountering her subject firsthand. Generally speaking, a rhetorical refusal's flouting of a genre should make clearer the alternative being embraced.

In part, I consider Croce's article a would-be review because, like most reviewers, she describes her subject. Although she hasn't seen *Still/Here*, she enumerates features of it, claiming a reviewer's familiarity with its sights and sounds:

> The cast members of "Still/Here"—the sick people whom Jones has signed up—have no choice other than to be sick. The fact that they aren't there in person does not mitigate the starkness of their condition. They are there on videotape . . . [as] prime exhibits of a director-choreographer who . . . thinks that victimhood in and of itself is sufficient to the creation of an art spectacle. (54)

Just from seeing the Moyers documentary, I find Croce's account misleading. The cast of *Still/Here* isn't limited to "the sick people whom Jones has signed up." Nor are these people Jones's "prime exhibits." Central to the production are his own dancers, who more than share the stage with the video screens where the workshop participants appear. Whether the tapes project "starkness" is, of course, open to interpretation. Reviewers may disagree about the mood. How, though, can Croce make claims about the tapes' function and effects? After all, she's failed to see *Still/Here* in the first place. By describing it, she exercises a reviewer's prerogative, even as she rejects a reviewer's usual duty.

In these circumstances, how does one establish rhetorical authority? Let's face it: most any rhetorical refusal requires shrewd deployment of ethos. The writer or speaker must labor to come across as entitled to defy protocol. This feat can be tricky, for it involves steering between arrogance and self-pity. Unfortunately, Croce drifts toward the latter.

Recall the subtitle to the essay: "A Critic at Bay." As this phrase implies, Croce seeks favor by presenting herself as besieged. "Victim art," she argues, leaves critics no meaningful role in culture. Like Othello's, her occupation is gone, ruined by Jones and his ilk. Actually, though, Croce's refusal is a reiteration of her long-established authority. She still wields considerable clout, remaining for many the preeminent dance critic of our age. Furthermore, the *New Yorker* was a conspicuous venue for her argument. Published there, her article was bound to be widely read. Indeed, the abiding stature of both her and the magazine made her piece noteworthy in the first place. Thus, her pose of vulnerability seems specious. People truly "at bay" don't have this public a voice.

A wounded tone is quite problematic when the rhetor seems bent on settling scores. Midway through her article, Croce recalls an experience with Jones that clearly rankles her still: "When I blasted an early work of his with the phrase 'fever swamps,' he retaliated by using the phrase as the title of a piece." For Croce, this behavior constituted "intimidation" (58). If anything, though, it seems mere impudence, and it hardly stopped her from criticizing Jones. By dwelling on this episode, she appears engaged in reprisal, not in the lofty pursuit of art. Her bruised ego seems to drive her present assault.

Her feeling of injury also leads Croce to contradict herself. While condemning "victim art," she more or less identifies herself as a victim of it. Thus, her own text seems part of the trend she decries. To be sure, she realizes the two can be linked: "[I] risk being taken for a victim myself" (55). Despite this admission, she proceeds to elaborate her impotence. Once again, she indicates, Jones is intimidating her. His current production disables her as a critic, for "I can't review someone I feel sorry for or hopeless about," and "with the righteous I cannot function at all" (55). She goes so far as to describe Jones with language usually applied to the AIDS virus, as if he himself were a lethally contagious mutation: "What Jones represents is . . . new and raw and deadly in its power over the human conscience" (55). Jones's physical condition aside, such wording seems a hyperbolic attempt to shift our sympathy from him to the author. That Jones is HIV-positive makes this attempt all the more noxious. Worse, Croce shows no self-consciousness about suggesting that *he* is a mortal threat to *her*. Right after acknowledging his condition, she proclaims that he endangers her, arguing that his "AIDS-focussed pieces . . . [revive] the permissive thinking of the sixties . . . and in the most pernicious form" (58). Surely the AIDS virus is more "pernicious" for Jones than *Still/Here* is for Croce! Her ethos seems tied to dubious ethics.

The most disturbing aspect of Croce's article is that it perpetuates a widespread tendency to generalize about people with AIDS without deigning to encounter their own testimonies. Their suffering has been exacerbated, in fact, by society's fear and loathing of them. Croce sustains this stigma. In shunning *Still/Here*, she upholds the invisibility imposed by our culture on stricken members of its population. Her rhetorical refusal fits the American tendency to discuss AIDS while ignoring its personal, human embodiment.

Croce's own willful ignorance is shown in her assumption that the people on *Still/Here*'s videotapes are doomed. In her second sentence, she calls them "terminally ill." In her first two paragraphs, she refers to them three times as "dying" (54). Yet several of these people may survive for years. As workshop participant Carol MacVey wrote in a subsequent letter to the *New Yorker*, "most of us are alive and still here." The piece's very title stresses endurance. By assuming these people's demise, Croce oversimplifies their experience, thus letting herself write them off.

Croce seems excessively reductionist, too, when she details the trend that she thinks *Still/Here* typifies. As I've noted, a key move in her article is her dissociation of genuine art from the meretricious "victim" sort. But arguments proceed through associations as well. To show that "victim art" exists as a broad cultural phenomenon, Croce squeezes under this rubric an inordinate variety of performers, creators, and productions. They include Jones, whom Croce explicitly identifies as a black gay man; Robert Mapplethorpe, a white gay man; the German New Wave choreographer Pina Bausch; dancers who present themselves as "dissed blacks, abused women, or disenfranchised homosexuals" (55); *Schindler's List* (60); and the NAMES quilt, which she refers to as "a pathetic lumping together" (60). Her own "lumping together" is not only extraordinarily eclectic but is also Archie Bunkeresque in its sweeping contempt for historically marginalized groups.

Mind you, I'm not faulting *all* rhetorical refusals. Inevitably, they vary in worth. Nor am I blasting the entire category that I've called refusing to see what one criticizes. Rather, my unease with Croce's text leads me to articulate standards of judgment. Many rhetorical refusals, I suspect, handle genre and ethos better.

Making Comparisons: Another Argument about Victims

Often we can evaluate a rhetorical refusal by comparing it with other texts on the same subject. Especially useful for this purpose is a more decorous text making similar claims. A good piece to compare with Croce's is "The Joys and Perils of Victimhood," a 1999 speech by Ian Buruma that appeared in the *New York Review of Books*. Buruma's text isn't a rhetorical refusal. Nowhere does he brazenly depart from procedural norms. But, like Croce, he regrets what he perceives as a new tendency to define oneself as victim. Increasingly, he thinks, people claim membership in a community of sufferers. Even if they are thriving more than its past members, they identify with these oppressed ancestors. Buruma worries that such affiliation distorts history. He fears that it is replacing patient and nuanced study of the past. "[W]hen a cultural, ethnic, religious, or national community bases its communal identity almost entirely on the sentimental solidarity of remembered victimhood," he argues, the result may be "historical myopia, and, in extreme circumstances, vendetta" (4).

To an extent, Buruma's concerns differ from Croce's. While she laments a trend in the arts, he criticizes a larger social development, which he sees taking multiple forms around the world. Still, their arguments largely accord. Both authors protest a burgeoning rhetoric of self-pity. For both, this discourse threatens a nobler endeavor. In Croce's view, it imperils true art; in Buruma's, real historical knowledge. Also, both authors object to an overall aesthetic they find becoming popular. Though Croce dwells more on this subject, Buruma touches on it, brooding in particular about the effects of Holocaust museums, memorials, TV shows, and films. Finally, Buruma joins Croce in faulting a range of historically marginalized groups. For example, he observes sarcastically that "the more emancipated women become, the more some extreme feminists begin to define themselves as hapless victims of men" (6). He is disturbed, too, that "[t]he idea of victimhood also haunts Hindu nationalists, Armenians, African-Americans, American Indians, Japanese-Americans, and homosexuals who have adopted AIDS as a badge of identity" (4).

Yet, Buruma's rhetoric is more persuasive than Croce's. Above all, he constructs a more admirable ethos. Whatever the excesses he finds in certain groups, he is also careful to register and praise their accomplishments. For example, he welcomes the progress that minorities have achieved: "It is surely good that nationalistic historical narratives have been discarded, that homosexuals can come out and join the mainstream, that women can take jobs hitherto reserved for men, that immigrants from all over the world enrich our cultures, and that we are no longer terrorized by religious or political dogma" (6). In addition, whatever his skepticism toward claims of victimhood, he carefully ponders what prompts them. For instance, he grants that associating oneself with oppressed ancestors "is especially appealing when few or indeed no other tags of communal identity remain, often precisely because of the survivors' desire to assimilate" (6). Moreover, he admits that on a visit to Auschwitz, he himself indulged in the sentiments that now trouble him: "I am not the child of Holocaust survivors. My mother was Jewish, but she lived in England, and no immediate relations were killed by the Nazis. And yet even I couldn't escape a momentary feeling of vicarious virtue, especially when I came across tourists from Germany. They were the villains, I the potential victim" (4). By implicating himself, Buruma avoids sounding arrogant. He attains, rather, a congenial air of modesty. By contrast, Croce scornfully keeps her distance from "victim artists." Repeatedly she declares they have alienated her. Indeed, she accuses Jones of personally affronting her. Thus, she exudes a self-pity that Buruma's essay lacks. Though Croce raises the possibility that she is playing victim herself, this prospect neither complicates her tirade nor softens its tone. Throughout, she depicts Jones and artists like him as betraying her aesthetic creed.

That Buruma doesn't perform a rhetorical refusal is significant as well. He spares himself an obligation that Croce incurs. Though she has to justify shunning *Still/Here*, he faces no such demand. Potentially, I think, Croce's stance is arguable. Another writer might have promoted it better. If some rhetorical refusals are lost causes, many may prove credible. As presented, however, Croce's refusal looks dubious. In the ways I have noted, she fails to make it acceptable. Meanwhile, Buruma's rhetoric is safer. It features no break with protocol that he must defend.

Instead, Buruma gains leverage by ruefully mentioning another rhetorical refusal. At the climax of his essay, he quotes with dismay the writer Edmund White, who in a piece for the *Nation* engaged in what I would call refusing to be criticized. Praising contemporary literature about AIDS, which includes his own works, White declares that "we will not permit our readers to evaluate us; we want them to toss and turn with us, drenched in our night sweats" (16). Of course, plenty of writers have groused about their past and prospective reviewers. Moreover, White's demand is unenforceable. Despite his edict, critiques of AIDS literature will appear. Nevertheless, it is strikingly rare for a writer to forbid assessment of his output. White's statement is a rhetorical refusal because it brazenly denies critics their usual role. Probably Croce would see it as proof that "victim artists" want to drive her out of business.

Yet Croce doesn't quote White as part of her argument. Rather, she must support the refusal she herself enacts. On the other hand, Buruma uses White to develop his case. The quotation helps him show that a new sense of victimhood threatens critical judgment. Indeed, White's statement seems a pledge of solipsism. Buruma looks more committed to open, reasoned inquiry than White does.

To be sure, Buruma is quoting selectively. Some readers may find White's statement more plausible in the context of his original piece. No doubt White would have enjoyed the chance to explain himself more to Buruma's audience. At any rate, Buruma's citing of White shows that, like all rhetoric, rhetorical refusals are subject to appropriation. Other rhetors may quote them for their own purposes. One task of rhetorical criticism, then, is to determine whether the quoter is fairly representing his or her source. Having read White's article, I think Buruma does convey its spirit. White's rejection of judgment is in keeping with the rest of his text, and his stand is no more or less palatable there. Thus, Buruma's quoting of White seems ethical. Needless to say, it's also a canny rhetorical move.

The Institution's Effort to Gain Attention

I've been arguing that Buruma is more prudent than Croce. He not only refrains from a rhetorical refusal but also criticizes someone else's. Yet Croce's article has been noticed much more than his. It has elicited vastly greater commentary and debate. One reason for this disparity is that the *New Yorker* has a much bigger circulation than does the *New York Review of Books*. Another factor is the two writers' different status. Though Buruma is a respected observer of international affairs, he doesn't loom in his field as much as Croce does in dance criticism. But it can be easily argued that Croce's piece also gained fame precisely because of her refusal. As Terry Teachout notes, probably she knew this move would produce "the maximum possible amount of journalistic noise" (60). Perhaps she even held the belief that Craig Seligman expresses in his analysis of another critic, Susan Sontag:

> You can't be a great critic—you can't even be an interesting critic—without a talent for provocation. . . . The aim is to make people think; the means is, much of the time, to make them mad. Judiciousness may be central to all criticism, but judiciousness without provocation of some sort is like nutrition without flavor. . . . Though angry responses to something you've written can be unpleasant, they're not nearly so demoralizing as *no* response. At least they're evidence—sometimes the only evidence—that the audience has listened. (95–96)

As things turned out, many did protest Croce's discussing a work she refused to see. Still, her boldness made her article hot, generating quite a bit of "buzz."

The latter term was a favorite of Croce's editor at the *New Yorker*, Tina Brown. In general, when we judge a rhetorical refusal, we'll do well to examine its institutional setting. In fact, most of these acts are worth analyzing as events within competitive media worlds. In Croce's case, her editor's love of "buzz" seems especially relevant. "Buzz" was what Brown very much wanted her magazine to spark, and Croce's refusal served Brown's dream, arousing interest in the *New Yorker* as a whole. Let's think about this larger context.[1]

Before assuming her position in 1992, Brown edited the fashion-oriented monthly *Vanity Fair*. In that role, she significantly increased readership, largely by turning her magazine into a dishy meditation on celebrity. Brown's manifest talent for producing "buzz" led to her post at the *New Yorker*. Its publisher hoped that her genius for publicity could reverse its decline in circulation. Veteran supporters and observers of the *New Yorker* shuddered at her hire. They worried that she would corrupt this legendarily classy periodical. No longer, they feared, would it be a polished, elegant, and intelligent arbiter of culture. After all, Brown had proven herself to be crassly pop. (Remember *Vanity Fair*'s cover photo of a naked, pregnant Demi Moore.) Thus, Brown now faced a potentially conflicting pair of challenges: she had to improve the *New Yorker*'s "buzz" while maintaining its sophistication.

Written soon after Brown's tenure began, Croce's article was a godsend. It defended high art, yet in startling fashion. By publishing it, Brown could be seen as upholding the magazine's commitment to taste, while at the same time she aroused public interest. Not that she relied on the article's content alone to get people talking about it. As she did regularly in her previous editorship, she waged a publicity campaign. One of her more devious strategies involved a section she added to the magazine. Whereas her predecessors hadn't published letters to the editor, she now did. Readers assumed that, as with most such columns, the correspondence in this one was unsolicited. Thus, it was interesting that Croce's piece garnered letters by major figures in the present culture wars, including Robert Brustein, Hilton Kramer, and Camille Paglia. With these voices weighing in, the "buzz" over Croce's article mounted. Actually, though, Brown had solicited their comments, a fact that only later emerged.

Probably Croce saw her article as more than a publicity gimmick. Most likely she was sincere in the beliefs she expressed. Even if, through her refusal, she was partly trying to gain notice, evidently she thought it proper to condemn *Still/Here* sight unseen. Besides, Brown would argue, seeking publicity is fine. "What's *buzz*," she has asked, "but another word, a pejorative, for discussion? . . . Do we really want a magazine that provokes no discussion?"(qtd. in Diamond 14). Rhetorical theory agrees that arguments must establish salience. They have to seem important or interesting enough to draw attention.

But an argument may rely too much on sensationalism. In particular, a rhetorical refusal is susceptible to this charge. It may be mostly a titillating scandal, whatever the rhetor's original intent. Such, I think, has been the fate of Croce's article. We can be more specific about the kind of "buzz" it created for the magazine. Its appeal, I would argue, reflects the new entertainment value of wounded wrath. Though Croce decried victim-centered media spectacles, her argument became one, much to the *New Yorker*'s profit.

It's useful, I think, to put this magazine's policies in historical perspective. Ironically, back in 1944, the *New Yorker* mocked another refusal to see. On that occasion, the satire was directed against James Agee's *Partisan Review* article "Pseudo-Folk." Recall that in his piece, Agee blasted *Oklahoma!*, *Carmen Jones*, and Margaret Webster's production of *Othello* while at the same time declaring his unwillingness to see them. The critical approach he took was noticed by the *New Yorker*'s "Talk of the Town" section. It poked fun at Agee by sardonically listing advantages that his stance gave him over normal reviewers. Among other things, the magazine noted, a critic like Agee is left with more time for composing reviews. Furthermore, he has a "mind uncluttered with detail." In addition, he's spared any physical discomfort involved in actually attending shows. For such reasons, the magazine pronounced "the Agee method" to be "a real honey" (11). The sarcasm is blunt. For the *New Yorker* of 1944, Agee's refusal was ridiculous, deserving merely a burst of contemptuous mirth. In contrast, the *New Yorker* of 1994 actually published Croce's refusal, implying that her revival of "the Agee method" deserved a serious hearing.

This change in attitude is significant. It reflects, I suspect, more than a change of editorships. Brown's contemporary success at creating "buzz" indicates that she grasped a shift in the zeitgeist. She could capitalize on Croce's refusal because she saw how it fit with a trend in popular culture. In the Brown era, which essentially remains our own, the *New Yorker* competed more than ever with other media outlets. At the same time, this competition involved their prizing much the same things. As we assess the institution behind a rhetorical refusal, we should identify what values the institution shares with its rivals. In this particular case, it's important for us to note how brash polemic is now a hot media commodity. It's the "real honey" of its day.

Possible examples of its popularity seem endless. For instance, the bestseller list regularly features the verbal combat of Ann Coulter, Michael Savage, and Sean Hannity. Meanwhile, plenty of television viewers relish the harangues of Bill O'Reilly, the *Real World* housemates, and the *Survivor* tribespeople, as well as the simmering tensions among Donald Trump and his would-be apprentices. As I write, a widely publicized feud rages between Trump and *The View*'s Rosie O'Donnell, boosting the ratings of both their shows. And each day, another ranting blog is born in cyberspace. Of course, consumers of this ire don't always agree with the views put forth. The bravura display of waspishness has grown popular in itself. My brother watches Fox News not because he shares its right-wing perspective but because he enjoys its pugnacity.

Much of this pervasive invective is tinged with personal grievance. Hence, in a way, Croce is right: cries of victimization abound. Still, her attack on leftist multicultural artists seems misdirected. If anything, the media resound with the howls of white conservatives, a company that Croce has apparently joined. If her rhetorical refusal was, in one respect, unorthodox, in another it matched dominant political discourse.

To be sure, dominant isn't the same as omnipotent, as the many protests against Croce's article show. Moreover, her attack on Jones's production boosted interest in it—an effect of her refusal that we should also bear in mind. In fact, *Still/Here* played to packed houses as its tour went on. Like Giuliani's war on the exhibition Sensation, Croce's effort to shrink Jones's audience made his production a commercial success. Recall Dave Hickey's remark that "the raw investment of attention, positive or negative, qualifies certain works of art as 'players' in the discourse" (111). Though Croce's article generated "buzz," it could do so only by conferring importance on Jones's piece as well.

So, did Croce actually do Jones much good? Well, this would be too simple a conclusion. Yes, she helped his box office, but he and his production became perpetually linked with her. Once her article appeared, even people who saw and liked *Still/Here* were measuring it against her depiction of it. Here, too, her magazine's competitors proved important: after the *New Yorker* published her piece, most every account of *Still/Here* mentioned Croce, most often in the first few paragraphs. Furthermore, any interview with Jones asked for his response to her. Though clearly he didn't agree with her, usually his comments about her were spare, as if he chafed at being constantly associated with her. Eventually, at a national conference of dance critics, he expressed full-blown anguish and rage over her treatment of him. From his point of view, her article was a curse, not a blessing.[2] But even if Jones had been able to take it in stride, he still would have had to address Croce's argument repeatedly. Though she made *Still/ Here* a "'player' in the discourse," nonetheless she shaped that discourse, in the sense that her condemnation of the work figured prominently in the media's subsequent discussions of it.

I may seem to have strayed from judging Croce's act in itself. But for rhetorical critics, the phrase "in itself" is questionable. Traditionally, we study attempts to influence audiences, so that separating "text" from "context" grows hard. Analyzing and assessing Croce's refusal, I've suggested, means considering the *New Yorker* as an institution. It also involves recognizing common topics of the media in general. In her case, particularly relevant is the media's focus on argument as spectacle. That her refusal sustains this emphasis is cause for concern.

When rhetorical criticism becomes cultural criticism, it hardly gets easier. Countering the media's commodification of polemic is especially difficult. Part of the challenge lies in imagining alternatives that aren't simply utopian. Several proposals call for replacing our "argument culture" (Tannen) with utter diplomacy, but some differences will inevitably lead to passionate debate. Nor is disputation inherently evil. Perhaps I would have appreciated Croce's argument had she been more cautious in pitying herself, in criticizing various groups, and in describing a production she had avoided. At any rate, the task is to distinguish between arguments worth mulling over and those that are inhumane engines of "buzz." Deciding which rhetoric is legitimate and which meretricious is, to be sure, a centuries-old project. But today's media make it urgent as ever, and refusals such as Croce's demand this scrutiny.

Her act has particular implications for the emerging academic field known as visual culture studies. Like any new field, this one teems with debates about its very definition. What should "visual culture" mean in the first place? The most productive answer, I think, is provided by Marita Sturken and Lisa Cartwright with the title of their textbook *Practices of Looking: An Introduction to Visual Culture*. Along with other charter members of the field, such as Mieke Bal and W. J. T. Mitchell, these theorists call for focusing on the processes through which individuals and institutions find certain phenomena worth seeing. I suspect these theorists would agree with Kenneth Burke's famous rhetorical dictum that "a way of seeing is also a way of not seeing" (*Permanence* 49). Hence, besides analyzing a gaze, they would ponder whatever limits accompany it. Bal reminds us that "far from being a feature of the object seen, visibility is also a practice, even a strategy, of selection that determines what other aspects or even objects remain invisible." Furthermore, she notes, "In a culture where experts have high status and influence, expert knowledge thus not only enhances and preserves its objects, it also censors them" (11). Croce's refusal to see *Still/Here* is a case in point. Although she can't actually censor the production, her attitude toward it is censorious. Besides rendering Jones's dance invisible to herself, she encourages other people to avoid it, and she mocks those who've already watched it. In the main, she aims to get *Still/Here* dismissed as mere "victim art." Indeed, if a way of seeing is also a way of not seeing, Croce's rhetoric shows that the reverse is true, too. Her way of not seeing is also a way of seeing, for her shunning of *Still/Here* is based on her classifying it as dross. As I've noted, her rhetoric drew attention to her own article. Therefore, a way of not seeing can be a way of getting seen oneself! All these principles at work in Croce's refusal seem pertinent to studies of "visual culture," especially if the term includes practices of disregard.

Although I've criticized Croce's move, I want to reiterate that not all rhetorical refusals are bad. Probably quite a few deserve praise. Clearly, though, we need to develop criteria for evaluation. In the previous chapter, I pointed out standards conceivably applicable to some cases resembling Croce's. Here, in assessing Croce's avoidance of *Still/Here*, I've focused on criteria that I realize are relevant to many sorts of rhetorical behavior. For example, I've called for us to gauge how accurately and fairly the rhetor treats whatever he or she criticizes. I've also suggested that we ponder how well the rhetor generally addresses issues of genre and ethos. With behavior such as Croce's—that is, with refusals to see what one criticizes—let's ask whether the rhetor is justified in ignoring typical features of a review. Let's wonder, too, whether the rhetor presumes knowledge that he or she actually lacks. With all rhetorical refusals, a good thing to weigh is their invocation of higher values. Is the refuser being principled or merely self-indulgent in defying the audience's norms? As I've suggested, the same question can be applied to the refuser's institutional backers.

PART TWO

Rhetorical Refusals and American Traditions

4 AGENTS, "TRUTH," AND SALIENCE

I concluded the last chapter by situating Arlene Croce's article within a larger media climate. More generally, I stressed the importance of attending to a rhetorical refusal's social context. I maintain this emphasis in part 2. Each of its chapters deals with a certain American ideal or tradition that rhetorical refusals can put into question, a possibility I demonstrate through one or more case studies. At the same time, each of these chapters continues developing a means of analyzing and evaluating *any* rhetorical refusal. For instance, in the present chapter I will suggest that our thinking about any such act can be aided by our considering (1) which element(s) of Kenneth Burke's pentad from his *Grammar of Motives* the refuser emphasizes; (2) the refuser's stance on the possibility and nature of "truth"; and (3) the salience that the refusal gives various parties.

The American principle on which this chapter focuses is openness to debate. Like the other political concepts I will go on to discuss, this one isn't voiced just by Americans, and the country's history includes several occasions when citizens have conspicuously ignored it. Nevertheless, free exchange of ideas is a central value of American ideology. In particular, as I noted when I discussed Maxine Hairston, many quarters of American higher education profess to worship debate. In the words of historian Deborah Lipstadt, they pledge "absolute commitment to the liberal idea of dialogue" (*Denying* 25). Though Lipstadt doesn't name any foundational texts for this tenet, one likely source of it is John Stuart Mill's *On Liberty*. In his manifesto, Mill stressed the value of testing our notions through free discussion with those who challenge them. When we have to deal with counterarguments, he thought, we develop a keener, livelier sense of the truth.

Mill was willing to leave some notions uncontested. He observed, for example, that "on a subject like mathematics . . . [there] is nothing at all to be said on the wrong side of the question" (98). Were he alive after Auschwitz, would he say the same about the claim that the Holocaust never occurred? Perhaps he would, in fact, endorse conversation with Holocaust deniers. At any rate, as Lipstadt has pointed out, many American colleges have provided these people a forum, believing it good for students to encounter their views. Lipstadt, though, feels differently. In this chapter, I examine the rhetorical refusal she performs when she spurns "dialogue" with deniers of the Shoah.

Lipstadt makes her position toward them clear in the following passage, which appears right on page 1 of her 1993 book *Denying the Holocaust: The Growing Assault on Truth and Memory*:[1]

> The producer was incredulous. She found it hard to believe that I was turning down an opportunity to appear on her nationally televised show: "But you are writing a book on this topic. It will be great publicity." I explained repeatedly that I would not participate in a debate with a Holocaust denier. The existence of the Holocaust was not a matter of debate. I would analyze and illustrate who they were and what they tried to do, but I would not appear with them. (To do so would give them a legitimacy and a stature they in no way deserve. It would elevate their antisemitic ideology—which is what Holocaust denial is—to the level of responsible historiography—which it is not.)

In recalling what she said to the television producer, Lipstadt gives the same message to her readers. She is announcing to them, too, that she won't debate Holocaust deniers. Moreover, besides applying this policy to talk shows, she won't tangle with deniers on campus. Again, this stance markedly violates the academy's codes. Officially, colleges prize exchange. Most scholars feel obliged to address, even court, interlocutors, including potential critics. Faculty who shirk this duty risk being called parochial or dogmatic. Yet Lipstadt takes the risk, and by rejecting debate at her book's very start, she makes her position emphatic.

To get a better sense of her daring, we might look at the following passage. I can imagine many people applauding its sentiments, which seem quite opposed to Lipstadt's. Moreover, the passage appeared in *Parade*, one of America's most popular magazines. Lending the passage further stature is the renown of its author, Elie Wiesel, one of the world's best-known and most-admired Holocaust survivors. Wiesel writes: "My experience is that the fanatic hides from true debate. The concept of dialogue is alien to him. He is afraid of pluralism and diversity; he abhors learning. He knows how to speak in monologues only, so debate is superfluous to him." The statement suggests that to eschew debate is to betray core values of the intellectual life: "dialogue," "pluralism," "diversity," "learning." Moreover, since he was addressing a broad public, probably Wiesel assumed most Americans share these values. Although Wiesel couldn't have Lipstadt in mind when he wrote—his article appeared a year before her book—he can be seen as condemning avoidance of Holocaust deniers. In fact, the passage from him now appears on a Web site about Lipstadt (*Lipstadt Trial Index*). In effect, the site praises Wiesel for being more open-minded than she. Unlike Lipstadt, the site implies, Wiesel would talk with those who label the Shoah a hoax.

But we should question the site's appropriation of Wiesel. After all, the site's operator is David Irving, whom Lipstadt has labeled a denier himself. He's one of the people she has refused to debate. Therefore, Irving considers Lipstadt his enemy. Affronted by her book, he sued her for libel in the British courts once it appeared in England. His bitterness toward her remained when he lost his case. Overall, Irving has a vested interest in tarnishing Lipstadt's reputation. He's anything but objective when he pits Wiesel against her.

Indeed, Wiesel is more apt to be Lipstadt's ally than Irving's. Having suffered through the Holocaust, Wiesel knows it happened. Would he even be willing to *argue* with Irving, a man who assaults Wiesel's sense of history? Actually, if we look at Wiesel's original article, we see that Irving has quoted him out of context. So have I, to show how selective Irving is. In Irving's case, citation amounts to distortion. To determine what Wiesel means with his statement, we need to observe what Wiesel says just prior to it. In his article, Wiesel has just been discussing how to deal with a fanatic. More precisely, he has declared that he will fight such a person. Now, he asks, "Does that mean I want to debate with him?" Clearly Wiesel is posing a rhetorical question. His implicit answer to it is no. What follows is the passage that Irving and I have quoted, but it isn't a call for debate. Rather, Wiesel is defending his decision *not* to debate with fanatics. When he says, "My experience is that the fanatic hides from true debate," he's claiming that such a person isn't worth arguing with. Note that Wiesel refers to "true debate." The opposite, he implies, is false or useless debate, and he accuses the fanatic of preferring this. More precisely, he thinks the fanatic ultradogmatic, thoroughly uninterested in "dialogue," bent on simply expounding pre-established views. Most likely Wiesel would put Irving in this category.

Certainly Lipstadt does. To her, Irving and other Holocaust deniers are merely anti-Semites with no respect for historical evidence or for scholarly reasoning. She thinks them incapable of "true debate" because they're indifferent to truth. And Irving's selective use of Wiesel seems to bear her out. Moreover, during the libel case, her legal team found numerous examples of Irving's willful misuse of documents. Time and again, he has distorted records.[2] Repeatedly, the ways that he's quoted and interpreted them have ignored or reversed their drift. His editing of Wiesel seems more mischief.

In my last chapter, I pondered at length how to evaluate Croce's rhetorical refusal. In this chapter, I admit straight out that I welcome Lipstadt's. And, as I proceed, I will try to justify it. But I will use this chapter mostly to examine Lipstadt's specific assumptions as part of my continuing effort to identify the sorts of premises that rhetorical refusals may entail. First, so that we don't make the mistake of thinking her refusal utterly unique, I will draw some historical parallels with it. Then, showing how Burke's pentad applies to rhetorical refusals, I will turn to Lipstadt's categorizing. I will discuss in particular how she bases her refusal to talk with deniers on a belief that they constitute an identifiable species. She thereby emphasizes, I will argue, Burke's "agent" slot, putting deniers into it. In the next section, I will trace the philosophical position Lipstadt takes with her concept of "truth," a term that can figure explicitly or implicitly in various rhetorical refusals. In the section after that, I will address issues of salience that can arise with many such refusals. Specifically, I will deal with the question of whether Lipstadt gives deniers too much publicity by discussing them at all. In a coda, I will turn to the classroom, using a personal teaching anecdote to consider premises that might guide faculty facing Holocaust denial there.

At various moments, I will refer to Irving's libel case against Lipstadt. Not that I will try to convey all its complexities. So plentiful were these that the verdict was decided by the judge, not a jury. Subsequently, the trial's details have occupied entire books, including one by Lipstadt herself. But I want to bring up the case somewhat, for a couple of reasons. In its own way, it suggests potential consequences of a rhetorical refusal. Although Lipstadt's

Denying the Holocaust spends only a few pages on Irving, he was angered by her branding him a distorter of history as well as by her unwillingness to debate him. In 1994, his ire led him to confront her during a speech she gave, and he even seized control of the discussion afterward. Admittedly, her snub of deniers wasn't the only reason he sued her. In 1996, she enraged him again when she and others called for St. Martin's Press to drop its plans for an American edition of his Goebbels biography. Still, her refusal was a big step in the path they both took to a London courtroom. Moreover, her refusal is itself illuminated by arguments made there. Especially significant were the debates in court about Irving's character, for these showed the importance of how Lipstadt conceived "deniers" as a group.

Lipstadt's Refusal in Historical Context

Even outside of political elections, rhetors other than Lipstadt have snubbed their opponents. I've already discussed Hairston's indifference to her critics. Repeatedly, you'll recall, she brushed them off by declaring that arguing with them would be pointless. But the evasion practiced by some other scholars has taken different forms.

One is a refusal to elaborate a foe's argument. An example appears in Janice Raymond's 1993 book *Women as Wombs: Reproductive Technologies and the Battle over Women's Freedom.* Throughout her book, Raymond is concerned with women who struggle to get pregnant. Relentlessly, she criticizes how various groups, including feminists, pressure them to invest in surrogacy or the latest clinical treatments. In her introduction, Raymond admits that

> [t]his book is a challenge to reproductive liberalism, including its feminist variety. It is positioned against the liberal consumer movement that supports new reproductive technologies and contracts. It is not a balanced approach to both sides of the issue, nor does it provide the supporters of these technologies equal time. Their position is dominant, well known, and widely publicized. . . . Radical feminist work on the new reproductive technologies has effectively been censored in the mainstream media and the mainstream feminist press. This book gives voice to these censored protests. (xii)

Many books on controversial topics don't thoroughly treat every side of them. As Raymond points out, several works on her subject emphasize a more positive view. Thus, perhaps they should practice her own truth-in-labeling. Right now, though, her blatant rejection of balance is unusual. Yet it reminds us that Lipstadt's refusal has counterparts in academe.

Also, some writers from the academy have resembled Lipstadt in proclaiming that certain subjects don't have multiple sides in the first place. In her 1996 book *Fatal Advice*, scholar and gay rights activist Cindy Patton objects to homosexuality's being presented as "an issue over which mutually loving family members can disagree" (169). Specifically, she is referring to the media's depiction of the troubled relationship between right-wing politician Newt Gingrich and his lesbian half-sister, Candace. By taking the latter for a spokeswoman, Patton argues, the Human Rights Campaign Fund sustains public interest in the Gingrich family drama. Patton would dissociate the topic of homosexuality from such quarrels. To her, everyone's sexual orientation should be unequivocally respected. "Some things are not debatable," she adds, "and to treat them as an 'issue' is to lay the ground for your own defeat" (169). It's with a similar view that Lipstadt refuses to debate whether the Holocaust took place.

Patton supports her stance by citing Frederick Douglass, recalling his "notorious refusal to debate the issue of slavery in his efforts at abolition" (169). Though she doesn't mention specific words of his, Patton could have quoted Douglass's famous 1852 Fourth of July address:

> [W]here all is plain there is nothing to be argued. What point in the anti-slavery creed would you have me argue? On what branch of the subject do the people of this country need light? Must I undertake to prove that the slave is a man? That point is conceded already. Nobody doubts it . . . .
>
> Would you have me argue that man is entitled to liberty? That he is the rightful owner of his own body? You have already declared it. Must I argue the wrongfulness of slavery? Is that a question for Republicans? Is it to be settled by the rules of logic and argumentation, as a matter beset with great difficulty, involving a doubtful application of the principle of justice, hard to be understood? How should I look to-day, in the presence of Americans, dividing, and subdividing a discourse, to show that men have a natural right to freedom? speaking of it relatively, and positively, negatively, and affirmatively. To do so, would be to make myself ridiculous, and to offer an insult to your understanding. ("Meaning" 190–91)

Douglass's references to division and subdivision show his familiarity with classic means of persuasion. He was, after all, a master speaker, well-versed in the precepts of *The Columbian Orator*. On this occasion and others, though, he scorned demands to elaborate a case against slavery. In his view, it was an indisputable evil. Of course, we can describe him as making arguments against it anyway, even in this Fourth of July address. In the passage I've quoted, he does give reasons for claiming that slavery is patently bad. Still, to call something a non-issue is a distinct rhetorical move, and Douglass's anticipates Lipstadt's notable refusal to put the Holocaust in doubt.

Lipstadt herself finds precedent for her stand in a remark made during the Vietnam War by the well-known intellectual Noam Chomsky. In his book *American Power and the New Mandarins*, she recalls, Chomsky depicted America's military involvement as unquestionably wrong. In the spirit of Douglass, he declared that "by accepting the presumption of legitimacy of debate on certain issues, one has already lost one's own humanity" (qtd. in Lipstadt 16). Yet, as Lipstadt points out, Chomsky has encouraged debates about the Holocaust's existence by writing the preface for one of Robert Faurisson's books. Faurisson is France's most prominent denier. Though not agreeing with all of Faurisson's arguments, Chomsky supported their airing. Lipstadt, however, thinks Chomsky had it right the first time. In her view, he loses his humanity when he makes the Shoah's reality contestable.

Of course, scholars sure of its existence may feel obligated to debate deniers, believing they're a danger that must be directly addressed. Michael Shermer, who has co-written an indictment of them called *Denying History: Who Says the Holocaust Never Happened and Why Do They Say It?*, argued with some deniers on *Donahue* (Shermer and Grobman 109–14). But other academics have, like Lipstadt, conspicuously avoided talking with them. For example, historian and Holocaust survivor Saul Friedlander did so at a conference on the Final Solution. In the question-and-answer period following his presentation, Friedlander notably ignored the raised hand of audience member Arthur Butz, whose book *The Hoax of the Twentieth Century* is a bible for the denial movement. In one sense, Friedlander's neglect of Butz wasn't an act of rhetoric. The slight was silent, not verbal. But surely it was deliberate. Berel Lang, on whose eyewitness report I'm relying, saw Friedlander as "consciously overriding the academy's commitment to open discussion" (312). Moreover, surely much of the audience perceived Friedlander as shunning Butz. He was clearly signaling that a denier's views didn't merit regard.[3]

French scholar Pierre Vidal-Naquet has taken a similar, if more articulated, position toward Holocaust deniers, including his own country's Robert Faurisson. Vidal-Naquet has become celebrated for exposing the ruses of Faurisson and his followers. At the same time, he has maintained that his campaign against deniers isn't the same as debate. Vidal-Naquet concludes his preface to his 1992 book *Assassins of Memory: Essays on the Denial of the Holocaust* by asserting that

> one can and should enter into discussion *concerning* the "revisionists"; one can analyze their texts as one might the anatomy of a lie; one can and should analyze their place in the configuration of ideologies, raise the question of why and in what manner they surfaced. But one should not enter into debate *with* the "revisionists." It is of no concern to me whether the "revisionists" are neo-Nazi or extreme left-wing in their politics: whether they are characterized psychologically as perfidious, perverse, paranoid, or quite simply idiotic. I have nothing to reply to them and will not do so. Such is the price to be paid for intellectual coherence. (xxiv–xxv, emphasis in original)

In *Denying the Holocaust*, Lipstadt registers somewhat different sentiments. She does care about the political background and psyches of the people she targets. Specifically, she aims to show that many are anti-Semites with ties to neo-Nazi or kindred organizations. But she and Vidal-Naquet are similar in refusing to debate them. Indeed, both authors declare this refusal in their opening pages.

Yet Vidal-Naquet expresses his refusal to debate in just one sentence at the end of his introduction. Lipstadt, on the other hand, elaborates her refusal, and she does so at her book's very start. For the paperback edition, she even added a preface reiterating her stand against debating deniers. There, she acknowledges pressures to "reconsider this policy," including an ad in which deniers themselves call her an "intellectual fascist" (xiii). But she continues to refuse direct encounter with such people, despite higher education's emphasis on debate. Indeed, by stating her refusal markedly, she prods her readers to rethink this norm. She tries to persuade them that, in the case of deniers, it should not apply.

The Term "Deniers"

Burke first proposed his pentad as a grid for analyzing various philosophies, but it can help us grasp the dynamics of rhetorical refusals, too.

The elements of the pentad are act, agent, agency, scene, and purpose. Let's imagine that Lipstadt is applying the pentad to the phenomenon of Holocaust denial. As she argues for not debating those who challenge the Shoah's reality, Lipstadt seems to attach greatest importance to the agent. I say this because her arguments rely so heavily on the term "deniers," as if she seeks to justify her refusal chiefly by describing the *people* making the claims she abhors. Of course, by underscoring the element of agent, Lipstadt obligates herself to address certain questions. What exactly do "deniers" deny? Why should we call them "deniers" rather than use one of their own favorite labels? What are the effects when we refer to "deniers" rather than to acts of "denial"? All of these issues figure in Lipstadt's declared avoidance of debate.

In her book, as well as in later documents prepared for the Irving trial, Lipstadt defines deniers as people who regularly distort history in specific ways. According to her, they typically make the following claims: that the number of Jews who perished under the Nazis fell well short of six million; that most of them died from disease or even from Allied bombings; that the Nazis never gassed Jews at Auschwitz or committed other mass exterminations; that many of the Jews supposedly dead are living secretly in Israel and elsewhere; that Hitler's policies were reasonable responses to the threat of Bolshevism; that, in fact, much of Germany's behavior was normal for war; that the Allies were at least as brutal as their enemies; and that basically "the Holocaust" is a Zionist fiction, concocted to gain reparations for Jews and moral support for the Jewish state. To a certain extent, she admits, deniers vary in their misrepresentations, but she sees most of them as spinning these particular tales.

As they propound their claims, Lipstadt argues, deniers also flout scholarly methodology. They prize the slightest detail that makes the Nazis seem civilized, declaring it clear and significant evidence. Yet, upon those who accept the Holocaust as fact, they place an impossible burden of proof. They demand, for example, that Auschwitz's mass gassings be verified by reports from the victims. Meanwhile, deniers willfully misconstrue, or try to discredit, witnesses and records that belie their views. In general, Lipstadt charges deniers with merely simulating a spirit of inquiry. For her, they're actually guilty of a dogmatic prejudice, a fierce close-mindedness, antithetical to academic life. To be sure, Lipstadt's analysis of them isn't idiosyncratic. Many scholars define and regard deniers as she does. Similar notions of them are maintained by nations that have made Holocaust denial a crime (for example, Austria, Canada, France, and Germany). Most important for Lipstadt, her thinking was eventually shared by Charles Gray, the judge in the Irving trial. Furthermore, like her, he wound up applying the term "denier" to Irving.

Lipstadt knows that the people she calls deniers prefer other names. As she points out in her book's first chapter, many of them want to be called "revisionists." This term sounds less inflammatory, more redolent of academic work. After all, often professional historians contribute to their discipline by revising predecessors' analyses. Actually, as Lipstadt notes, "revisionist" has been a name for two specific schools of historical thought. One held that Germany was blamed excessively for World War I, while the other looked askance at America's behavior in the Cold War. Lipstadt observes that whatever we think of these schools, both of them undertook genuine scholarship. But, she argues, the denial movement pursues no such thing. Similarly, though historians challenge one another's interpretations, deniers reject basic, well-documented facts. Their use of the term "revisionist," then, is for Lipstadt "a tactical attempt to acquire an intellectual credibility that would otherwise elude them" (20).

Of course, her calling them deniers is tactical on her part. Not only does this label ignore their pose as serious historians; it also implies that they aim to wipe out proven events. On numerous occasions, Lipstadt has even compared them to those who deny the earth is round. To be sure, not everyone who shares Lipstadt's view of them labels them deniers. Even among her allies, she is exercising a rhetorical option. For example, a member of her legal team, architectural historian Robert Jan van Pelt, prefers the term "negationists." However she feels about his choice, her own is certainly blunter. In its very crispness, "deniers" is strategic, describing the likes of Irving more plainly than van Pelt's word does.

Even before Irving's suit against her, Lipstadt felt obliged to pinpoint how this term fits him. Her book's discussion of him helps us see what she means by the word. In *Denying the Holocaust*, she distinguishes between two phases of Irving's career. Lipstadt acknowledges that Irving hasn't always rejected key elements of the Shoah. But at a certain point, she argues, he stopped being a respectable—if provocative—scholar. Rather, he turned into a full-fledged denier, a change that for her amounts to a difference in kind. More precisely, Lipstadt dates Irving's conversion to 1988, when he no longer conceded that the Nazis had systematically slain Jews. Before then,

Irving had written many books that tended to exonerate Hitler by arguing that he didn't know about the Final Solution. Nevertheless, until the late 1980s, Irving had basically acknowledged the reality of this extermination program. According to Lipstadt, his thinking shifted when he served as a witness in Canada's second trial of Ernst Zundel, a brazen Holocaust denier. And Irving admits that this trial was pivotal for him. He was captivated by one of the defense's documents, in which alleged engineer Fred Leuchter reported his chemical investigation of Auschwitz ruins. On the basis of his analyses, Leuchter concluded that no gas chambers had operated in the camp. Subsequently, Leuchter's research has been exposed as perversely mistaken, and the man himself, as it turns out, had little scientific or technical training. But the Leuchter Report persuaded Irving, so much that he published it in Britain. In recent years, Irving seems to have developed misgivings about this study, especially after friends of his noted flaws in it. Nevertheless, Irving has yet to repudiate the report in public, and even during his lawsuit against Lipstadt, he hesitated to condemn it. Throughout the proceedings, he still refused to concede the epic barbarism of Auschwitz.

Irving himself objects fiercely to being called a "Holocaust denier." In his opening statement to the court, he preferred to describe himself as "an historian and as an investigative writer." In one respect, his attempt to identify with the discipline of history is ironic, for often he has scorned other members of it. Not having been formally educated as a historian, he's proceeded to portray himself as more knowledgeable than the academically trained. In particular, he's declared himself superior to other scholars of the Third Reich. His opening statement stressed that he has found, translated, and published previously neglected documents of the regime. Overall, Irving's professional role has been that of gadfly. When he defines himself as a "historian," he's claiming to be the ideal kind while expressing contempt for lesser incarnations. No wonder, then, that he thinks "Holocaust denier" a term that impugns his professional legitimacy. For him, it not only ruins his right to entitle himself a "historian"; it also fails to recognize that he's a brilliant one. Indeed, throughout the trial, Irving downplayed his role in denier conferences. He didn't want to concede that he'd often spoken at such meetings. Moreover, he did refer to the "Holocaust," as if the word *might* denote a real event.

Significantly, though, Irving climaxed his opening remarks by declaring "Holocaust" an "artificial label." True, he went on to observe that it is "commonly attached to one of the greatest and still most unexplained tragedies of this past century." But with this comment, he was hardly conceding that systematic mass slaughter had occurred. The word "unexplained" still put the reality of the death camps in doubt. And, as the trial proceeded, Irving tried to make it a debate about Auschwitz. Repeatedly, he mocked the idea that hundreds of thousands had been gassed there. By the time of the verdict, few had trouble agreeing with Judge Gray: Irving was a Holocaust denier, even if he denied his being so.

Irving's bitterest protest against this label came at the climax of his opening statement. There, he used highly charged analogies to discredit the very term "Holocaust denier," claiming that it "is a poison to which there is virtually no antidote, less lethal than a hypodermic with nerve gas jabbed in the neck, but deadly all the same: for the chosen victim, it is like being called a wife beater or a paedophile. It is enough for the label to be attached, for the attachee to find himself designated as a pariah, an outcast from normal society. It is a verbal Yellow Star." Here, Irving engages in what Burke describes as "the stealing back and forth of symbols" (*Attitudes* 358). Burke is referring to the practice whereby one group appropriates images or slogans that another group has claimed for itself. Chiefly, Burke has in mind how this strategy is often used by the powerless—"the Outs" (*Attitudes* 358)—to gain leverage over the dominant. In his 1935 address to the American Writers' Congress ("Revolutionary"), he himself recommended that his audience of leftists adopt their country's traditional exaltation of "the people." Irving's declaration, on the other hand, was an effort to protect his present status. As yet, he wasn't an utter outcast, but he feared becoming so. By linking himself to the yellow star, he dramatized his sense of danger. He suggested that, just as the Nazis stigmatized Jews, so Lipstadt's label threatened him.

Lipstadt did attack Irving's sheer self. By calling him a denier, she scorned who he is, not just what he does. Recall the specific language of the passage from her book that I quoted at the start of this chapter. There, she reports herself telling the TV producer "that I would not participate in a debate with a Holocaust denier." Subsequently, she notes, she did express her willingness to discuss "who they were." This language is ontological. It evokes deniers as a particular breed whose existence should worry us. In her writing, the denier looms as a distinct—and threatening—human type. Clearly, this concept of them is the heart of her refusal to debate them.

Keep in mind that she might have phrased her policy differently than the way she puts it at her book's start. She might have told the TV producer, and her readers, that she won't join a forum where statements denying the Holocaust get uttered. Had she expressed her position this way, she would have been refusing to brook particular speech acts. Instead, she rejects certain people. Then, she proceeds to name several of them and explain how to identify their ilk.

The Irving–Lipstadt trial perpetuated this focus on the Holocaust denier as an identifiable figure. For one thing, Irving represented himself in the courtroom, thereby putting his personality much on display. Moreover, as revealed in his "verbal Yellow Star" remark, that personality is provocative in the extreme. Most important, the trial became a probe of Irving's integrity. This development reflected differences between the American and British legal systems. Had Irving sued Lipstadt for libel in America, he would have had to prove her guilty of false statements and malice. Therefore, the trial would have been a study of her. In England's libel cases, however, the burden is on the defendant, which is why Irving sued her there. As a result, Lipstadt had to prove that her claims about him were valid. Given this situation, her team extensively researched Irving's record, including documents and videotapes acquired from him in the court process known as discovery. Then, her chief lawyer, Richard Rampton, grilled Irving about this archive throughout the trial. Meanwhile, exercising a legal right, Lipstadt didn't even take the stand, so Irving couldn't interrogate *her*.

As she watched silently, colorful statements of his that he might have preferred to repress came back to haunt him. On opening day, for example, Rampton recalled for the court Irving's 1991 claim "that more people died on the back seat of Edward Kennedy's car in Chappaquiddick than ever died in a gas chamber in Auschwitz." Right from the start, then, Rampton painted Irving as a wielder of noxious hyperbole. Significantly, Rampton went on in his opening statement to declare the following: "My Lord, this is obviously an important case, but that is not however because it is primarily concerned with whether or not the Holocaust took place or the degree of Hitler's responsibility for it. On the contrary, the essence of the case is Mr. Irving's honesty and integrity as a chronicler—I shy away from the word 'historian'—of these matters . . ." To a great extent, the media ignored Rampton. They did frame the proceedings as a debate about whether the Shoah occurred. To cite the title of a book about the case, they saw it as

The Holocaust on Trial (Guttenplan).[4] At issue, though, was indeed "Mr. Irving's honesty and integrity." Hence, Judge Gray devoted his statement of findings mostly to this topic. When he largely condemned Irving, while basically exonerating Lipstadt, he supported her emphasis on deniers as a discrete—and abhorrent—category of persons.

Further Questions about Lipstadt's Term "Denier"

Despite her victory over Irving, Lipstadt's emphasis on the term "denier" raises additional questions. First, is there *any* validity to Irving's suggestion that invidious labeling of a person's essence has something in common with anti-Semitism? Is the word "denier" comparable at all to a "yellow star"? Well, even after the court verdict against him, Irving is better off than the Holocaust's victims. Besides remaining alive, he retains many sympathizers, including some distinguished historians. In this respect, his analogy is vile. Still, it *is* possible for agent-centered criticism to become bigoted and even genocidal. This is, in fact, what the Nazis demonstrated! As Burke, however, signals by including "agent" in his pentad, describing and evaluating someone's personality isn't necessarily inhumane. When they discuss this tactic in *The New Rhetoric*, Chaim Perelman and Lucie Olbrechts-Tyteca also treat it as potentially acceptable. Actually, they note that we can relate someone's acts to that person's essence in various ways. Analyzing how the person behaved on a given occasion, we may deem such conduct out of character. Then again, we may argue that it's typical of him or her and in this sense reflects the person's real self. Perelman and Olbrechts-Tyteca observe that usually a key premise of the latter argument is intention. When we declare behavior characteristic, we also think it purposeful, thus allowing ourselves to judge "the morality of the agent" and not just "the morality of the act" (301). By calling Irving a denier, Lipstadt is making a claim that by now seems unquestionably true: namely, that he regularly and deliberately seeks to eradicate basic facts of the Holocaust.

Lipstadt's approach is somewhat akin to that taken by journalist Gitta Sereny when she interviewed Treblinka commandant Franz Stangl. Throughout their talks, Sereny reports, Stangl focused on individual incidents, wrangling about details of atrocities he'd committed or supervised. Meanwhile, he didn't welcome her suggesting that these events showed that he'd become *fundamentally* bad. To Sereny's frustration, he spoke as if "what a man *does* on isolated occasions" is more significant "than what he *is*" (124, emphasis in original). Here, Sereny isn't making a philosophical point about human nature. Nor, clearly, is she promoting genocide. Rather, she's trying to undermine a rationale adopted by Stangl and other engineers of mass murder: the belief that they remain essentially innocent no matter what killings they launch.[5] So, too, is Lipstadt's agent-centered discourse hardly equivalent to the Nazis'. For one thing, they defined Jewishness in racial terms, as an inborn, inescapable trait, whereas she thinks Irving willfully turned himself into a denier over time. With her label, she holds him accountable for a project he chose to pursue.

Irving seems the very prototype of a Holocaust denier, and Lipstadt's book shows ways of detecting his kin. But presumably no surefire instrument exists for determining if someone is quintessentially Irving-ish. We lack the equivalent of a Breathalyzer. How freely, then, should the term "denier" be applied? Imagine a person who briefly and casually expresses doubt about the Holocaust. Should we automatically call this skeptic a denier? Imagine someone who acknowledges the Shoah but who doesn't treat it as a major event. Might denier still be a fair term in this case?

Such issues of classification have recently arisen with actor-director Mel Gibson's defense of his father, Hutton. The latter is unmistakably a Holocaust denier, repeatedly calling the Shoah a Zionist hoax. In a February 2004 radio interview, a couple of days before the official opening of his son's movie *The Passion of the Christ*, Hutton himself drew national attention by mocking the historical record. Claiming that "there were not that many Jews under Hitler's power under his sway," he scorned the idea that Germany murdered six million: "They simply got up and left! They were all over the Bronx and Brooklyn and Sydney and Los Angeles." Far from acknowledging the slaughter at Auschwitz, he asserted that the Nazis "did not have the gas to do it." About the Holocaust, he concluded that "it's all—maybe not all fiction—but most of it is." Of course, the perpetrators of the deceit are Jews, who plan to cash in on it. After all, he said, "they have to go where there is money." In fact, they were the real owners of the Nazi railroads and banks, and even the Rockefellers were actually Jewish. With this religion, he stressed, "it's all about control." Besides killing Christ, the Jews are "anti everyone else." In fact, now they aim to overthrow the Catholic Church, and they already have agents in the Vatican serving their "plot" ("Partial"). Ironically, the interviewer to whom Hutton made these remarks was Jewish, as was the organization sponsoring the show.

No matter: Hutton reveled in anti-Semitic distrust of the Shoah, content to present himself as Denier Supreme.

Is Mel ideologically his father's son? Both men have identified themselves as ultratraditional Catholics, loathing the reforms of Vatican II. But does Gibson the Younger join Gibson the Elder in being a Holocaust denier? This question became especially pertinent in the furor over *The Passion*, a film that itself elicited charges of anti-Semitism. Hence, Peggy Noonan understandably brought up the Holocaust when she interviewed Mel for *Reader's Digest*. When she invited him to comment on his father's skepticism toward the Shoah, he was initially evasive. He preferred to sketch his father's biography in glowing terms. He did assert, though, that "the man never lied to me in his life" (93), a statement hardly comforting to those afraid that Mel is a denier, too. Therefore, with her next question, Noonan sought to clarify his views: "The Holocaust happened, right?" (93). His answer:

> I have friends and parents of friends who have numbers on their arms. The guy who taught me Spanish was a Holocaust survivor. He worked in a concentration camp in France. Yes, of course. Atrocities happened. War is horrible. The Second World War killed tens of millions of people. Some of them were Jews in concentration camps. Many people lost their lives. In the Ukraine, several million starved to death between 1932 and 1933. During the last century, 20 million people died in the Soviet Union. (93)

With this response, Mel Gibson seems to admit that the Holocaust happened. But, as confirmations go, this one is suspiciously mild. Bear in mind that Noonan was, in essence, offering him an opportunity—inviting him to relieve people's concerns by acknowledging the Shoah took place. Only in the middle of his answer, though, does he refer to Jews. Even then, he mentions them in just one sentence. Furthermore, to say of the Nazis' victims that "Some of them were Jews in concentration camps" is to fall well short of recognizing the number of Jews who died. Nor does Mel acknowledge the Nazis' systematic effort to eliminate *all* Jews. Indeed, by relying on the term "concentration camp," he ignores the reality of intentional death camps. On the whole, he relativizes the Holocaust, insinuating that its Jewish victims were just one group among many who've suffered. Noonan's reaction catches his drift: "So the point is that life is tragic and it is full of fighting and violence, mischief and malice." As a "lesson" to draw from the Holocaust, this is quite general and abstract. It sweeps away all of the disaster's specific details—not only the persecution of Jews but that of other particular groups, including Gypsies and homosexuals. But Mel likes Noonan's summary of his remarks. Has she captured his "point"? "Absolutely" (94).

To *New York Times* columnist Frank Rich, Mel Gibson's remarks about the Holocaust in this interview are chillingly familiar: "This is the classic language of contemporary Holocaust deniers, from David Irving to Mr. Gibson's own father. . . . Their rhetorical strategy is to diminish Hitler's extermination of Jews by folding those deaths into the war's overall casualty figures, as if the Holocaust were an idle byproduct of battle instead of a Third Reich master plan for genocide" ("Mel Gibson"). I like Rich's critique. So, too, I suspect, would Lipstadt, who voices similar misgivings about Gibson's comments in her book *History on Trial*.[6] Still, I wouldn't yet proclaim Mel Gibson a Holocaust denier. My take on the interview is this: he's more inclined than Dad to admit the Holocaust, but he also wants to show filial love. I think this balancing act fails. It raises more questions than answers. Above all, it leaves us guessing how much the son does share his father's anti-Jewish paranoia. After Mel Gibson's notorious 2006 episode of drunk driving—during which he spouted anti-Semitic slurs—we have more reason than ever to think "like father, like son." But in order to decide whether Mel is, in fact, a denier, I'd need more comments from him about the Holocaust—a subject he's apt to avoid in the future! At the moment, we can turn back to his *Digest* interview, analyzing and evaluating his use there of deniers' "classic language." Indeed, if we're to confront Holocaust denial, we should probe any use of such discourse, even when we're unable to pigeonhole the person deploying it. We ought to study the words of people other than the movement's hard core.

When Lipstadt refuses to debate deniers, though, she does have chiefly in mind the most dedicated: those strongly committed to proclaiming the Holocaust a fraud. They are, after all, the ones bent on publicity. At the same time, Lipstadt doesn't seem to think the world is neatly divided between them and "Holocaust believers." Some of humanity, she suggests, occupies middle ground. Early in *Denying the Holocaust*, she identifies figures who resort to elements of Holocaust denial without, in her view, fully embracing it. One is pundit Patrick Buchanan. She notes that he questions whether Treblinka had a gas chamber and that he often scoffs at survivors' testimonies. Elsewhere in her book, she discusses people who acknowledge the Shoah but who minimize its significance by insisting it was no worse than other modern atrocities. Her examples include Andreas Hillgruber and Ernst Nolte, leading participants in Germany's "historians' debate" of the 1980s who argued that "it was historically and morally incorrect to single out the Germans for doing precisely what had been done by an array of other nations" (211). Similarly, lawyers representing Klaus Barbie at his war crimes trial asserted "that it was no more of a crime to murder millions of Jews than it was to fight against Algerians, Vietnamese, Africans, or Palestinians who were attempting to free themselves from foreign rule" (11). While clearly Lipstadt regards the Holocaust as uniquely horrific, she recognizes that a legitimate historian may think it comparable to some other events. But she sees people like the above as sheer propagandists. In her view—and many would concur—they emphasize equivalency because they seek to exonerate Germany. Even so, she doesn't call them deniers. She assigns Barbie's lawyers, for instance, to a slightly less invidious class: "those who hover on the periphery of Holocaust denial" (11).

Meanwhile, Lipstadt broods about yet another group. Though she distinguishes them from hard-core deniers, she worries about their own current tendencies. More and more "good-hearted people," she points out in *Denying the Holocaust*, have partly succumbed to deniers' rhetoric. Though they may still find Holocaust denial "ugly, reprehensible, and extremist," they now consider it "an other side nonetheless" (3). Hence, they're willing to give deniers a hearing, and on several occasions, they've felt compelled to provide it. In part, Lipstadt attributes this new tolerance to deniers' change of tactics. Now, they pose as serious historians up against their field's rigidity. Also, they present themselves as crusaders for free speech. The latter, of course, is central to the American political imagination. Similarly, the academy presents itself as receptive to a broad range of views.

Lipstadt observes that this hallowed openness, along with other factors, has led deniers to exploit the academy as a venue. "One of the primary loci of their activities," she reports, "is the college campus, where they have tried to stimulate a debate on the existence of the Holocaust" (24). Although her book was published by a trade press, Lipstadt is an academic. Moreover, she seems to assume her readers will consist largely of college faculty and students. To a great extent, then, her rhetorical refusal is a tactic aimed at this community. She hopes it will join her in shunning dialogue with deniers. In her view, academics shouldn't offer them a forum in the first place.

As Lipstadt notes throughout her book, she was stirred to write it partly by a campus trend. In the early 1990s, several college and university newspapers had published an ad by Bradley Smith, cofounder of the Committee for Open Debate on the Holocaust. Under the headline "The Holocaust Story: How Much Is False? The Case for Open Debate," the ad questioned several facts about the Shoah. In addition, it protested the academy's reluctance to have them challenged. This absence of debate, the ad claimed, amounts to a conspiracy of silence. "America's thought police" are overthrowing academic principles; "the ideals of the university itself are exchanged for intellectual taboos" (qtd. in Lipstadt 189). The newspaper staffs that printed Smith's ad believed he had a point, insofar as the academy proclaims debate a good thing. Devoting a whole chapter to this development, Lipstadt argues that Smith and his cronies are corrupt manipulators of the campus press.

To understand better her rhetorical situation, let's return to Perelman and Olbrechts-Tyteca's idea in *The New Rhetoric* that "audiences pass judgment on one another" (35). Earlier, in elaborating this point, I observed that rhetorical refusals evoke two audiences. One, which the refuser thinks may be his or her actual audience, expects rhetorical norms to be followed. The other accepts the refuser's defiance of these norms. Basically, I suggested, the refuser aims to convert the first group into the second. Success, in this respect, would mean that members of that audience now criticize the audience they used to be. In Lipstadt's case, the first group would be made up of people dismayed by her refusal to argue with deniers. They might not expect her to begin her book with a Bush-like "Bring 'em on!" Nor might they demand that she dive into such exchanges herself. But her refusal would chagrin them anyway, for with it she objects to these debates' taking place. The very ethos of academe, this audience would feel, requires more receptivity. Given audience members' stance, Lipstadt must coax them to become the second sort of audience. Those in the latter appreciate her refusal, share her anti-debate stand, and deem the first audience mistaken.

As with Croce, the notion of audiences judging audiences can go further. Recall that Croce pushes her readers to scorn those who actually did attend *Still/Here*. Similarly, Lipstadt hopes her readers will scorn the audiences for deniers—people, that is, who pay respectful attention to a Bradley Smith. These people include the newspaper staffs who published his ad. Even if it revolted them, they thought it worth printing, thereby ensuring that much of their community would see it.

Whatever the existence of other groups, Lipstadt's book is mainly an exposé of deniers. In chapter after chapter, she describes them as a movement. In particular, she draws attention to their anti-Semitic backgrounds and motives. Throughout, she portrays them as hateful, irrational, and deceptive ideologues. Indeed, though surely she knows that some of them will read her book, she doesn't deign to address them in it. Instead, the book is *about* them, a warning to the rest of us that they exist. Similarly, she refuses to debate them because of their basic mindset. Their approach to the Holocaust, she submits, is devious rather than credible. Therefore, the academy as well as the media shouldn't give them an audience at all.

Conceptualizing "Truth"

Still, Lipstadt knows that some of her academic readers are inclined to grant them an audience, due to higher education's valuing of debate. Again, Perelman and Olbrechts-Tyteca clarify what she's up to as she raises her concern. Recall their observing that rhetoric often entails dissociations, especially appearance/reality splits. Lipstadt's remarks about dialogue are a good example. She dissociates appearance from reality by distinguishing between two definitions of the academy's essence. One was voiced by the *Ohio State Lantern* in defending its publication of Smith's ad. The paper declared "repulsive" the assumption "that the quality, or total lack thereof, of any idea or opinion has any bearing on whether it should be heard" (qtd. in Lipstadt 197). Lipstadt abhors this refusal to gauge, and take seriously, the relative soundness of ideas. To her, it "contravenes all that an institution of higher learning is supposed to profess" (197). For the same reason, she is disturbed by how Frank Rhodes, president of Cornell University, justified its newspaper's printing of Smith's ad. Rhodes asserted that "free and open debate on a wide range of ideas, however outrageous or offensive some of them may be, lies at the heart of a university community" (qtd. in Lipstadt 207). Although Lipstadt thinks debate important for a campus, she has a different vision of the academy's "heart." Colleges and universities, she contends, don't exist to foster any and every sort of dialogue. Rather, their central goal is rational dialogue, in which participants carefully analyze evidence, genuinely listen to one another, try to surmount their biases, and basically seek truth. For Lipstadt, this particular kind of debate is the academy's real priority, and members of it, like Rhodes or the *Lantern* staff, mistakenly seize upon a lesser one in their call for unlimited tolerance. As with many dissociations, then, she identifies a principle and elevates it over its rivals. Indeed, her move bears out what Alan Gross says about dissociations: they are "a way of taking the argumentative high ground" (320).

Lipstadt elaborates her position in the preface to the paperback edition of her book. There, she says that "although the academy must remain a place where ideas can be freely and vigorously explored, it must first be a place that differentiates between ideas with lasting quality and those with none" (xvi). Perhaps this statement poses too simple a binary. Plenty of ideas now circulating in the academy may fall short of "lasting" value but, for the moment, deserve respect. Let's face it: any quest for *enduring* wisdom may be doomed! Yet Lipstadt's unwillingness to privilege debate over all other practices does correspond with much academic habit. In general, higher education hasn't deemed every idea worth entertaining on campus. As the late British philosopher Bernard Williams said of universities, "People cannot come in from outside, speak when they feel like it, make endless, irrelevant, or insulting interventions, and so on; they cannot invoke a right to do so, and no-one thinks things would go better in the direction of the truth if they did" (217). Perhaps Williams overstated the case with his "no-one," for maybe some people do wish campuses were anarchist playgrounds. Nevertheless, most schools have established, implicitly or explicitly, certain intellectual standards and have felt no duty to provide rhetorical space for people who disdain them.

Endorsing Lipstadt's claim that academe needn't welcome deniers, Stanley Fish points to the American Association of University Professors' classic 1915 report on academic freedom. The AAUP defined this tenet, he observes, as "a freedom peculiar to the academic enterprise and a freedom whose boundaries are to be determined and patrolled *by* academics" ("Holocaust Denial"). Thus, the document allows colleges and universities to dismiss various ideas as absurd, no matter how much certain parties extol them. Generally, the principle of academic freedom has helped the academy resist outside pressure groups, including several with blatantly partisan agendas. Even as I write, I and many faculty are alarmed by two proposals that challenge the AAUP's understanding of academic freedom by demanding that colleges and universities turn rightward. David Horowitz's so-called Academic Bill of Rights pushes for an increase in conservative faculty, while a federal government initiative would de-fund area studies programs that are insufficiently pro-American. Quite possibly these measures would result in oversight power for nonacademics of an anti-liberal bent. At any rate, as foes of these steps emphasize, the academy has never sought to honor the entire spectrum of existing notions. Rather, each school has developed criteria for evaluating research, teaching, and student work. Moreover, usually these criteria accord with the various academic disciplines, reflecting their standards for achievement. Therefore, most astronomy departments ignore the charge that America's moon landings were faked. Most biology departments refuse to hire creationists. Most exams in American history don't ask whether slavery was, all in all, a good thing. Of course, intellectual life is apt to thrive on campus only if a range of views gets voiced, and many a field has come to accept perspectives it once marginalized. But a school doesn't have to be an utterly open agora. Although several of the papers that printed Smith's ad claimed that the First Amendment required them to, Lipstadt observes correctly that it outlaws censorship by the government, leaving most campus publications free to decide their contents. In fact, as she points out, many papers that published the ad had previously rejected ones they found sexist or racist.

Lipstadt splits appearance from reality in another way, once again undertaking *The New Rhetoric*'s prototypical kind of dissociation. She argues that although deniers claim to want rational debate, they are faking interest in it, for actually they have no commitment to its principles. Instead, they aim to promote their anti-Semitic causes, regardless of documented historical facts. Insisting there is "a significant difference between reasoned dialogue and anti-intellectual pseudoscientific arguments" (25), Lipstadt proceeds to show how deniers "confuse and distort" (28). Indeed, she proclaims as her main imperative this piercing of their facade: *"above all, it is essential to expose the illusion of reasoned inquiry that conceals their extremist views"* (28, emphasis in original).

If we engaged in this debunking, most of us would feel tempted to make epistemological pronouncements. We'd be inclined to express our views about the nature of truth, and more specifically about whether there are objective historical facts. Probably we'd opine, too, about how truth fares in today's academy. Sure enough, Lipstadt comments on these matters. In doing so, however, she occasionally gets facile. Especially dubious are statements she makes about the academy's turn to postmodern thought. Lipstadt contends that such theory has corrupted students as well as faculty. For example, she accuses Fish and other reader-response theorists of mistakenly arguing that "texts had no fixed meaning" (18). She scolds neopragmatist philosophers such as Richard Rorty and Nelson Goodman for "rejecting the notion that there was one version of the world that was necessarily right while another was necessarily wrong" (18). She blames deconstructionists for fostering "an atmosphere of permissiveness toward questioning the meaning of historical events" (18). In general, she criticizes these various intellectual movements for holding that "no fact, no event, and no aspect of history [have] any fixed meaning or content. Any truth can be retold. Any fact can be recast. There is no ultimate historical reality" (19).

Yet postmodern theory hasn't had the mass influence that Lipstadt claims. Like Ishmael Reed, she overestimates its impact. A likelier instigator of relativism is postmodern *media*. For example, numerous Web sites float conspiracy theories, finding devious cabals behind previously established facts. At any rate, relativism has always thrived among students, and if hordes of them now embrace it, they are ignorant of the thinkers whom Lipstadt cites.

Moreover, even many a traditional scholar doubts that a fact, event, or text can be permanently assigned a single "meaning." These scholars may be limited in their pluralism, but they assume no interpretation is definitive, and they see their own analyses as contributions to debates that will likely persist. Lipstadt fails to recognize, too, that most postmodern theorists believe interpretation is constrained. Instead of assuming that "any truth can be retold" and "any fact can be recast," they often point out how all sorts of forces shape our understanding. For example, with his notion of "interpretive communities," Fish has stressed that readers are influenced by groups to which they belong.[7] Finally, Fish and many other postmodern thinkers can be said to posit an "ultimate historical reality." At least, they believe the past actually occurred, and they consider certain features of it to be so widely accepted as to merit being called facts. Where these theorists chiefly differ from Lipstadt is in their insistence that the past isn't directly available. More than she, they maintain that we interpret it, we represent it, and we try to persuade others that our view of it makes sense.

To be sure, if we're dealing with Holocaust deniers, postmodernists aren't necessarily our best coaches. Fish, for one, takes questionable positions in his article "Holocaust Denial and Academic Freedom," where he examines

Lipstadt's approach. Fish agrees with Lipstadt that the academy needn't give deniers entrée. Also, he sanctions her refusal to debate them. Nevertheless, he objects to her claim that while she relies on historical evidence, deniers ignore it. To Fish, what constitutes "evidence" and "objectivity" is a matter of community norms. Our preexistent beliefs, shaped by the groups we're tied to, lead us to decide what counts as proof. Thus, Fish holds that Lipstadt doesn't really have an epistemological advantage over deniers: "Deniers' pages are no less full of evidence and reasoning than are her pages; it is just that what is evidence for them is absurdity for her and what is evidence for her is Zionist blindness for them." In the main, Fish asserts, "Neither party reaches its conclusion by sifting the evidence on the way to determining the truth of the matter; rather, each begins with a firm conviction of what the truth of the matter is, and then from inside the lens of that conviction receives and evaluates (the shape of the evaluation is assured) the assertion of contrary truths." Fish insists that he and Lipstadt are still justified in arguing that deniers distort history. But all knowledge claims, he declares, are legitimate only within particular groups. Yes, Lipstadt's version of history makes more sense than deniers', but not because she's in direct contact with the truth. Rather, her version is sounder because it reflects the scholarship of professional historians, who as a collective agree that the Holocaust happened. To Fish, this grounding in the academic discipline of history suffices. Lipstadt shouldn't aspire to more.

In addition, he submits, she makes a *tactical* blunder when she claims to possess sheer facts. This pose of utter objectivity is risky, Fish contends. Deniers can demand that their case be heard until believers in the Holocaust do produce absolute proof of it. And unfortunately, Fish asserts, such proof isn't possible: "If the standard of validation is the establishment of a truth that is invulnerable to challenge, no one, including Lipstadt, could meet it." Fish thinks she's better off simply invoking the consensus of scholars, for then she can focus on showing how deniers diverge from it.

Ironically, Fish's advice to Lipstadt contradicts one of his long-standing principles. He is famous, or notorious, for asserting that theory has no consequences. Our positions on philosophical issues, Fish claims, don't actually affect our conduct. In debates about epistemology, we may see facts as socially constructed, but in our daily behavior, we treat them as real. Even if we're armed with a brilliant theory of truth, it won't make us more skillful than others at handling the contingencies of existence. Thus, to Fish, assuming that one's theory *does* have effects is presumptuous. Fish himself defines truth as a product of discourse; in his view, it emerges through practices of persuasion. Deirdre McCloskey calls theories like his "Big Rhetoric," for rather than considering rhetoric one particular art—a conception that McCloskey terms "little rhetoric"—they see it as a central element of human life.[8] If theory lacks consequences, however, Fish's theory doesn't entitle him to mentor Lipstadt. Yet he does advise her on strategy, as if his "Big Rhetoric" doctrine authorizes him to propose "little rhetoric" moves. Fish seems especially presumptuous when we look at his article's original circumstances. He first gave it as a paper at a conference honoring Lipstadt's courtroom victory over Irving. Although he isn't known for humility, one might have expected him to ponder her triumph. As things stand, though, Fish doesn't examine how her rhetoric helped her win.

Indeed, Fish treats deniers too generously when he gives their use of evidence the same epistemological status as Lipstadt's. Her legal team showed that Irving had been consistently *deceitful* in his use of historical documents, slyly distorting them to fit his own agenda. Her lawyers demonstrated, for instance, that he egregiously mistranslated a memo from Himmler. Rather than an order to exterminate Jews, it became a stay of execution for them. Pointing to this example, Michael Bernard-Donals observes that "Irving tried here, and at countless other points in the trial where he was caught in the same sorts of blatant lies about evidence, to simply make something up out of thin air" (253). Lipstadt chronicles such deception throughout her book, exposing how it is practiced by Irving and the company he keeps. As Bernard-Donals points out, though, Fish doesn't take enough account of this lying. Contrary to Fish's claim that deniers hold some standards of "evidence," Irving's habitual deceit suggests the concept means nothing to him. Rather, he seems devoted to toying with other people's criteria for proof.

Fish is also too simplistic when, at the climax of his essay, he urges foes of Holocaust denial to seek their data from "government agencies, official commissions of inquiry, standard works of scholarship, and the received wisdom of professional bodies and associations." Professional scholars are only one factor in how society grasps the Shoah. If our image of the past is influenced by interpretive communities, these aren't limited to the "guild authority" that Fish exalts. Various forces have led to the mass conviction that the Holocaust happened. Fish indicates as much when, early in his piece, he briefly recalls how he first learned of the disaster: "I grew up in a culture (postwar, American, and Jewish) where the Holocaust (then not named) was a given, with relatives who had survived it, and a father who spent time and money bringing those relatives to the United States." With the term "culture," Fish suggests that a whole ensemble of elements shaped his historical awareness, including family members who told of their experiences under Hitler. Clearly he hasn't relied on trained historians alone. Neither, then, should Lipstadt feel restricted to them.

As I've indicated, I'm disturbed by some of her book's language. To me, Lipstadt's slurs on postmodern theory aren't fair. Like Fish, then, I feel that she's not all that cogent as a philosopher. She's more impressive as an investigator of deniers' biases, backgrounds, and acts. The difference, I suspect, results from her choice of genre. Obviously she doesn't intend her book be a philosophical treatise. As I've said, she designs it as an exposé. Given the book's main drift, she's not disposed to elaborate her assertions about truth and its academic career. Besides, she may feel that the more she explains and justifies these claims, the more she'll suggest that truth is a complicated concept, one that has been theorized in diverse ways. This implication can be a resource for deniers, eager as they are to challenge the historical record. Still, Lipstadt takes a risk by only glancing at issues of epistemology. She leaves herself open to Fish's charge that she's naive about them.

As always with rhetoric—Big or little—determining what authorities to cite and what arguments to make depends on one's specific circumstances and audience. For the Irving trial, Lipstadt's legal team did enlist the testimony of academic historians. After all, their expertise made them shrewd analysts of Irving's pseudoscholarship, and their credentials impressed the judge. By the same token, her lawyers didn't solicit testimony from Holocaust survivors, for Irving would have pounced on gaps and errors in their memories. Outside of courtrooms, however, Lipstadt has a larger repertoire of tactics. Potentially she can invoke numerous sources of information that have shaped public knowledge of the Shoah. So, too, might she build on the common belief that we've established key aspects of the past. Of course, Holocaust deniers will reject much of her argument, but rarely will she be addressing them. Certainly they're not the target audience of her book. There, she tries to convince those who do acknowledge the Holocaust that deniers don't merit respect.

Again, Lipstadt's book focuses on the basic character of deniers. In a way, her concern is less with *truth* than with *truthfulness*, which she finds deniers lack.[9] Analyzing the two terms in his book *Truth and Truthfulness: An Essay on Genealogy*, Bernard Williams submits that truthful people care about accuracy, even to the point of accepting facts at odds with their wishes. Moreover, Williams notes, truthful people are sincere, refraining from conscious deceit and distortion. But, as Lipstadt details, Holocaust deniers flout these standards. They automatically dismiss all documents that plainly conflict with their fantasies, including confessions by administrators of the death camps. In addition, many deniers—including Irving and Smith—conceal their ties to hate groups. Although he isn't referring to deniers, Williams could be describing them when he observes that such a radically untruthful being "does not care enough about the effect of what he says on the component of trust in the relations that he has to other people, and does not mind carelessly or deliberately manipulating them." By refusing to debate a denier, Lipstadt enacts what Williams says is the only sensible response: "[I]f you can, you will ignore him, do such things as warn other people about him, and generally treat him with less respect" (120).

Is Lipstadt's notion of debate utopian? Does she shun deniers because she holds an ultra-idealistic view of dispute? If she's nervous about "the liberal idea of dialogue," is this because few dialogues meet her standards? Someone might argue that she's too concerned with achieving "the ideal speech situation," Jurgen Habermas's term for fully rational exchange. Habermas himself has been criticized for cherishing this model, even though he gives it counterfactual status. Indeed, he knows that most interactions fall short of it. Similarly, Lipstadt seems to accept that debates often involve people behaving badly. She sees Holocaust deniers, though, as worse than uncivil. To her, they're fundamentally unconcerned with truth. This is why she declares them unworthy of a forum.

We can further clarify Lipstadt's position by turning to Paul Grice's theory of speech acts. Among rhetoricians, linguists, and philosophers of language, Grice is well known for hypothesizing the premises that steer informal conversation. Imagine two people talking. What assumptions, Grice wondered, must they make if they're to see their dialogue as rational? Above all, he concluded, they must assume that each of them accepts what Grice termed the Cooperative Principle: "Make your conversational contribution such as is required, at the stage at which it occurs, by the accepted purpose or direction of the talk exchange in which you are engaged" (26).

From this principle, Grice derived certain maxims, which he thought the speakers relied on as they talked. For example, under the rubric of Quality, Grice put the following tenet: "Try to make your contribution one that is true." From this, he drew corollaries: "Do not say what you believe to be false" and "Do not say that for which you lack adequate evidence" (27).

Grice realized that, as they talked, speaker A may perceive speaker B as defying a maxim. Because he admitted this perception is possible, and because he analyzed what A might do with it, Grice's theory of discourse seems more nuanced than Habermas's. Grice noted that A may decide to be charitable. That is, A may strive to understand how B is, in fact, observing the maxim in question. To achieve this interpretive feat, A would have to make various inferences. Grice called these "conversational implicatures," and his analysis of them is perhaps the most-discussed aspect of his work. But, as he pointed out, A may decide that B really is wayward. Throughout their conversation, for instance, B "may quietly and unostentatiously *violate* a maxim." If A isn't quick to catch on, B is even "liable to mislead" (30, emphasis in original). Grice implies that B may be deviating from several maxims at once. Insofar as B misleads, though, B isn't being truthful, and so B is violating at least one of the maxims of Quality.

Essentially, Lipstadt accuses Holocaust deniers of violating all three maxims in this category. She argues that they *don't* try to make contributions that are true, for their wild claims about the Shoah are just weapons in their war on Jews. Moreover, she asserts, they *do* say what they believe to be false, posing as neutral and objective scholars instead of the anti-Semites they are. Also, they *do* say things for which they lack evidence, hardly bothering to support their charge that Zionists invented the Holocaust. Consequently, Lipstadt resists talking with deniers at all. Nor, she believes, should others engage with them.

Grice had critics, who led him to reflect on his points. He acknowledged that many conversations seem oblivious to his maxims, the speakers evidently not caring how logically they proceed. Also, he admitted that he focused on a certain kind of discourse. He was concerned, he said, with the assumptions of people who did attempt rational talk. In a more value-laden way, Lipstadt focuses on such dialogue as well. For her, it's a supreme ideal, and she wants society to pursue it. She thinks that colleges and universities in particular should make it their prime aim. If they did, she believes, they wouldn't welcome deniers, who lack the truthfulness that rational exchanges need. Interestingly, Grice came to regard as vital the maxim "Try to make your contribution one that is true." He saw that it appears "to spell out the difference between something's being, and (strictly speaking) failing to be, any kind of contribution at all." In other words, "False information is not an inferior kind of information; it just is not information" (371). Basically, Lipstadt agrees. This is why she avoids those who dispute the Holocaust's existence.

Most notably, she's been unwilling to give deniers a hearing on campus. Moreover, her book begins with her refusal to appear with them on TV. Thus, when Lipstadt didn't testify in the Irving trial, observers weren't surprised. She was commonly thought to be upholding a personal policy. Actually, though, she was willing to debate Irving in court. In this particular venue, she believed, he couldn't use deniers' usual ploys, for the judge would identify and control nonsense. As things turned out, Lipstadt's legal team did leave her off the stand, much to Irving's consternation. They decided that they didn't need her to testify and that the wiser move was to keep spotlighting the plaintiff. At any rate, her attitude in this instance is significant. Presumably, she still refuses to debate deniers in most forums. But apparently, she's more open when she thinks the site is one where Grice's maxims are enforced. Whether such places really exist is less clear.

An Issue of Salience

When Lipstadt opens her book with her rhetorical refusal, she's aware that much of her audience likes "the liberal idea of dialogue." Hence, she knows that she must explain why she won't talk with deniers. The rest of her book elaborates her stand. But she's aware, too, that some people would have her ignore deniers completely. These advocates of neglect remind us that when a rhetorical refusal expresses animosity toward its subject, it still makes that topic salient, which not everyone may want. Of course, to devote a whole book to the topic—as Lipstadt does with deniers—may cause even greater unease.

Lipstadt's critics include people who accept that the Holocaust occurred but who feel that Americans have grown obsessed with it. Historian Peter Novick takes this position in his much-discussed 1999 book *The Holocaust in American Life*. Novick faults American Jews for pivoting their history around the Shoah. He thinks their preoccupation with it has led them to identify themselves just as victims (shades of Croce!) and to overlook other ways of strengthening their religious and cultural bonds. But Novick also faults Americans in general, claiming that our whole society broods about the Holocaust too much. By dwelling on it as a unique horror, he argues, we avoid precise analysis, and we ignore lesser forms of violence that we might actually curtail. Consistent with these assertions, Novick doesn't welcome *Denying the Holocaust.* He suggests that Lipstadt exaggerates the danger that deniers pose. Though he grants that the movement exists, he doesn't see it as a threat. Rather, he submits that her book reinforces Americans' fixation on the Holocaust, a habit of mind that he considers unhealthy.

People who do fear deniers are also capable of questioning Lipstadt's approach. Any reader of her book is bound to realize that, rather than praising deniers, she exposes their sins. Nevertheless, some opponents of the movement worry. Why, they ask, must Lipstadt pay *any* attention to deniers? Doesn't she thereby suggest that they're a major intellectual force? Might her criticisms of them even gain them recruits? To appreciate such concerns, recall Dave Hickey's remark from chapter 2: "The raw investment of attention, positive or negative, qualifies certain works of art as 'players' in the discourse." As deniers themselves proclaim, bad publicity is still publicity. Why, then, provide them a spotlight at all?

In her book, Lipstadt acknowledges that she risks appearing to "give the deniers a certain stature" (27). Specifically, she grants that she may make them seem the "other side" (27) of a real dispute. Van Pelt raises a similar concern in his book on the Irving lawsuit. As a member of her legal team, van Pelt welcomed Lipstadt's victory. But he regrets that, during the trial, Irving had a platform equal to hers. The deniers' cause did seem an "other side." This parity, van Pelt observes, helped the media suggest that on trial was the Holocaust itself, as if its occurrence hadn't already been proven (xv).

At the start and close of *Denying the Holocaust,* Lipstadt notes why someone might avoid her topic. Nonetheless, the book exists, and in it she defends her choice of subject. Mainly she claims that the public needs to learn about deniers, whatever the risks. On a superficial level, this argument resembles the "light of day" one put forth by some editors who ran Smith's ad. Their excuse for printing it was that it would make readers aware of Holocaust denial as a growing evil. To Lipstadt, however, this reasoning is specious, for publishing Smith's ideas implied they might be valid. Thus, in her own book, she discusses the ad but doesn't reproduce it. Moreover, she clearly portrays deniers as a menace. Specifically, she registers the pain they inflict on Holocaust survivors as well as on relatives of the dead. Also, she points out that if deniers can reshape history, so will others. In addition, she observes that today's students flirt with doubts about the Shoah, especially now that deniers pose as respectable scholars. For these reasons, Lipstadt feels justified in writing about the movement, even as she refuses to debate its members.

To me, Lipstadt makes a strong case for her project. And since the original publication of *Denying the Holocaust*, more rationales for the book have emerged. In the next chapter, I will consider at length the history of certain rhetorical refusals, tracing changes of context they have undergone. Here, I will simply point out that contemporary conditions make Lipstadt's book seem as pertinent as ever, giving it the aura of what rhetorical theory refers to as *kairos* or timeliness. Needless to say, the Irving lawsuit has gained *Denying the Holocaust* many new readers interested in learning the background to this now-famous trial. So, too, has there been interest in books about the trial itself by Lipstadt and her legal team. But meanwhile, Lipstadt's triumph over Irving hasn't killed the denial movement. It remains a force to be countered. In the Middle East, it has actually grown, fueled by rage against the state of Israel. Most prominently, the current president of Iran insists the Holocaust is a Zionist fiction. At the same time, Smith has revived his ad campaign, and some campus papers have published an entire pamphlet of his.

Just as disquieting was C-SPAN's initial plan for dealing with Lipstadt's book about the trial. Not content simply to air a talk by her about the book, at first the network insisted on following this broadcast with a talk by Irving. Quite rightly, Lipstadt and others objected to his being giving equal time, as if Holocaust deniers deserved it. Subsequently, the network changed tack, saying it had never intended to give Irving the same coverage. But many parties suspected C-SPAN was now being disingenuous. As things turned out, it didn't show a talk by either of the two combatants. Yet the whole affair, together with the others I've mentioned, seems a reason to join Lipstadt in feeling that deniers remain a threat.

I must admit that, at this very moment, Irving himself doesn't *seem* menacing. As I write, he has just been released from an Austrian prison, where he'd been serving a term for breaking that country's laws against Holocaust denial. Furthermore, at his sentencing, he showed a new willingness to admit that gassings had occurred at Auschwitz. In a later BBC interview, however, he was more his usual self. He refused to concede the existence of the camp's major gas chambers. He argued that the number of people executed at Auschwitz was rather low. As always, he claimed that Hitler never authorized mass extermination of Jews ("Irving Expands"). Even now, therefore, he remains largely unrepentant, as anyone can tell from his still-active Web site. Indeed, his imprisonment enables him to pose as a martyr for free speech.

But less extreme words than his are also cause for concern. Remember, for one thing, the *Reader's Digest* interview with Mel Gibson. Whatever his real thoughts, he tapped deniers' language and swore fidelity to his extremist father. That a widely read magazine published his remarks with scarce comment makes them all the more chilling. Similarly scary is John Sack's article "Inside the Bunker," originally published in the February 2001 issue of *Esquire* magazine. I want to dwell on this text a bit, not only because of its slant but also because it has won respect. Sack reports on his trip to a conference held by the Institute for Historical Review, a leading denier organization. Because he'd written about Jewish reprisals against the Germans, he'd been invited to speak at this gathering. Though not a denier himself, he accepted. Rather than avoid such people, Sack addressed them and mingled with them. In other words, he challenged Lipstadt's policy of non-debate. Of course, her stand is disputable, and his greater openness might have yielded insights. But his report seems willfully naive about the meeting's participants. Sack is content to depict them as oppressed and charming eccentrics. Thus, his article's appearance in a major periodical is disturbing. Worse, Stephen Jay Gould then selected it for the volume *Best American Essays 2002*.

Sack does convey amazement that deniers resist verified facts about the Holocaust. For the most part, though, he treats them kindly. He insinuates that the conference attendees aren't anti-Semitic, given that they didn't speak that way. He even distinguishes between deniers and "the true Jew haters of the world" (292). But, as Lipstadt and others have shown in exhaustive detail, the Institute for Historical Review has been thoroughly anti-Semitic since its founding. Two of the people that Sack met, Irving and Zundel, have been especially scornful of Jews. In fact, Irving came to this conference after the libel trial, during which his anti-Semitism was well documented. Sack doesn't acknowledge this record. Rather than consider what the trial revealed about Irving, he complains at length about abuse of deniers. He goes so far as to suggest that, if treated better, they might drop their cause. Yet there's no reason to accept Sack's claim that "the deniers survive because they are persecuted" (292). Just as absurd is his effort to equate deniers with less malicious groups. To the charge that deniers are anti-Semitic, he responds that Jewish leaders are "anti-denieric" (291), as if opposition to a certain set of cranks was the same as contempt for an entire religion. This penchant for equalizing marked Sack's conference speech, where he declared that "we all have it in us to become like Nazis" (294). Although his statement doesn't exonerate Nazis, it reinforces the idea that they weren't unusually bad. Naturally his audience cheered. Indeed, Sack ends his article by reporting that he's agreed to be keynote speaker at the institute's next meeting.

When Gould included this article in *Best American Essays*, he knew he had to defend his choice. After all, he himself was a scientist, one who regularly debunked pseudorational accounts of history. In his introduction to the volume, Gould admits that he "struggled with" Sack's analysis of deniers, and he adds that "I disagree with his decision to speak at their meetings." Nonetheless, he says, "The deniers do remain (unlike the actual perpetrators) within the category of human beings, and I supposed that we therefore need to understand them as well as we can" (xvi). As a rationale for honoring an essay, this seems halfhearted. It hardly amounts to a ringing endorsement. Nor does Gould specify how Sack helps us "understand" deniers. In fact, Sack downplays their nastiness, even though he could have evoked them as "human beings" while still probing their moral flaws.

As a counterexample, Sack underscores the wisdom of Lipstadt's stance. Better to avoid deniers, his behavior suggests, than to dialogue with them. True, another writer might talk with them and proceed to describe them more shrewdly than Sack does. But I suspect it's his relative lack of judgment that led *Esquire* and Gould to publish him. Sack's approach seems a fresh take on Holocaust denial, especially after the Irving–Lipstadt case. Many of the reports on the trial portrayed Irving as a mean conniver. In today's competitive market, though, the media pursue novelty, and after the trial a charitable portrait of deniers fit the bill. Will more texts like it appear? The possibility exists. Hence, there's continuing merit in Lipstadt's ill will.

In the Classroom

Though clearly Lipstadt resists debating them, *Denying the Holocaust* doesn't spell out how a school should handle deniers in its midst. She does acknowledge that under the First Amendment, such people "have the absolute right to stand on any street corner and spread their calumnies. They have the right to publish their articles and books and hold their gatherings" (17). Moreover, she seems uninterested in establishing laws against them, as some countries have done. Early in her book, though, she evidently approves one university's firing of a teacher who preached Holocaust denial. Also, recall that despite her remark about deniers' right to publish, she later sought to dissuade St. Martin's from issuing Irving's book on Goebbels. Her own book may leave its readers guessing, then, just how far she would go to thwart deniers on campus. For example, she fails to say whether she'd urge dismissal of every professor who respects them as a legitimate "other side." To be sure, her reticence may be strategic. If she did present specific, detailed policies, readers might brood about each, wondering whether it preserves academic freedom or makes hash of the concept. As her book stands, it mostly analyzes the deniers themselves as a menace, with her opening gesture—her refusal to debate them—signifying that campuses should beware them.

An especially vexing matter is what professors should do with students who espouse or support Holocaust denial in class. Gerald Graff has touched on this problem. Advocating a conflict-centered curriculum in his 1992 book *Beyond the Culture Wars*, he remarks that a number of people would "rightly be offended by proposals to debate questions like 'Did the Holocaust really happen?,'" for this would be a case where "no reputable scholar considers the question open" (14). Even in an essay years later, Graff makes pretty much the same comment. Yet he adds to the later piece a significant observation. While reiterating that the Holocaust's existence *shouldn't* be disputed, he points out that students may feel differently, questioning this and other facts during class. As a result, Graff notes, "teachers may find themselves forced to open . . . [such truths] to debate" ("How I Learned" 37). Here, Graff makes an assumption that I and many faculty share. Normally, we believe, we should enlighten our students, not scold them. Even when they express skepticism that seems foolish, we should strive to educate them rather than dismiss them. Needless to say, this ideal may be hard to enact. For one thing, we may be hazy about how to define it. What exactly occurs in a genuine "teaching moment"? In particular, we may be uncertain about *who* is to learn *what*.

In part, I bring up these considerations because I wrestled with them one day in class. In the early 1990s, when Lipstadt's book first appeared in paperback, I was teaching at the University of Maryland–College Park. One of my undergraduate courses was on modern women essayists. As you might expect, most of the students were female. But a few men did enroll, including a student I'll call Fred. Throughout the semester, Fred was resolutely antifeminist, objecting to the essayists' ideas and to his classmates' remarks. He was one of those students that theorists of critical pedagogy have in mind when they refer to student "resistance." Often, he exasperated me. Still, usually I didn't show him my real feelings. Rather, I gently pushed Fred to support or modify his claims, and I invited other students to respond. In fact, some students privately complimented me for being so patient with him.

On this day, however, Fred went too far for me. As I entered the classroom, the students were buzzing about the latest issue of the campus newspaper. The *Diamondback* had published Bradley Smith's ad, just days before Jews' annual memorializing of the Shoah. My class included several Jewish students, among them the head of the Jewish Student Union. But virtually all of the students were disturbed by the ad, and they were discussing how to protest it. Not Fred, though. He was brazenly contemptuous of their reaction: "All the guy is saying is show him a gas chamber! Just show him a gas chamber! Prove there was any gas chamber at all!" Perhaps Fred just wanted to be ornery. But quite possibly he was sincere. At any rate, the class grew tensely quiet. To make things worse, Fred looked to me for help. Apparently he thought I would treat his demand as legitimate. After all, hadn't I always listened to him respectfully? Meanwhile, I sensed the other students waiting to see if I'd respect him now, even though he was supporting a Holocaust denier. Indeed, to accept Fred's outburst as reasonable would be to accept Smith's ad as such.

Ultimately, I rejected both. "I'm sorry, Fred," I said. "I'm willing to tolerate all sorts of opinions, but I draw the line at Holocaust denial! The gas chambers are a proven fact. There's no real debate about them." This response clearly startled him. For once, Fred was at a loss for words. Any minute now, I thought, he'll snap back at me—but he didn't. Nor did anyone else say anything. So, I plunged into the day's assignment: "Let's turn to Adrienne Rich's essay." And in the weeks that followed, my behavior toward Fred didn't have any clear repercussions. We continued to study modern women essayists as we'd done before.

I consider my response to Fred a rhetorical refusal. In reacting as I did, I pointedly violated his expectations. Most likely, he hadn't assumed I'd agree with him, but surely he thought that once more I'd tolerate what he'd said. This time, however, I scoffed, in a break from habit that registered with him and with the rest of the class. I'd decided that my responsibility as a teacher was to certify the gas chambers' existence, even if this meant ruling a particular student out of bounds. Whether or not I managed to convince Fred—and I don't know if I did—I felt obligated to reassure the other class members about a historical fact.

To this day, I'm fairly happy with how I handled the situation. I remind myself that my response wasn't—and isn't—my common practice. In my classes, I face many fervent displays of opinion. As I've noted elsewhere (*Between* 155), conservatives who accuse faculty of imposing political correctness ignore how often *students* use class to promote their own ideologies. Most of the positions that my students advance do strike me as worth mulling over. Therefore, I use their opinions as springboards for debate. For each class that I teach, I try in this way to establish a certain ethos. I want the students to feel that I'll usually respect their views. Once I manage to develop this reputation, however, I'm willing to risk it occasionally. That is, because I've accumulated quite a bit of moral "capital," I can dare to dismiss absurd proclamations like Fred's.

Still, I'm not thoroughly ecstatic about my approach to him. In one of her book's few comments on pedagogy, Lipstadt proposes another move. Although she wouldn't have students consider whether the Holocaust occurred, she says that "it is crucial that they be shown *how* we know what we know, e.g., how oral testimony is correlated with historical documentation; how testimony is evaluated for its historical accuracy; and how artifacts are determined to be genuine" (xiv). We can take her to mean that with the likes of Fred, I should be more patient and methodical. I suspect this approach is more feasible in history courses, especially those focused on the Shoah. In my course, only briefly did the Holocaust come up, and it did so because of Smith's ad. At any rate, Lipstadt's proposal keeps me wondering whether I treated Fred right. She reminds me that rhetorical refusals are debatable—including the one I performed that day. True, this chapter has defended Lipstadt's own refusal to contend with Holocaust deniers. But even I see her act as needing to be continually reviewed and pondered, especially given developments like the libel suit. My next chapter focuses on what can happen when rhetorical refusals do encounter new contexts.

5 WHEN A REFUSAL'S CONTEXT CHANGES

David Irving's lawsuit has enlarged Deborah Lipstadt's audience. By attacking *Denying the Holocaust*, he's won the book new readers, curious about this text that sparked an epic courtroom battle. Naturally, their awareness of the legal proceedings shapes their reading experience. They open the book knowing Lipstadt was sued. The same goes for previous readers of the book now revisiting it. The first time round, few of us guessed it would land its author in court. When she wrote it, Lipstadt herself didn't expect to end up there. But now, rereading the book, we're mindful she went on trial for it. Thus, we see her rhetorical refusal in a new light. As we read once again her stand against debating Holocaust deniers like Irving, we know that later she had to contend with his libel charge. The context of *any* rhetorical refusal may change significantly, a possibility that studies of such acts should consider. In this chapter, therefore, I want to focus on what can happen to a rhetorical refusal's impact over time.

With the passage of time, many a rhetorical act faces new audiences whose lenses may differ from those of the original target group. In his 1965 book *Rhetorical Criticism: A Study in Method*, Edwin Black urged his field to examine this kind of development. He proposed that rhetorical studies "assess all the differences a rhetorical discourse has made in the world and will make, and how the differences are made and why" (74). Black hasn't been the only scholar to set such an agenda. In the next couple of decades, for example, Jacques Derrida emphasized how an utterance's context may prove unstable ("Signature," "Limited"), and Edward Said stressed that theoretical claims may get reinterpreted as they "travel."[1] Similarly concerned with textual itineraries is the rhetorician Steven Mailloux. Since the 1980s, he's called for tracing the multiple contexts a literary work moves through.[2]

Black was challenging the typical way that rhetorical critics analyzed an oral or written text. Quite rightly, he saw them preferring to dwell on the text's first appearance. Nowadays, there are several exceptions to this practice. I've just referred to Mailloux, who still cultivates "reception histories" (the title of his 1998 book). Another example is Jeanne Fahnestock, who examines how articles in science journals are misrepresented in the popular press. In the area of visual rhetoric (another sort of "text"), Robert Hariman and John Lucaites analyze appropriations of iconic photographs. Meanwhile, in the field of rhetoric and composition, John Trimbur has called for studies of how works circulate. That Trimbur demands such scholarship, though, suggests he feels it's lacking. In fact, most rhetorical critics continue to fixate on primal scenes.

To be fair, their habit is understandable. They take on an important and often complex task when they research a rhetorical act's first milieu. To grasp what occurs in a rhetorical refusal, we must study its first occasion and constituency. After all, these acts deliberately defy their original audience's norms. In general, though, a rhetorical utterance's later treks also merit analysis. If we analyze them, we'll grow more alert to the utterance's specific features, and we'll better sense how, with shifts in time or place, it's been variously perceived. Hence, we should examine a rhetorical refusal's long-term fate.

True, not every act of this kind will change much in meaning and impact. Take Arlene Croce's "Discussing the Undiscussable." Six years after its publication in the *New Yorker*, it reappeared in her collection *Writing in the Dark*. This book's recycling of her article does provide a somewhat new framework for it. "Discussing" is one of the volume's last three pieces, and the final two join it in lamenting a decline of standards in the dance world. Indeed, in the book's preface, Croce declares that 1989 was "the last year of ballet, the end of the wonderfully creative and progressive ballet I'd known all my life" (9). Thus, "Discussing" has acquired an air of valediction. Now, it seems part of Croce's overall farewell to her field. Nevertheless, public response to it hasn't altered dramatically. Croce's refusal to see *Still/Here* is still controversial. Reviewers of the volume singled out the article as if it remains grounds for dispute. As I noted earlier, this reaction was even encouraged by Croce herself, for in her book's preface she declares that "Discussing" is her "most notorious piece" and that she would not "have written it differently" (8). The latter statement is bound to keep her fans content, her critics irked.

Plenty of rhetorical refusals, though, have been more significantly re-packaged. Consider another text I analyzed earlier, Maxine Hairston's address at the spring 1985 national meeting of the Conference on College Composition and Communication. Recall that after she presented it as a speech, Hairston published it in the October 1985 issue of the journal *College Composition and Communication*. On both occasions, presumably, she defined her target audience as writing instructors. Certainly her rhetorical refusal was a recommendation that they cease talking with literature faculty and even consider seceding from English departments. Also in the fall of 1985, however, Hairston's text appeared in another journal: the *Association of Departments of English (ADE) Bulletin*. My university's library even received the *ADE* issue before the *CCC* one. The audience for the *ADE Bulletin* includes literature specialists. Much of its readership consists of English department chairs, many of whom are in their positions because of their literary background. How did Hairston expect these people to react when they saw her arguing that composition specialists—including herself—weren't in a rhetorical situation with them? Should they have considered themselves helpless spectators at a composition conspiracy? Or, was Hairston indeed trying to converse with them, albeit through a warning: "We will snub you and eventually leave you if you don't treat us better"? She does seem to draw *ADE* readers into a rhetorical situation even as she declares they can't share one with her. And so, while her message to her target audience is plain, her message to the *ADE* audience is ambiguous. She demonstrates that when a rhetorical refusal shifts venue, mixed signals may arise about its aims.

In the rest of this chapter, I look at the migrations of three specific refusals. I examine an interview given by Michel Foucault; an essay by the literary theorist Jane Tompkins; and grand jury testimony by President Bill Clinton. In each instance, the writer or speaker notably defied the audience's norms. But the subsequent "public career" of these refusals involved major shifts in context, another reason I gather them together. Their fate reminds us that we should look beyond a rhetorical refusal's debut. We need to consider its later adventures, how it has fared in shifting circumstances. We must also decide what to *do* with such acts when their contexts change.

Furthermore, each of the refusals I discuss in this chapter challenged reigning distinctions between public and private. More generally, the cases of Foucault, Tompkins, and Clinton show how rhetorical refusals can trouble attempts at separating these realms. Distinguishing them has been a task pursued by average citizens as well as political leaders. In fact, American history has seen many efforts to define these spheres in ways that will keep them clearly, permanently apart. Ironically, the result is that boundaries between private and public have often been contested and redrawn.

Deborah Nelson makes this point about the contemporary United States in her 2002 book *Pursuing Privacy in Cold War America*. Nelson is especially interested in showing that debates about privacy have become something of an American tradition. As her title implies, Nelson focuses on the three or so decades after World War II. In this era, she observes, the nation saw privacy as distinctly American. Our love of it, supposedly, made us better than the Soviet Union and other totalitarian states. Yet, our government's fear of Reds led to increased surveillance; cultural critics decried Big Business's influence over consumers; and, eventually, Watergate led to new scrutiny of the government's own secrecy. In addition, Nelson recalls, the classic idea of privacy as a male-ruled home came to face women's protest against their restriction to that space. Indeed, with *Roe v. Wade*, the Supreme Court honored a more female-oriented notion of privacy by affirming women's control of their bodies. Later, though, in *Bowers v. Hardwick*, the Court condoned laws against homosexual conduct; police could still invade a gay man's bedroom. Nelson concludes that together, these developments show that privacy isn't a settled concept. Fairly consistently, Americans have argued over its meaning, value, and scope. Moreover, at any point in the deliberations, the specific issues may shift. As I was writing this book, one hot topic was brain-damaged Terri Schiavo, whose husband was legally empowered to remove her feeding tube. Among the controversial features of her case was the federal government's intervention, its bold effort to get the tube restored. Meanwhile, other government infringements on privacy have aroused opposition. Nelson wrote prior to the terrorist attacks of September 11, 2001, so she doesn't refer to the Bush administration's security measures since, yet debate rages over the surveillance authorized by steps like the Patriot Act. Also, there's increasing fear of privacy's being erased through technology. Some worry that their very identity will be snatched by scam artists of the Internet. Some groan when they must overhear cell phone users' romantic or medical woes. To be sure, worry has also arisen over certain *retreats* into privacy. Some fear that the common good will be harmed by various *withdrawals* from public space. For example, increasingly people object to iPod users' aural cocoons. Uneasiness has grown, too, over the seclusion adopted by America's gated enclaves of the rich.

Though Americans have repeatedly squabbled over the relation of private to public, they can always stand to be reminded of these terms' instability, especially while efforts to reify them persist. Moreover, rhetorical refusals like Foucault's, Tompkins's, and Clinton's suggest that public/private dichotomies are not only temporary but tactical. This isn't to say that the terms are merely elements of discourse. Institutions have deployed notions of them to regulate behavior, with quite material effects. But the refusals I will discuss here do call attention to how a public/private binary may be rhetorically revised.

Foucault

The interview with Foucault was first published in a 1980 issue of *Le Monde*. It was part of the newspaper's then-weekly series of dialogues with prominent thinkers. On this occasion, Foucault wanted readers to forget his stature, to draw their own conclusions, and to note that intellectual developments can emerge from mass movements instead of from master pundits. He worried about the power exerted by his own public repute, fearing that people were captivated by him as a figure and not prone to grapple with his theories. "A name makes reading too easy," he complained. In a ludic vein, he even proposed that "for a year, books would be published without their authors' names" (321). Consistent with these sentiments, Foucault insisted on anonymity for the interview. In a rhetorical refusal, he kept his identity private, even though published interviews usually make the interviewee known. The article's title: "The Masked Philosopher."

By now, however, its subject's name has become quite public. You can find Foucault's originally anonymous interview in *Ethics, Subjectivity, and Truth: The Essential Works of Michel Foucault 1954–1984, Volume 1*. It appears, too, in another "Greatest Hits" collection, *The Essential Foucault*. In both volumes, Foucault's identity is by no means secret. Moreover, both books encourage us to see his *Le Monde* remarks as a key part of his public oeuvre. In the *Ethics* collection, the editors even end with the interview, implying that it sums up important tenets of this entire Foucault anthology. To be fair, they faced a no-win situation. They would have had trouble keeping Foucault anonymous in this piece if they included it in any collection devoted to his works at all. Besides, they were hardly the first to reveal his name. The masked philosopher had been unmasked years before. In any case, wherever the interview appears now, this Lone Ranger is known. Hence, we can't look at his refusal the way its original readers did.

One of our tasks, then, becomes tracing specific differences and similarities between this refusal's first context and our own. In part, such inquiry entails further probing of Foucault's career. His masking of himself in the interview was philosophically consistent with certain other texts of his, even though he disclosed his identity in those. In particular, his anonymity in *Le Monde* reflects ideas he expressed in "What Is an Author?," his essay from a few years before. Interestingly, that piece ends with Samuel Beckett's question "What difference does it make who is speaking?" (120), an issue that Foucault's rhetorical refusal in the interview raises as well. In "What Is an Author?," Foucault examines various roles—social, historical, institutional, ideological—played by the "author function," our habit of classifying and interpreting certain texts by tying them to their creators' names. He emphasizes that this focus on the author's personal identity isn't a timeless and universal routine. As he concludes the essay, he even foresees an era that isn't concerned with the author: "[F]iction and its polysemous texts will once again function according to another mode, but still with a system of constraint—one which will no longer be the author, but which will have to be determined or, perhaps, experienced" (119). Thus, when he ends with the words "What difference does it make who is speaking?," he's envisioning a society that poses this question with a shrug. Nevertheless, Foucault held that his own society had yet to enter this phase. He believed that it was still preoccupied with identifying and publicizing authors. Hence, when he masked himself in *Le Monde*, he aimed to alter the status quo. He hoped to shift his readers' attention from names to ideas.

In fact, as I've noted, the Foucault who talked with *Le Monde* was beleaguered by his personal fame. His biographer James Miller reports that "in Paris, he could not venture out at night without being mobbed by fans." Moreover, "even in America, he had become a star of sorts, particularly on many college campuses" (320). Though many theorists would have welcomed this public attention, Foucault regretted it. A few months after the *Le Monde* interview, Miller reports, he displayed his chagrin just before a lecture he gave at the University of California–Berkeley. Unsettled by the crowd awaiting him, Foucault had his friend Hubert Dreyfus make the following announcement: "Michel Foucault says this is a very technical lecture, and difficult, and, I think, he wants to imply, boring; and he suggests that it would be better for everyone to leave *now*" (qtd. in Miller 321). I wouldn't call this warning a rhetorical refusal, if only because Foucault was trying to get rid of his audience rather than to change its beliefs. But the announcement did show he rued his celebrity. Given this mood, his anonymity in the interview is even more understandable. There, too, he was expressing dismay at his own renown.

Of course, audiences are more apt to find a mask thought-provoking if they assume that the person is actually famous. Throughout history, though, numerous authors have never become celebrated in the first place. And often, their obscurity results from discrimination against some group they belong to. When Virginia Woolf hypothesizes in *A Room of One's Own* that "Anon, who wrote so many poems without signing them, was often a woman" (51), she's intimating that the oblivion of many female artists is due to centuries-old male supremacy. Indeed, while feminist theory can learn much from Foucault, he was sketchy on the topic of gender. Male supremacy has shaped notions of authorship more than he admitted.

Still, would *any* literary or cultural theorist today feel suffocated as he was by public attention? Probably not. While the American academy hopes to breed public intellectuals, it seems to be producing few. Granted, some of its members have managed to seize the larger world's regard. African American intellectuals Henry Louis Gates, bell hooks, and Cornel West enjoy a wide readership. Deborah Tannen's books on gender differences have become best-sellers. Stanley Fish writes op-ed columns for the *New York Times*. Still, I have trouble imagining an American professor besieged by hordes of fans. Nor does it seem possible that a newspaper in this country would run a series of interviews with college faculty. The biggest glare of publicity most can aspire to is an appearance on C-SPAN's weekend *Books TV*. Were he still alive, probably Foucault himself would again attract a mob at Berkeley, and so might certain other Continental theorists such as Jurgen Habermas and Jean Baudrillard. But they wouldn't become utter American idols. Our culture isn't like France in the 1980s, keenly attuned to the High Priests of Theory. It's more guarded toward the professional sages in its midst.

This cautiousness isn't necessarily bad. It may even be seen as what Foucault was advocating in his 1980 interview. Though his anonymity is now gone, we can still adopt the attitude he expressed when he declared that "the right to knowledge [*droit au savoir*] must not be reserved to a particular age group or to certain categories of people" (326). By keeping his identity private, Foucault was basically protesting the mandarin tendency to accuse the masses of false consciousness. To be sure, he never sentimentalized them. Actually, he could sound quite gloomy about the prospects of social change. He did believe, though, that vital ideas and acts can emerge from populist movements, and this prospect is worth taking seriously. Had Foucault lived past 1984, he might have felt reinforced by some later events: say, the overthrow of Communist regimes or the protests at capitalist economic summits.

Foucault's masking in *Le Monde* might also spur us to continue the academic tradition of blind review. When they have scholars assess a manuscript, most academic presses and journals withhold its author's name. Furthermore, many of them never tell the author who the evaluators are. The habit of blind review isn't deeply entrenched everywhere in the academy. Not until 1980, the year of Foucault's interview, was a policy of anonymous submission adopted by *PMLA*, the leading journal in literary studies. And that decision has had its critics, most notably Fish.[3] Nor is blind review foolproof: some judges of manuscripts have proved able to detect their authors, and vice versa. Still, generally speaking, scholarly publishers have joined Foucault in valuing authorial anonymity, at least when they're seeking preliminary appraisals of a writer's work.

That last clause is important, though, for certainly reputations have counted in academe. Whatever a preliminary reader says, scholars are more apt to get published if they're already exalted in their field. Thus, Foucault's secretiveness back in 1980 does challenge academic mores that survive. Indeed, besides historicizing his gesture, we might take it as an invitation to critique lingering scholarly habits. Yes, the masked philosopher's cover was blown, but Foucault's willful disguise should move us, I think, to examine and question how each field remains a "star system," David Shumway's term for literary studies. True, our chances are small of making the academy utterly democratic. Fish is right when, in his essay criticizing blind review, he argues that no manuscript can be judged only on its "intrinsic merit," for social forces will always influence how we interpret and evaluate it. In reading texts by established scholars, we're bound to consider their personal reputation. Whether we revere these people or are prejudiced against them, we won't encounter their work with a wide-open mind. Nevertheless, we can strive to curb their fame's effect on our reading, not letting their identity shape our entire response.

Moreover, we can be skeptical toward other academic forms of stargazing. For example, though supposedly the humanities have entered a "post-theory" phase, many members of these fields still like to support their arguments simply by citing Foucault, along with a few other theorists. That is, they write as if sheer invocation constituted evidence. The masked philosopher would frown upon these ritualistic uses of his name.

Admittedly, Foucault hid his identity only in the 1980 interview. If we're going to put the latter in historical context, we should note that, before and after, Foucault courted attention. If he wasn't the Paris Hilton of theory, he wasn't its Garbo either. He may have tried to repel the crowd at Berkeley, but he didn't tell it to stop reading his books, and he went on with his lecture. Whatever lessons for the present we find in his moment of anonymity, let's acknowledge that Foucault himself didn't always uphold them.

Of course, we're hardly required to take his *Le Monde* interview as germane to our current lives. Though the anthologies I've referred to make it central to the Foucault canon, there's no evidence it ever won admirers far and wide. Furthermore, many studies of Foucault don't even mention it. On the other hand, we *can* view this conversation as more than a historical document. In particular, Foucault's self-masking may prove relevant to us. A rhetorical refusal's first circumstances certainly merit study, but the act may inspire additional audiences later on.

Tompkins

Foucault's concealment of his identity in *Le Monde* remains pretty startling. But other rhetorical refusals don't remain "abnormal discourse," to use Thomas Kuhn's term. In some circles, at least, they become conventional, even if not every member of these groups approves. A clear case in literary theory is Jane Tompkins's essay "Me and My Shadow." Originally it appeared in a 1987 issue of the journal *New Literary History*. Tompkins then expanded it for publication in Linda Kauffman's 1989 volume *Gender and Theory: Dialogues on Feminist Criticism*. (This is the version I'll quote from here.) The essay's appearance in Kauffman's book—just two years after its debut—suggests that it had swiftly gained the field's attention. Eventually, Tompkins's kind of writing proved quite influential in literary studies.

Today, we can associate it with Kuhn's term "normal discourse," for it has entered the discipline's standard set of genres.[4]

In its first appearance, "Me and My Shadow" was part of a symposium that *New Literary History* organized around Ellen Messer-Davidow's essay "The Philosophical Bases of Feminist Literary Criticisms." Officially, Tompkins was one of nine respondents to Messer-Davidow. Yet, in contrast to the other respondents, Tompkins spends much time on matters other than Messer-Davidow's claims, thereby departing conspicuously from protocols of response. She admits, "My response to this essay is not a response to something Ellen-Messer Davidow has written; it is a response to something within myself" (128). Above all, Tompkins uses the occasion to repudiate the then-current discourse of literary theory, which she finds too impersonal and stifling:

> The problem is that you can't talk about your private life in the course of doing your professional work. You have to pretend that epistemology, or whatever you're writing about, has nothing to do with your life, that it's more exalted, more important, because it (supposedly) *transcends* the merely personal. Well, I'm tired of the conventions that keep discussions of epistemology, or James Joyce, segregated from meditations on what is happening outside my window or inside my heart. The public-private dichotomy, which is to say, the public-private *hierarchy*, is a founding condition of female oppression. I say to hell with it. (122–23)

"I say to hell with it" is a good example of a rhetorical refusal. In Tompkins's climactic proclamation, the immediate referent for "it" is the privileging of the public over the private, which Tompkins feels especially damages women. But her "it" refers, too, to literary theorists' conventional mode of writing, which Tompkins also disputes. In general, she enacts the principle of "to hell with it" by consciously swerving from her assigned task, which was to weigh Messer-Davidow's argument.

Much of Tompkins's piece is candid autobiography, a series of reflections on her personal experiences, concerns, and sentiments. She brings up such topics as her therapy, her father's illness, her relationship with her husband, the suicide of a friend, encounters she's had with Messer-Davidow, the weather outside as she writes, and even her contemplated trip to the bathroom. At the time, these subjects were rare for an academic journal such as *New Literary History*, let alone for a colloquy on a philosophical treatise. Nancy Miller recalls that she "was electrified by this piece when it first appeared" and that for her, "its will to be personal was surprising, even in the critical context of a feminism that historically has included and valorized testimonial writing" (4). As she points out, "Me and My Shadow" was especially unusual in its forthright expression of female rage (22–23). Historically, anger has been a male prerogative, with hostile women denounced as monsters. When she makes statements like "to hell with it," however, Tompkins defies this stigma. She asserts women's right to vent.

Yet, Tompkins's essay soon became popular in various quarters, most especially literary studies. There, an early sign of its increasing stature was its prominent inclusion in Kauffman's book. Though that volume also featured Messer-Davidow's essay, Tompkins's appeared in a different section, and it was followed by two responses to its own remarks. A year later in the journal *College English*, Olivia Frey began an article by praising Tompkins's essay as "revolutionary" and "brave," declaring that it "raises several important issues that those of us in the community of literary scholars cannot afford to ignore" (507). Subsequently, Frey included the essay in *The Intimate Critique*, a collection she edited along with Diane P. Freedman and Frances Murphy Zauhar. By now, in its amplified form, it has entered a host of anthologies, becoming an ur-text for scholars ready for their own close-up.

Granted, Tompkins's stand has been criticized. In his article "Secrecy and Disclosure as Rhetorical Forms," Black observes that "we may have a general distaste for secrecy, but it does not follow that we are uniformly comfortable with disclosure" (147). Several theorists have expressed "distaste" for Tompkins's revelations. Scorned, among other things, is her mention of going to the bathroom. Charles Altieri, for example, finds this reference "melodramatic" (67), while David Simpson mocks her for conveying the sentiment "I pee, therefore I am" ("Speaking" 86). A more serious charge is that Tompkins perpetuates gender stereotypes. Several theorists regret that she disdains theory as a hopelessly masculinist enterprise. They're bothered, too, that she links women with the emotive memoirs she favors. Toril Moi, for example, objects to this dualism. She recalls that Simone de Beauvoir was passionate about philosophy, committed to deploying it on behalf of women. Moi herself believes theory *can* serve feminist ends. Meanwhile, other critics of Tompkins fault her for preaching essentialist feminism. Ironically, these opponents include Kauffman. Though she put "Me and My Shadow" in *Gender and Theory*, she thinks it narrow-minded. Women, she argues, are more diverse than Tompkins recognizes. In a piece she published later ("The Long Goodbye"), she scolds Tompkins for dwelling on her own bourgeois life. Further, she attacks Tompkins's basic concept of identity. To Kauffman, the self isn't as legible and stable as Tompkins thinks (137–38).

In the expanded version of "Me and My Shadow" that she wrote for Kauffman, Tompkins herself reports such complaints. She notes that she's been accused of advocating "a return to the 'rhetoric of presence,' to an 'earlier, naive, untheoretical feminism'" (121). Remember that she made this observation in 1989, not long after her piece premiered. Already, it had provoked much debate. And even if the controversy around it has ebbed, it has yet to be universally praised.

Nevertheless, the essay has had many admirers, and its critics have felt obliged to contend with it. Thus, it deserves to be called canonical. Indeed, Tompkins's rhetorical refusal has become a rhetorical touchstone. Meanwhile, Messer-Davidow's essay—the subject of Tompkins's "response"—has dropped out of sight. Nowadays, probably most of Tompkins's readers are unacquainted with it or know it only from her account. To use a sports analogy: Bobby Richardson is legendary for his grand slam in the 1960 World Series, but few recall that the pitcher was Clem Labine.

How did Tompkins's refusal wind up achieving wide acceptance? We need to address this question if we want to play historian—and as we ponder whether and how to emulate Tompkins now. In part, the impact of "Me and My Shadow" mirrors developments in the world beyond academe. As Nancy Miller notes, the second wave of feminism had already been privileging testimonials. More generally, identity politics was on the rise. Increasing numbers of people defined themselves in terms of their gender, race, sexual orientation, and the like while insisting that others declare how these things shaped their views. But a development in commercial publishing was significant, too. In the late 1980s and 1990s, plenty of autobiographies gained a wide audience. Cultural commentators referred to "the memoir boom." Even today, it shows no sign of collapsing. Though "Me and My Shadow" is an academic essay, its fans no doubt include those also beguiled by best-selling revelations: for example, *The Liars' Club*, *Angela's Ashes*, and *The Kiss*. Tompkins has benefited, I suspect, from this larger trend in literary taste. An issue for more research, of course, is *why* this taste exists. Aside from identity politics, what prompts it? What has led our society to peer into formerly walled interiors—lately, by means of "reality" TV? Various factors seem relevant. One is the weakening of traditional social bonds, especially those of family and place. Many cultural analysts argue that the result has been increased feelings of isolation, so that we lust for any human links. At the same time, developments in communications technology—from TV to e-mail to cell phones—whet our appetite for glimpsing other lives. Meanwhile, the West's general loosening of moral codes has given the media more freedom. Now, they can make tawdry circuses out of ordinary citizens' struggles: for example, the issue of who'll sleep with whom on *Big Brother*. Forced now, in fact, to compete with dozens of other channels, TV networks actively look for sensational true dramas, especially since they're fairly cheap to air.

But these are only a few possible reasons for the efflorescence of voyeurism. Indeed, hordes of books examine why privacy is gone. Therefore, let me return to particular conditions of the academy, where Tompkins's piece has circulated most. One reason for its impact there was her professional standing. Only a person already esteemed by her field would have been asked to respond in the first place. Moreover, this status enabled her to take rhetorical risks. If a less-known scholar had mused about going to the bathroom, she might have elicited only snorts.

Yet, also important are the limits of Tompkins's daring. As a literary theorist, she isn't altogether subversive. Her rhetorical refusal accords with some forces already at work in her field. As David Simpson ("Speaking") and Jane Gallop point out, literary scholarship has always let its practitioners display some subjectivity, even if they have had to control its presence. Moreover, as Tompkins observes in her essay, her stress on the subjective accords with the post-1960s movement called reader-response theory (135), a trend that she herself had helped develop. Her emphasis can be linked as well to poststructuralism, which by 1987 had already encouraged creative analyses of texts. Also by then, politically minded theorists were protesting literary scholarship that claimed to arrive at sheer truth. In their view, literary criticism and theory should be explicitly self-reflective. That is, scholars should probe how they're influenced by their biases and social positions.

Noteworthy, too, as I've observed elsewhere (*Between* 181), is that Tompkins does insert a traditional academic critique. True, she spends just two pages pointedly analyzing Messer-Davidow's argument, less than the journal's audience probably expected. Moreover, she couches her evaluation in the subjunctive mode. Announcing "This is how I would reply to Ellen's essay if I were to do it in the professionally sanctioned way" (124), Tompkins attempts some distance from academic discourse. All the same, she employs that discourse, and she makes her judgment of Messer-Davidow's piece clear. "Messer-Davidow assumes," she observes, "that if we change our epistemology, our practices as critics will change too." In Tompkins's view, this position is wrong. Epistemology can't affect practice, and any hope that it does "stems from a confused notion of what an epistemology is" (124). According to Tompkins, "Epistemology, strictly speaking, is a *theory* about the origins and nature of knowledge" (124–25). That is, it may *account for* our particular convictions, but it won't actually *shape* them: "Knowing that my knowledge is perspectival, language-based, culturally constructed, or what have you does not change in the slightest the things I believe to be true" (125).

Whether or not Tompkins's critique is sound, what's significant is that she provides one. She's rendered a judgment of Messer-Davidow's logic. Yes, Tompkins quickly goes back to questioning the academic response as a genre, preferring personal testimony once more. But her rhetorical refusal hasn't proved consistent. She's interrupted it, if briefly, with a show of loyalty to discursive norms. In effect, she reminds us that rhetorical refusals never just convey "to hell with it." As attempts at persuasion, they resist mocking all of their audience's standards. Some, they treat as more or less divine.

Nevertheless, theorists such as Simpson and David Shumway ("Solidarity or Perspectivity?") exaggerate when they claim that "Me and My Shadow" is ultratraditional. There's an important sense in which Tompkins *isn't* being misleading when she declares "to hell with it." In their stark personal fury, these words do flout her discipline's previous mores. It's easy to see why Nancy Miller was "electrified."

Throughout her essay, Tompkins is engagingly clear and passionate. As we explore why her essay has been appealing, we ought to consider her language, for clearly much of her audience liked it. Even critics of her content may appreciate her style. At any rate, many of her readers have been drawn to her essay's personal voice. Moreover, since the voice belongs to a person of high status, they take it as authorizing their own disclosures. One of the essay's goals is to encourage testimonies like hers; Tompkins tells her audience that she hopes her piece "will express something you yourself have felt or will help you find a part of yourself that you would like to express" (126).

For women readers, her example was especially catalytic. After all, Tompkins sees herself breaking with a discourse of male supremacy. At the end of her new introduction, she reports that "I now tend to think that theory itself, at least as it is usually practiced, may be one of the patriarchal gestures women *and* men ought to avoid" (122). In both the original and amplified versions of her essay, though, Tompkins mostly cares about women. She stresses that theory-talk harms *them*. She holds that it aims to be impersonal, logical, competitive—traits, she notes, deemed male. She argues, too, that it discourages affect, traditionally thought of as women's realm. Thus, when Tompkins engages in blatantly emotional confession, she depicts it as feminist. Although, as I've noted, some women object, many others have cheered. Within academe, Tompkins has inspired several to write about themselves, thereby joining her war on theory's masculinist bent. While hers wasn't the only text spurring this craze, "Me and My Shadow" helped launch it.

Since much writing in literary studies is now explicitly personal, the context for Tompkins's essay has changed. Her piece could even appear in a journal called *Fairly Old Literary History*. At first, Tompkins's rhetorical refusal was an act of resistance, an intervention in her professional scene. Today, because literary scholarship teems with autobiographies, her refusal no longer shocks. To be sure, certain pockets of her discipline remain leery of such writing. If you're in literary studies, don't get intimate with a journal like *Modern Philology*, and don't expect your memoir to win you tenure at Yale. Nevertheless, Tompkins's case raises the issue of what to do with a rhetorical refusal that's become something of a convention.

For one thing, we can evaluate the refusal's influence. Was it good that so many in literary studies felt enlightened by "Me and My Shadow"? Is their field better because they welcomed, even imitated, this essay? These questions return us to the text's possible faults. In my earlier book *Between the Lines*, I myself criticized Tompkins's piece, finding three main problems with it (179–82). First, Tompkins is misleading when she claims to display her genuine self. Though she feels stifled by the literary theorist's typical persona, her alternative is a construction, too. It's an artful, strategic performance of authenticity rather than a baring of soul. In other words, Tompkins overlooks the *rhetoric* of personal writing, its particular tactics and aims. Second, she hardly confronts her own professional status, though it largely protects her from harm. In the 1980s, confessional prose could be risky for junior academics. Even now, it's not always a good career move for them. Whatever the merits of self-expression, Tompkins ignores her institutional power, the leverage she's already achieved. Finally, her focus on individual will neglects the importance of social movements. Toward the end, she does imply that it's good to "write the letters, make the phone calls, [and] attend the meetings" (138), but generally she disregards the need for collective action.

I still feel these criticisms are fair. Furthermore, I'm willing to turn them into imperatives. If you're a literary scholar tempted to imitate Tompkins, acknowledge that personal writing is rhetorical! Examine the relevance of social status! Recognize the value of groups! But let's go beyond such prescriptions. If a particular rhetorical refusal no longer comes across as daring, then we might imagine replacements for it—alternatives that do seem bold. Because Tompkins's discourse has become common in her field, let's consider what would be unconventional in literary studies today. If members of the discipline were to startle their audiences, what would they have to do now?

One possibility is to reverse gear. If Tompkins's field has pretty much come to accept the confessional mode she advocated, then a truly rebellious move today would be clinical detachment. Moi wryly remarks that "subjectivity can become a prison-house from which a few moments of impersonality can be a delightful respite" (155). Yet, the whole objective/subjective opposition—which tends to coincide with the public/private one—can be confining in itself. Rita Felski, among others, points us toward a middle ground, observing that "the best feminist work on reading interweaves the scholarly and the personal, the critical and the confessional, using each to illuminate the other" (56). Besides, all such binaries may get distracting. After all, plenty of issues can be raised about the rhetoric of literary studies. Several of the field's writing practices merit debate.

An example is the way many literary critics conclude their articles. They end by implying they've definitively analyzed whatever text they've discussed. They don't suggest that understanding it requires more thought and research. To be sure, they may propose ways of applying their methods to other subjects. Basically, though, they rest content with the interpretation they've produced. As I've noted elsewhere ("Scholarship" 26), this air of finality is rare in the sciences and social sciences, where most articles end by proposing ways of further studying their topic. At present, then, a rhetorical refusal in literary criticism might entail acting like these other fields. The critic wouldn't treat textual analysis as a discrete and perfect triumph. Rather, it would come across as a collective, ongoing project—as a public conversation that the critic has joined.

To show what I mean, I turn to the ending of a recent article, James Annesley's "Pure Shores: Travel, Consumption, and Alex Garland's *The Beach*," which appears in the Fall 2004 issue of *Modern Fiction Studies*. If you're familiar with Garland's 1996 book or if you've seen the film version, you'll remember that it's about a remote island community in present-day Thailand. The story's hero is attracted to this seeming paradise, but finally it is attacked and wrecked by drug lords. For Annesley, the hero is quixotic to hope he can flee our global economy for nature. Long ago, Annesley argues, capital invaded our alleged Edens. Inspired, however, by Michael Hardt and Antonio Negri's emphasis on agency in their 2000 book, *Empire*, Annesley searches *The Beach* for means of resisting the new world order. Ultimately, he's heartened by the characters' references to popular culture, for these show how people can tailor dominant discourse to their own aims. Annesley's conclusion:

> *The Beach*'s style thus offers a solution to some of the dilemmas explored in the novel's content and gestures toward the existence of creative dynamics that both survive processes of incorporation and draw nourishment and strength from those same processes. The point is that these elements are not only central to the analysis of the novel, but significant in terms of the implications they raise for the interpretation of the relationships between culture and capital. Reflecting on the significance of Garland's language and recognizing the connections that tie these elements with the ideas raised by Hardt and Negri thus generates a wider perspective on the developing debates around aesthetics, culture, and globalization. It is this sense of the ways in which the text can be read in terms that prompt an analysis of these broader issues that stands, this paper argues, as the most significant feature of Alex Garland's *The Beach*. (567)

By focusing on a contemporary novel, by relating it to the current economy, and by invoking Hardt and Negri's recent book, this conclusion seems resolutely postmodern. Yet, Annesley is old-fashioned when he ends by announcing that he's discerned the novel's "most significant feature." True, he refers to ongoing "debates" about "aesthetics, culture, and globalization," as if he hasn't resolved social issues dramatized in *The Beach*. Like many critics, though, he claims success as an interpreter, implying that he's settled the meaning and import of this text. Tompkins, perhaps, would say that he's traditional as well in his style, for his sort of prose is what she had in mind when she scorned her field's abstractness. At any rate, Annesley's form of closure is classic.

What if he were to end in a way that, for his field, would be more daring? That is, what if he were to provide an additional paragraph that reads as follows?

> Nevertheless, I refuse to sound as if I am an absolute authority on Garland's novel. Frankly, I'm tired of the conventions that force literary critics to write as if their interpretation of a particular text is the best. As far as this pretense is concerned, I say to hell with it. Actually, I think other critics should test my argument about *The Beach* by conducting further inquiries into this novel, its author, and its real-life social context. I, for one, would be interested in analyses of *The Beach* that compare its political implications with those of Garland's other novels, which I lack the space to investigate here. Also worth looking at, I suspect, are interviews that Garland has given. While we should not take the author as the perfect guide to his book, he may have said things about *The Beach* that support my analysis or undercut it. Helpful, too, would be studies of reactions to this novel, both from professional reviewers and from "ordinary" readers (e.g., comments that appear on Amazon's Web site). One question worth pursuing is whether British and American responses to the novel reflect different political ideologies. In addition, I think there is a need for empirical research on real-life uses of popular culture, so as to test my claim that such discourse can be subversive. Of course, I do believe that I have accomplished much in this article, but I cannot in good conscience claim to have the last word on *The Beach*.

This Annesley isn't completely modest. He grants himself some interpretive prowess. All the same, he presents his analysis as a tentative feat, which other scholars must weigh and supplement. Thus, he resists the literary critic's normal pose of wisdom. He won't claim such mental superiority. In fact, his stand recalls Tompkins's protest against academic competitiveness. To some extent in "Me and My Shadow," and at greater length elsewhere, she rejects literary studies' love of rivalry. Yet, the love survives, even as the field has grown more personal. And so, the ending I've created would surprise its readers. For now, *this* rhetorical refusal has kick.

Clinton

Nevertheless, my variation on Annesley's ending may, like Foucault's interview and Tompkins's essay, come to seem less provocative as the years pass. Actually, to have much impact, a text can't be frozen in time or space. It must be appropriated—and newly interpreted—by multiple groups. Furthermore, nowadays plenty of texts wander uncontrollably, for media such as the Internet, cell phones, and faxes can send them far and fast. Should we, then, bother to predict all the contexts our words may face? Certainly a reasonable answer is no. Yet, sometimes the stakes are so high that we must engage in this guessing. It can even influence how a rhetorical refusal is phrased. For an example, I turn to a refusal made by President Bill Clinton in which he insisted on keeping private some details that his interlocutors technically had a right to know.

The refusal was part of the grand jury testimony that Clinton gave on August 17, 1998.[5] The panel was investigating whether Clinton had lied in his deposition for the Paula Jones case. Was he being deceptive when he denied having sexual relations with Monica Lewinsky? In question, too, was whether he had obstructed justice by pushing associates to distort the truth. Throughout the four hours that Clinton testified, the matter of his audience was complex. As is typical of such proceedings, he engaged two groups while he spoke. One consisted of independent counsel Kenneth Starr and his staff. The second was the grand jury itself. In this case, however, the latter's role was unusual. There was little chance this grand jury would issue indictments. Although Clinton might face charges once he left office, for now the next move would be up to Starr, who could (and did) urge Congress to unseat him. Another limitation on the jurors was physical. While they could query the president, they weren't in the same place as he. As Clinton met with Starr's team in the White House Map Room, the jurors were in a federal courtroom, watching on one-way, closed-circuit TV. Furthermore, while they did raise questions for Clinton, they had to transmit these to Starr's team. That is, they weren't able to address the president directly. In important respects, then, he was spared the embarrassment of having to confront the grand jury. Still, there was a trade-off: he could only imagine jurors' reactions to whatever he said.

Meanwhile, the president was well aware of prospective audiences. Normally, grand jury testimonies are sealed, but Starr would cite Clinton's in his report to Congress. And with this report, Starr would probably try to get Clinton ousted from office. Also, since one juror was absent, Clinton's interrogation was videotaped, and he had reason to fear it would eventually show up on national TV. As things turned out, this is exactly what happened. After only a month, the Republican-led House Judiciary Committee released the tape. Three days later, it was widely broadcast.

Thus, during his testimony, Clinton had to consider both law and politics. Starr's staff and the grand jury were testing his claims that he hadn't perjured himself in the Jones case and that he hadn't told others to lie. Unfortunately for him, his perjury defense seemed weaker than ever, given new evidence that he and Lewinsky had been physically intimate (for example, the notorious semen-stained dress). Once Starr reported to Congress, it too would decide whether Clinton had broken laws. And someday, an ordinary court might put him on trial. As important, though, as the legal framework was the world of political factions. For one thing, Congress is never objective and neutral as a judicial body. Inevitably, both chambers' judgments of Clinton would reflect party struggles, which in turn would be fueled by the press and by the public mood. At the moment, Clinton did have significant national support. Despite the legions who hated him, a majority were willing to keep him president, whether or not they believed all he said. Still, he couldn't assume this appeal would persist. His testimony had to make Americans feel he should remain in power.

All of these factors led to his offering the grand jury "a limited confession," Jeffrey Toobin's term for Clinton's main genre (312). In a prepared statement that he read aloud soon after the hearing began, Clinton finally admitted that he'd repeatedly had "inappropriate intimate contact" with Lewinsky (Kuntz 361). Thus, he acknowledged something he could no longer hide. At the same time, he stressed that his actions "did not constitute sexual relations as I understood that term to be defined at my January 17th, 1998 deposition" (Kuntz 361). In this way, Clinton presented himself as still obeying the law. Meanwhile, he withheld details of his frolics: "While I will provide the grand jury whatever other information I can, because of privacy considerations affecting my family, myself, and others, and in an effort to deserve the dignity of the office I hold, this is all I will say about the specifics of these particular matters" (Kuntz 361). Clinton's declaration is what I have been calling a rhetorical refusal. Whereas traditionally grand juries and associated prosecutors have the right to pursue their own questions, here Clinton denies them this. To be sure, a witness can always invoke the Fifth Amendment. But Clinton didn't do so, maintaining he'd committed no crime. What was extraordinary, then, was that he nevertheless proceeded to assert control over the scope of the hearing. He acted as if he were entitled to decide what he might be asked at all. As Toobin reports, some of his audience shouldn't have been surprised by his strategy. Just prior to the hearing, Clinton's lawyer David Kendall told Starr what the president would do (312). Nevertheless, Clinton did defy expectations in the sense that he defied the court's prerogatives.

Sensitive to this effrontery, his interrogators pressed Clinton to defend it. At one moment, when he balked at demands for particulars of the Lewinsky affair, examining attorney Sol Wisenberg pointed out that "there's no general right not to answer questions." "And so," Wisenberg added, "one of the questions from the grand jurors is on what basis, what legal basis, are you declining to answer these questions?" (Kuntz 406). Later, when Clinton again refused to divulge the intimate facts, Wisenberg reiterated the protocol he was flouting:

> Mr. President, one of the, one of the nice things about—one of the normal things about an investigation and a grand jury investigation is that the grand jurors and the prosecutors get to ask the questions unless they are improper, and unless there is a legal basis. As I understand from your answers, there is no legal basis for which you decline to answer these questions. And I'll ask you again to answer the question. I'm unaware of any legal basis for you not to. (Kuntz 411)

By this point, surely Wisenberg knew that Clinton would never yield more details. He shouldn't have been shocked, shocked by the president's stubbornness. By getting Clinton's stonewalling repeatedly on the record, however, Starr and his team were being strategic, building support for a claim they might later decide to make. Even in this hearing, they might want to argue, Clinton broke the law. Meanwhile, Wisenberg's scolding of Clinton shows how the term rhetorical refusal applies here. When Clinton restricted what the jurors and prosecutors could ask, he was rejecting their established authority.

Significantly, Clinton didn't justify this boundary-setting by appealing to a greater *judicial* principle. Throughout the hearing, he basically ignored demands that he cite legal grounds for his reticence. Perhaps he did so because he realized that no such grounds exist. But he seemed to be thinking of the whole country, where his remarks were apt to travel. Were he to describe his affair graphically, masses of Americans might shudder. All the same, he had to convince them to accept his vagueness. This rhetorical task, he probably felt, required him to invoke big ideals, not quibble over fine points of law.

In the passage I've quoted from his opening statement, Clinton brought up two such ideals. As one reason for limiting his disclosures, he cited "the dignity of the office." Here, Clinton was underscoring his position as Chief of State. He was claiming the presidency would suffer if he had to specify his carnal acts. Of course, it can be said that his affair had already harmed "the office," especially because much of it occurred literally in the West Wing. At any rate, he was counting on Americans' desire to preserve the aura of their leader. At the same time, he was tying that position's stature to his own. Each would be degraded, he was implying, if he had to tell all.

The second ideal he mentioned was "privacy considerations." Here, as Michael Kramer and Kathryn Olson point out, Clinton was shifting stases—that is, the kinds of issues supposedly relevant. Prior to his testimony, his comments on his behavior with Lewinsky had more or less focused on a question of fact. Above all, he denied—or seemed to—that they'd been physically intimate. In his testimony, he basically gave up this pretense. But he foregrounded other issues. In bringing up "privacy," Clinton was emphasizing what Kramer and Olson identify as an issue of jurisdiction. With this term, the president was pointing to a value that many Americans cherish. More specifically, though, he was making his own distinction between the private and public realms. In addition, he was associating his adultery with his personal, not political, life. Nevertheless, he took care to seem ashamed about his behavior with Lewinsky. He didn't speak of "privacy" as the individual's right to gratify lust. Rather, he equated the term with a set of connections: his ties to family and friends. What he'd done, Clinton said, was betray these people. And, he'd make it up to them, if Starr would stop interfering.

As we know, Clinton's recalcitrance in the hearing *didn't* prove consequential. Once the limits he'd put on his confession became widely known, they weren't especially damned or praised. His impeachment and Senate trial focused on other alleged crimes. So, too, did the media's reports. In this sense, Clinton's rhetorical refusal failed to have a prominent afterlife. We're left to analyze why.

As Kramer and Olson remind us, Clinton's testimony was only a stage in a whole series of defensive maneuvers. Before and after, he spoke several times in an effort to halt the scandal. If his rhetorical refusal were to preoccupy the public, it had to stand out from this chain of statements. Yet it didn't. Far greater discussion was sparked by the speech he gave shortly after the hearing, when he addressed the country that evening on TV. After all, now he was admitting to the whole nation something he'd concealed: that he'd had "a relationship with Miss Lewinsky that was not appropriate." In addition, the speech fiercely developed the jurisdictional claim he'd made earlier that day. On this new occasion, Clinton stressed that Starr was improperly invading his personal life. He went so far as to *condemn* Starr's inquiry, declaring it "has gone on too long, cost too much, and hurt too many innocent people" (qtd. in Toobin 318–19). By going on the attack and by apologizing minimally for his own wrongdoing, Clinton struck many politicos and pundits as inadequately contrite. Thus, the speech became notorious for them. It so pained Clinton biographer David Maraniss that he wrote an entire book about it. If, as Anne Freadman suggests, rhetoricians should trace "the genres that constitute public memory and the uptakes they condition" (51), we must acknowledge the extensive chatter that Clinton's evening address provoked.

True, the speech didn't seem to disconcert many average citizens. Polls showed that Clinton's general approval rating stayed high. Whatever the masses' reaction, though, the media's sheer attention to the speech pushed Clinton's grand jury remarks to the background. Besides, the nighttime address failed to mention his earlier rhetorical refusal. Clinton even misled the country about what he'd said to the jurors and prosecutors. "I answered their questions truthfully," he reported (qtd. in Toobin 318), not revealing that he'd refused to answer certain questions at all.

The real extent of Clinton's compliance was, of course, fully on display when the videotape of his grand jury testimony was eventually broadcast. Now, the world could see him deny his examiners the details they'd sought.

Yet his rebuff of them still didn't excite the larger public. For one thing, only some people had the patience to watch the entire tape. Quite a few settled for excerpts. Furthermore, many viewers didn't *want* to know each lusty feat performed by their president. Caring about "the dignity of the office" themselves, they preferred not to learn the particulars of his dropping trou. In other words, they exemplified Black's point: "it does not follow that we are uniformly comfortable with disclosure." Meanwhile, Clinton made a better impression on the tape than had generally been expected. He seemed more dignified, confident, and reasonable than many people thought he'd be. To be sure, helping him shape this image was the position of the camera, which stayed on him alone. Starr's team may have scowled at Clinton's remarks, but their faces remained offscreen.

Clinton's rhetorical refusal didn't rock the country for another reason. By the time Americans saw the videotape, many had already decided what should happen next. Even after Clinton's testimony aired, polls showed a majority would keep him president. These findings reflected widespread agreement with his call for "privacy." But they indicated, too, that much of the nation dissociated two sides of the man. A great number assumed that Clinton *had* perjured himself in his Jones deposition, and they thought his fling with Lewinsky was tawdry. In short, they'd already concluded he was a sleaze. Yet, they also found him quite adept as president. In the terms of Burke's pentad, such reasoning dwells on the "agent." While it may attend to the person's "acts," ultimately it determines and judges character. This is Lipstadt's approach to Irving: though *Denying the Holocaust* specifies his ploys, mainly it argues he's a "denier." With Clinton, many Americans relied on their sense of his psyche. Again, they didn't yearn to know his every grope and spurt.

Their thinking has important implications for a study of rhetorical refusals. One is that although these refusals are acts, their audiences may attend more to the refuser's self. Further, this focus may result from familiarity with the refuser's whole career. After all, people may be acquainted already with much that the refuser has said—and with much else he or she has done. The Clinton example shows, too, that when a rhetorical refusal travels, groups may respond differently to it. This is especially so when they have different priorities. The late social theorist Niklas Luhmann maintained that society is composed of various systems, each with its own values and mapping of reality. Because the independent counsel was bent on building a judicial case, Starr and his staff pounced on Clinton's refusal as a possible crime. Americans at large, though, cared less about bringing Clinton to the bar of justice. Even if they thought him immoral, they wanted the country to move along, not try him for his ethical lapses.

A separation of spheres emerged in other ways. Many Americans disregarded Clinton's political foes for pushing what seemed an ultrapartisan line. Many also grew dismayed with the press's inclination to make the Lewinsky episode a long-running series. As Luhmann observed, the media do have their own priorities. Their favorite subjects, he pointed out, include "norm violations," especially the kind that "take on the character of *scandals*" (29, emphasis in original). Within the media, Luhmann noted, "The way morality is imagined and its ongoing renovation [are] linked to spectacular cases—when scoundrels, victims, and heroes who have gone beyond the call of duty are presented to us" (31). Earlier, I suggested this habit is evident in the spectacles of "reality" TV. Luhmann's remarks suggest why the Clinton scandal, too, enchanted cultural producers. But much of the public wasn't as entranced. Thus, Clinton's rhetorical refusal seemed to them minor news.

One remark he made in the grand jury proceedings did arouse public interest. Even as I write, a columnist in our local paper refers to this comment. Answering a reader's question about a construction project, Dave Horn writes the following: "With apologies to former President Bill Clinton, whether or not work is under way to widen West Third Street depends on what the meaning of 'is' is." Clinton used such words in the early hours of his grand jury hearing. At that point, he faced an accusation from one of Starr's lawyers. Wisenberg was arguing that Robert Bennett, Clinton's attorney in the Jones case, had been deceitful when he'd claimed that "there is absolutely no sex of any kind" between Clinton and Lewinsky. Clinton wanted this claim to seem valid in some respect, and Bennett's use of "is" *had* been honest in the sense that Clinton's affair with Lewinsky had ended. Therefore, Clinton parried Wisenberg with "It depends on what the meaning of 'is' is" (Kuntz 387).

Why, out of all his testimony, did this retort become immortal? The answer, I think, is that it starkly defied a distinctly American faith in the existence and value of plain language. How absurd Clinton was to declare ambiguous a common little word! Of course, Americans also know that slipperiness abounds. They're constantly on the lookout for tricksters. And, as I've said, the public had already framed Clinton as such. In its crisp way, his remark confirmed the country's image of him as "Slick Willie," a contemporary version of Melville's confidence man.

That *this* moment of his testimony got so much notice tells us something about rhetorical refusals. Because they're the subject of my book, I've treated them as noteworthy, but they may not be the most memorable feature of the text where they appear. Current or future audiences for the text may dwell more on other parts of it. Indeed, they may focus on these other sections exclusively, forgetting the rest of the work. I suspect that although many Americans remember Clinton's remark about "is," most of those who recall it are hazy about its original setting. They don't realize it comes from Clinton's grand jury hearing. For them, it's just a bizarre, if revealing, thing he once said.

On Privacy

To be sure, a rhetorical refusal is worth analyzing even when another utterance has eclipsed it. In the case of Clinton's testimony, his insistence on "privacy" continues to raise important questions. How *should* we define this term? What things *should* remain within one's own circle? How do we balance the right to "privacy" with the public's need to know? Notice that all three of this chapter's main figures compare privacy with publicity, attaching importance to how society conceives and balances them. Black concludes his article with a statement that's relevant here: "Rhetorical forms are elements in that system of assent that defines a public consciousness. The rhetorical forms of secrecy and disclosure are especially definitive: They reflect the ways in which people assimilate themselves to those two sovereign antonymies, the public and the private" ("Secrecy" 149).

The three theorists I've focused on do put different spins on these terms. By refusing to disclose his identity, Foucault tries to limit the effects of his fame. At the same time, he protests the general habit of exalting professional theorists. On the other hand, Tompkins seeks to demolish academe's public/private divide, chiefly by plunging readers into her personal life. Obviously, Clinton isn't nearly so interested in disclosure. Yes, he does reveal his name, but he's nowhere as frank as Tompkins. Though he tells some things about his dalliance, he denies Starr's right to all. The three differ, too, in the definitions they appear to sketch. In particular, their refusals support different meanings of "privacy." In Foucault's case, the term would refer to the hiding of identity. The "private" details that Tompkins reveals, though, are sundry intimate topics, from the suicide of her friend to the stirrings of her bladder. As I've mentioned, Clinton takes care not to make "privacy" seem self-centered. He associates the term with his ability to make up to his loved ones.

Maybe Clinton wasn't sincere in his promise to make such amends. Still, it's significant that he put forth his own private/public distinction. That Foucault and Tompkins did so as well points to a feature of rhetorical refusals. Often, as they defy audiences, these acts re-envision public space. At the same time, they may hold some things private.

Probably these present controversies will ebb. Yet, privacy will still be debated, even if the disputes concern new features of it. Moreover, previously contested aspects of privacy may end up discussed again. For a lot of commentators, the Schiavo story recalls other stormy cases of euthanasia. And some day, surely, Americans will face another Washington sex scandal, once more wrangling about whether to probe a politician's flings. At any rate, the lines between public and private are perpetually negotiated, often in response to rhetorical exigencies. And many rhetorical refusals signal this fact, in part through the ways successive audiences respond to them.

So far, I have tended to speak of rhetorical refusals as if they dominated the texts containing them, becoming those texts' most important element. An example is Arlene Croce's declaration that she won't see *Still/Here*. This pronouncement is, I would say, her most notable move in "Discussing the Undiscussable." Certainly it's her article's most discussed part. The rest of the piece is largely an attempt to justify her stand. Thus, to call her whole text a rhetorical refusal seems fair.

Yet, certain texts that feature a rhetorical refusal can't be reduced to this term. As they proceed, they perform various speech acts, some perhaps at odds with the refusal. Studies of rhetorical refusals need to recognize that such tensions can exist. Therefore, I turn to the possibility of them now. In the previous chapter, I traced how some rhetorical refusals changed in impact as they met with new audiences. Here, I consider how a rhetorical refusal may change in effect even on the same occasion, due to words that follow it in the text. In cases like this, it matters that the refusal occurs within a larger work, for the writer or speaker shifts to complicating the refusal's thrust.

The example I will investigate in this chapter is an 1876 speech that Frederick Douglass made about Abraham Lincoln. In the midst of his oration, Douglass voices complaints about Lincoln that his listeners wouldn't have expected. But he doesn't remain in this critical mode as the speech continues. Rather, he shifts toward a more positive view of the country's fallen leader. Increasingly, his portrait of Lincoln brightens. It's inaccurate, then, to describe his address as a rhetorical refusal alone. Instead, we must relate his refusal to the speech's other parts. We're left to determine how to connect the text's discordant sections, and we must figure out which of its passages should occupy us most.

Faced with this task, the speech's readers have responded in a number of ways. As we'll see, some dwell on the speech's acerbic moments, some on its kinder notes. When a text with a rhetorical refusal subsequently shifts tone, audiences may devise various frames for the entire work, especially if they come to it from disparate social sites. Douglass's speech is interesting to study for this very reason. Its eliciting of different reactions calls for analysis, both of its language and of the contexts in which it has been received. In particular, responses differ over what Douglass does with epideictic. An issue that emerges is exactly how flexible this genre of rhetoric can be.

But I have another motive for focusing on Douglass's speech. However we decide to characterize his overall address, he demonstrates how rhetorical refusals can provocatively disrupt memorial events through which a nation tries to consolidate itself *as* a nation. For the last few decades, the United States in particular has often used ceremonies of collective memory to affirm that it remains one people indivisible. Consider, for example, the memorial event at Ground Zero a year after the September 11, 2001, attacks. For the occasion, New York political leaders read aloud famous American texts: the Gettysburg Address, the Declaration of Independence, and Franklin Roosevelt's "Four Freedoms" speech. Bradford Vivian points out that "the ceremonial recital . . . appeared to rehearse audiences, however implicitly, in foundational civic precepts as a means of rededicating the community to their pursuit in light of national tragedy" (5). Such attempts at reunification through memory are not without cost. They risk obscuring differences—especially social inequalities—among the citizens discursively yoked together. Vivian observes that the "seemingly nonpolitical speech" at the 2002 Ground Zero ceremony actually served "to annul the myriad cultural, political, and economic disparities inherent to contemporary U.S. pluralism while accommodating the sensationalist culture of corporate media" (8). In his book *9/11: The Culture of Commemoration*, David Simpson elaborates how America's ways of remembering the World Trade Center attacks have reinforced nationhood while slighting difference. For one thing, he notes, these practices establish a stark binary between the United States and mysterious, demonic foreigners: they reflect "nativized pressures to imagine terror as the absolute other, the enemy, the ultimate incarnation of a model of 'them and us'" (9). Moreover, by depicting the victims of the attacks as martyrs for the American nation, these modes of remembrance forget that "the multinational (seventy or so nationalities) and multiethnic workforce that was inside the

Towers on that terrible morning would have subscribed either to a whole range of patriotisms or to none at all" (48). Simpson points out that even the *New York Times*'s celebrated "Portraits of Grief" series imposed on the dead a questionable uniformity, engaging in "the projection of an all-American wholeness of spirit" (46). At the same time, Simpson argues convincingly that these memory practices are part of a larger American tradition: "The deaths of 9/11 . . . occurred within a culture of commemoration that was already primed to resort to sanctification and personalization in the cause of upholding the image of a flourishing civil society and a providential national destiny, and one that inadvertently signals, as the Gettysburg Address signals, that it is doing exactly that" (31).

Note that the Gettysburg Address was, in fact, read at the 2002 Ground Zero ceremony. Its recitation there confirms Simpson's link between 9/11 memorializing and a nationalist heritage that includes Lincoln's speech. In composing his oration *about* Lincoln, Douglass had to decide whether his memorializing of the president would depict the country as a blessed unity, with Lincoln as its people's shared icon. At this moment in time, 1876, his hearers were quite keen to celebrate national identity, aware that it remained fragile after the Civil War. But Douglass wound up expressing a complex view of Lincoln and of the nation. For part of his speech, he emphasized racial disparities and faulted Lincoln's approach to them.

Douglass's Refusal

Douglass gave the speech on April 14, 1876, at the dedication of a monument to Lincoln in Washington, D.C. Sponsored and funded by ex-slaves, the memorial was established to honor Lincoln as their Great Emancipator. This aim was deemed so important that Congress had declared a national holiday. A parade was even held in Washington. Moreover, the dedication was attended not only by African American dignitaries but also by many a white government official, including President Ulysses S. Grant as well as Supreme Court justices, senators, and congressmen. That the date was the anniversary of Lincoln's assassination was further reason to commemorate him. Besides, despite their periodic disagreements, Lincoln and Douglass had been allies. When the president was slain, Douglass grieved. For all these reasons, his audience figured his speech would be adulatory.

We might say that his listeners expected Douglass to engage in epideictic, the classical term for rhetoric of praise or blame. Dale Sullivan observes that epideictic discourse often involves "acts of unveiling," thereby "exposing the value system of a text or person to the gaze of spectators" (342). Douglass spoke at a literal unveiling, for at this ceremony, the Lincoln monument was undraped. But the audience also expected from Douglass a metaphorical "unveiling": a laying bare of Lincoln's character. More specifically, they thought Douglass would treat Lincoln fondly, conveying their own love for him. Chaim Perelman and Lucie Olbrechts-Tyteca have expectations like this in mind when they say of epideictic that "the speaker tries to establish a sense of communion centered around particular values recognized by the audience" (51).

Douglass's speech turned out, however, to depart from this model. At first, he does encourage his audience to praise Lincoln. He refers explicitly to Lincoln's "exalted character and great works" ("Oration" 311). But, as he goes on, Douglass grows more critical. At length, he elaborates the proposition that Lincoln "was preeminently the white man's President, entirely devoted to the welfare of white men" (312). Turning biographical with this idea in mind, he says that Lincoln "was ready and willing at any time during the first years of his administration to deny, postpone, and sacrifice the rights of humanity in the colored people to promote the welfare of the white people of this country" (312). Lincoln was prepared, Douglass notes, "to execute all the supposed guarantees of the United States Constitution in favor of the slave system anywhere inside the slave states" (312). Even as Douglass begins to speak better of his subject, he lists ways in which Lincoln frustrated African Americans:

> When he tarried long in the mountain; when he strangely told us that we were the cause of the war; when he still more strangely told us that we were to leave the land in which we were born; when he refused to employ our arms in defence of the Union; when, after accepting our services as colored soldiers, he refused to retaliate our murder and torture as colored prisoners; when he told us he would save the Union if he could with slavery; when he revoked the Proclamation of Emancipation of General Fremont; when he refused to remove the popular commander of the Army of the Potomac, in the days of its inaction and defeat, who was more zealous in his efforts to protect slavery than to suppress rebellion; when we saw all this, and more, we were at times grieved, stunned, and greatly bewildered; but our hearts believed while they ached and bled. (313)

Though it ends with a declaration of trust in Lincoln, this passage is a litany of flaws. Anaphorically, it recalls that often he dashed Black America's hopes. If eulogistic addresses normally amplify the deceased's virtues, here Douglass stresses Lincoln's faults. In short, this is not the exposure his audience anticipated.

Consistent with several other definitions of epideictic, Perelman and Olbrechts-Tyteca point out that "one has an impression of misuse when . . . [the speaker] turns the argument toward disputed values and introduces a discordant note" (53). Douglass does both these things. Not only does he treat Lincoln, man of the hour, with less than absolute awe, but he also calls attention to divisions within his audience by stressing their different races and histories. This emphasis is evident in his choice of pronouns. In many epideictic speeches, "we" means everyone present, but Douglass applies it mostly to his own race. Furthermore, he distinguishes African Americans from his white listeners, in one section addressing the latter as "you." For Lincoln, he says, "The race to which we belong were not the special objects of his consideration." Instead, he tells his white audience, "You and yours were the objects of his deepest affection and his most earnest solicitude." Then, Douglass even sharpens the contrast: "You are the children of Abraham Lincoln," while "[w]e are at best only his step-children; children by adoption, children by forces of circumstance and necessity" (312). With this remark, Douglass identifies white and black Americans as now, in a sense, kin. Far from being a racial separatist, he himself sought an America of diverse groups. Yet here he suggests that Lincoln was slow to implement this vision—that only gradually and reluctantly did Lincoln let blacks join the national family. Because such comments were quite unorthodox for this sort of occasion, I call them a rhetorical refusal.

Why, midway through, did Douglass choose to criticize Lincoln? Surely one reason is that he couldn't bear to hide his own nuanced view of history. To him, Lincoln hadn't consistently helped Black America. Just as important, though, is that Douglass wanted to stress his own race's achievements, which he might have obscured had he represented Lincoln as the slaves' absolute savior. Significantly, his speech ends by emphasizing his people's worth, industry, and civic sense: "When now it shall be said that the colored man is soulless, that he has no appreciation of benefits or benefactors; when the foul reproach of ingratitude is hurled at us, and it is attempted to scourge us beyond the range of human brotherhood, we may calmly point to the monument we have this day erected to the memory of Abraham Lincoln" (319). As this final sentence suggests, an orator can at once commend Lincoln *and* praise African Americans. Logically, the two acts aren't mutually exclusive. But clearly Douglass wanted to leave his audience mainly aware that blacks had become major contributors to the nation. Apparently, too, he thought utter worship of Lincoln would undermine this rhetorical goal.

Historian David Blight points out that Douglass set his particular agenda because he worried that popular memory would distort the war. Increasingly, Southerners were portraying it as a noble Lost Cause, while Northern Republicans repressed its racial aspects to unite the country. Douglass was also conscious that racism had by no means vanished. As he notes in his conclusion, its vicious stereotypes survived. So, too, did white supremacist violence. Therefore, though slavery was no longer a clear foe, Douglass had strong exigence for insisting on African Americans' public value. Deifying Lincoln was a less urgent task. Blight even proposes that the chief importance of Douglass's speech "lies in its concerted attempt to forge a place for blacks in the national memory, to assert their citizenship and nationhood" (1165). This claim accords with Douglass's own recollection of the day. In what was to be his final autobiography, he says of the ceremony that "occasions like this have done wonders in the removal of popular prejudice, and in lifting into consideration the colored race" (*Life and Times* 855).

Douglass's speech hid some of his negative feelings. Most important, perhaps, is that he didn't reveal his dismay at the monument's design. As he disclosed to others privately, he disliked that it showed Lincoln freeing a kneeling slave. To him, this image misleadingly implied that African Americans were passive. So, in a sense, the speech was an effort to raise the memorial's slave from his knees, "lifting" him "into consideration" as an active member of the realm. At the same time, this mission encouraged him to "lower" Lincoln's stature.

Homi Bhabha argues that, through various sorts of "pedagogical" acts, nation-states encourage their citizens to identify with the regime. Speeches memorializing the state's past leaders are, I would say, good examples. Bhabha also contends, however, that during such acts, something may undercut the state's authority. Douglass's criticisms of Lincoln in the midst of his dedication speech illustrate Bhabha's point. Indeed, Bhabha suggests these acts may be disrupted by "minority discourse." With this term, Bhabha has chiefly in mind the rhetoric of colonial and postcolonial populations, but the term can be applied as well to the rhetoric of African Americans like Douglass. To Bhabha, "minority discourse . . . acknowledges the status of national culture—and the people—as a contentious, performative space of the perplexity of living" (*Location* 157). Again, Douglass's refusal seems a pertinent case. By asserting that Lincoln didn't always treat African Americans well, he called attention to their "perplexity of living," thereby prodding his listeners to make America's culture truly just and harmonious.

A More Positive Tone

In significant respects, the Lincoln speech resembles Douglass's most famous, his 1852 oration dealing with the Fourth of July. Then, too, he challenged the celebratory air associated with a particular occasion. Rather than simply affirm Independence Day, he reminded his largely white audience that slavery still thrived at the time he spoke. Thus, he argued, the holiday belonged to whites, not blacks. Moreover, as he would do in the 1876 speech, he directly addressed his white listeners, noting they were free while his race remained chained.

Nevertheless, I suspect that anyone comparing the 1852 and 1876 speeches will find the earlier text bolder—surely one of the reasons why the Fourth of July address has been analyzed more often. From beginning to end, it bristles with anger over the state of the country, while the Lincoln speech seems to turn benign. Much of this difference stems, of course, from the difference in time period. In 1852, with slavery persisting, Douglass sought to eradicate it. Hence, though normally Fourth of July speeches treasured the American heritage, he turned his into social critique. To a great extent, the oration was patently deliberative: pitched, that is, toward inciting change. Among other things, Douglass pushed his audience to revive the radically democratic spirit he associated with the Founders. More specifically, he called for seeing the Constitution as advocating racial equality, even as defenders of slavery and quite a few abolitionists read it otherwise. In 1876, however, with Emancipation and the Civil War behind him, slavery was gone as an enemy. At this point, dangers to African Americans couldn't be as precisely defined. In addition, Douglass knew that Lincoln had played a major role in ending slavery. He was also proud that his own people had funded the monument to Lincoln, thereby playing the biggest part in its history. Thus, he was inclined to talk longer about the past than about the future and to speak better of Lincoln than he did of the Fourth of July.

Remember that Douglass's rhetorical refusal is, indeed, only part of his 1876 address. As he continues, he refers much more positively to Lincoln, honoring him as strongly as the occasion seems to demand. Having used anaphora to enumerate Lincoln's faults, Douglass now uses it to amplify his accomplishments:

> [U]nder his wise and beneficent rule we saw ourselves gradually lifted from the depths of slavery . . . ; under his wise and beneficent rule . . . we saw that the handwriting of ages, in the form of prejudice and proscription, was rapidly fading away from the face of our whole country; under his rule, and in due time, about as soon after all as the country could tolerate the strange spectacle, we saw our brave sons and brothers laying off the rags of bondage, and being clothed all over in the blue uniforms of the soldiers of the United States; under his rule we saw two hundred thousand of our dark and dusky people responding to the call of Abraham Lincoln . . . ; under his rule we saw the independence of the black republic of Haiti . . . ; under his rule we saw the internal slave-trade, which so long disgraced the nation, abolished, and slavery abolished in the District of Columbia; under his rule we saw for the first time the law enforced against the foreign slave trade . . . ; under his rule . . . we saw the Confederate States . . . battered to pieces and scattered to the four winds; under his rule, and in the fullness of time, we saw Abraham Lincoln . . . penning the immortal paper . . . making slavery forever impossible in the United States. (314–15)

Even in this passage, Douglass recognizes African American agency. He recalls, for instance, that numerous black men fought in the Union Army. But certainly the passage is a hymn to Lincoln, repeatedly noting the marvelous events that occurred "under his rule." And later, Douglass goes so far as to celebrate Lincoln's prudence, a virtue championed by rhetoricians and moral philosophers alike. More precisely, Douglass praises Lincoln for being a political realist, admitting that "had he put the abolition of slavery before the salvation of the Union, he would have inevitably driven from him a powerful class of the American people and rendered resistance to rebellion impossible" (316). Then, as if to head off charges that Lincoln was *merely* pragmatic, Douglass avers that the man himself "loathed and hated slavery" (316). From this point on, the speech seems largely an encomium.

From grudging praise for Lincoln, we move to sheer enthusiasm. "[H]is memory," Douglass proclaims, "will be precious forever" (319).

Responses

Aristotle observes of epideictic that it focuses on the present. He points out, however, that it may deal as well with the past and future (48). To varying extents, Douglass ponders all three. Thus, a main subject of his speech is actually time itself. The present appears in Douglass's oration whenever he refers to the statue's unveiling, the ceremony for which his listeners have gathered. The future plays a fairly small role, but it does loom at the speech's end. There, Douglass predicts this memorial created by African Americans will refute slanders against them. As for the past, throughout the speech he looks back on history. He even starts by noting that this racially mixed gathering couldn't have gone smoothly a few years before. As I've shown, he then recalls his people's relations with Lincoln, including ways that this leader vexed them. The role of history in this speech is, in fact, complicated. Though Douglass turns to commending Lincoln's racial policies, he does so only after a long and sharp account of the man's delays. Douglass winds up acclaiming Lincoln as a leader, but the history he sketches beforehand is a gloomier tale.

The dissonance between these two currents of the speech can be labeled *ironic*. John Lucaites recalls that in classical rhetoric, irony "often served to configure dialectical tensions within a text, or between a text and its context," so that the text became a vehicle for "managing or resolving the apparently problematic oppositions in a given situation" (56). Along with other rhetorical critics, Lucaites finds irony a hallmark of Douglass's oratory. These critics invoke the term especially with respect to his famous Fourth of July speech. The 1852 address is, for Lucaites, ironic in two main respects. First, Douglass registers the absurdity of his delivering Independence Day remarks while his people are still slaves. Second, even as Douglass insists on a common heritage for the country, he is willing to let black political activism remain somehow distinct. Lucaites plausibly argues, however, that Douglass resolves these tensions. He exhorts his audience to see that the Founders were committed to equality—that they used the Constitution to continue, not cancel, the Declaration's pledge of it. Furthermore, he evokes America as a democracy allowing racial difference rather than demanding all citizens act alike.

Does irony lead to a clear, untroubled conclusion in the Lincoln speech, too? Certainly the 1876 address brings up conflicting perspectives, this time on the president who is its subject. And, on the surface, the outcome of irony here is endorsement of Lincoln, support that seems to override the earlier criticisms of him. Yet whether Douglass actually forgoes these reservations is, I would say, not certain. Should we just ignore the fact that the speech *mixes* praise and blame, not focusing on one as most epideictic does? Is it possible that by dilating on Lincoln's slow pace toward black emancipation, Douglass means to subvert his final claims? Consciously or unconsciously, is he actually protesting Lincoln's belatedness? Let's consider existing and possible answers to these questions.

It's hard to determine exactly how Douglass's listeners reacted to his speech. According to William Safire, the waspish remarks about Lincoln "shocked the Republicans present" (168), but he doesn't identify sources for this claim. Unfortunately, the speech took place before the age of C-SPAN, so we can't examine a videotape for possible scowls and gasps. Probably, though, Douglass disconcerted much of the crowd when he swerved from pure homage. No doubt, too, many of the gathered felt relief when he did move to sheer tribute. His finale may have even led some of those assembled to forget or downplay his barbs. As I've noted, the bulk of Douglass's audience valued national unity, especially because it was still a precarious achievement after the war. For these listeners, idolizing Lincoln as the Union's preserver was a key way to bolster the Union itself.[1] No wonder, then, if they chose to disregard the speech's harsher claims about Lincoln, preferring to focus on its eventual warmth.

For those encountering the speech today, the situation is different. First of all, no one alive has experienced Douglass's delivery of it. True, some may have heard it orally rendered, but not by the author himself. Actually, most people discover the speech only in written form. This shift in medium comes with costs. I, for one, would love to have heard Douglass's vocal play of affect, how he audibly glided from anger at Lincoln to apparent contentment. There's at least one advantage for us, though, in his temporal performance's becoming a spatialized text. Now, we can move back and forth among its parts. Again and again, we can revisit and brood on Douglass's refusal. This ability encourages present audiences to consider whether his refusal is, actually, outweighed by his concluding remarks.

The social context has changed, too. In 1876, political circles certainly thought Douglass worth hearing on the subject of Lincoln; this is one reason the white establishment attended his speech. Now, however, Douglass's stature can be described as absolutely mighty, while there's growing interest in deciphering Lincoln's intricate, shifting attitudes toward blacks. Hence, many people value Douglass's thoughts on Lincoln's racial views. Recent evidence of this esteem appears in the July 4, 2005, issue of *Time* magazine, which celebrated Independence Day by presenting several articles on Lincoln. Given Douglass's currently high reputation, and given the widespread desire to gauge Lincoln's philosophy of race, it's almost inevitable that the issue included an article on the two men's relationship. Nor is it surprising that the piece focuses mostly on Douglass's assessment of Lincoln's racial beliefs rather than the other way round. In fact, author John Stauffer ends by citing Douglass's 1876 speech.

To be sure, Stauffer depicts the speech as a vindication of Lincoln. As if determined to keep *Time* a voice of mainstream American pieties, he suggests the address essentially amounts to a paean. Though he alludes to Douglass's less enthusiastic comments, he sums up the address as "a tender verdict from the perspective of someone who had been converted" (65). Stauffer even closes with Douglass's most glowing remark about Lincoln: "[M]easuring him by the sentiment of his country, a sentiment he was bound as a statesman to consult, he was swift, zealous, radical, and determined" (qtd. in Stauffer 65).

This slant on the address is presented, too, at the new Lincoln Museum in Springfield, Illinois, specifically in a film called *Lincoln's Eyes*. As one would expect from an institution devoted to Springfield's favorite son, the film basically honors him. Yet, in a nod toward historical realism, it cites gruff statements from Douglass's speech. After these, though, comes the accolade that Stauffer quotes. The latter, in fact, leads into the film's own ecstatic finale, which celebrates Lincoln as unequivocally great.

Plenty of modern scholars, though, have other takes on the speech. A prominent example of another perspective is that of Philip Foner, editor of Douglass's papers. Like Stauffer, Foner finds the speech basically positive, but he's dismayed by this drift. A radical leftist himself, he thinks the oration too tame. "No other Negro had ever had so great an opportunity to reach the American people with his message," Foner argues, but "Douglass remained silent on the crucial issues facing his people," including "the fact that everything Lincoln had achieved for the Negro was being wiped out in state after state in the South" (99).

To me, Foner's verdict seems excessively harsh, as if he expects Douglass to have foreseen Reconstruction's demise a year later. At any rate, numerous scholars see his speech as more a brief against Lincoln. They linger on his rhetorical refusal, relishing the speech's ambivalent moments. Indeed, after countless Lincoln hagiographies, many of us like his being portrayed as flawed and complicated. Of course, as I've noted, we can afford to dwell on this president's negative traits. Unlike much of the first generation after the Civil War, we feel able to do more than exalt him. Thus, concerned to expose Lincoln's racism in his recent book *What Lincoln Believed: The Values and Convictions of America's Greatest President*, Michael Lind underscores Douglass's lament that Lincoln "was preeminently the white man's President." He even ends a chapter with this dour remark, thereby giving it emphasis (232). Similarly, Jenny Franchot applauds Douglass's speech as "a penetrating indictment of Lincoln" (150). On a more measured note, Eric Sundquist finds in the address "a subversive current," so that Douglass is "ambiguously embracing America's martyred hero while struggling with him at the same time" (17).[2]

Certain popularizers of history share Sundquist's view. The Web site of Facing History and Ourselves, an organization that provides resources for teachers, stresses that "the oration touched on incongruities and complexities in Lincoln's record—in a sense, the messiness of historical facts that at times seem to get smoothed over or carefully sorted and selected in the process of creating monuments" ("Freedmen's"). In his anthology *Lend Me Your Ears: Great Speeches in History*, Safire makes much the same point as he introduces Douglass's text. Because he's a conservative, Safire might be expected to focus on and adore the pro-Lincoln moments. Yet, in his own political writings, he's often the spunky iconoclast, so perhaps it's not surprising that he lauds Douglass for assuming this persona. The speech, Safire enthusiastically reports, shows Douglass's refusing "to join the line of those creating the Lincoln myth." Douglass thereby became "one of the lone observers in a century that followed who saw Lincoln without tears—as a man and politician, not as a martyred saint" (168).

Given these diverse reactions, what should present readers of the speech think? What *does* Douglass's ultimate acclaim of Lincoln imply about his prior complaints? As I trust that I've shown, there isn't and can't be a definitive answer to such questions. Were we to find detailed notes by Douglass about the speech's aims, it could still be argued that the actual text has a different slant, as if he unconsciously swerved from his original plan. Personally, I find myself lingering on Douglass's refusal, thinking it deserves major pondering despite his rosy conclusion. Though Douglass may well have intended to emphasize the latter, I tend to think that he remained beset by a sense of grievance. Meanwhile, the story of friendship that Stauffer finds in the speech strikes me as Hollywood. In sketching this scenario, he seems influenced by contemporary interracial buddy films: movies where a black man and a white man bicker but ultimately harmonize. Douglass plays Morgan Freeman's role, while Lincoln takes on Clint Eastwood's.

Dialoguing With and Within Traditions

A more nuanced view of Douglass's speech would attend to its dialogic aspect. I don't mean its negotiation of the audience but rather its relationship to earlier texts. Such intertextuality is what Mikhail Bakhtin is referring to when he observes that "the work is a link in the chain of speech communion. Like the rejoinder in a dialogue, it is related to other work-utterances: both those to which it responds and those that respond to it" ("Problem" 76). Douglass takes a critical stance toward two rhetorical traditions. One is the series of tributes to Lincoln already voiced since his slaying. Douglass was well aware that Lincoln had been mourned adoringly in numerous addresses. "That ground," he announces, "has been fully occupied and completely covered" (315). His own speech occupies the same ground in the sense that he, too, pays Lincoln homage. But even as he moves into this territory, he challenges some of its commonplaces, most notably the idea that Lincoln always shared black Americans' sense of their plight. Meanwhile, Douglass troubles some of the more general conventions of epideictic, insofar as he doesn't constantly laud the man he is eulogizing. His speech is an intervention, then, in these two oratorical canons. It does participate in them, but critically. Indeed, through this edgy engagement, Douglass tries to steer the whole "cultural conversation," Steven Mailloux's term for a society's main debates. Specifically, he intervenes in discussions about the ideal postwar republic, his own model stressing African American progress.

Though he tampers with established forms of oratory, Douglass can be seen as perpetuating another rhetorical tradition, the African American one known as *signifying*. I'm not the first to associate him with this particular kind of "minority discourse." In the much-discussed 1988 book *The Signifying Monkey: A Theory of African-American Literary Criticism*, for example, Henry Louis Gates calls Douglass "a masterful Signifier" (66). Gates has in mind the style of Douglass's autobiographies. He thinks, too, of these books' content, for Douglass can be seen as commenting on how other black Americans signify. As a literary theorist, Gates ignores Douglass's speeches. Several of the latter, though, support the label of "masterful Signifier," the 1876 Lincoln address being one.

To be sure, "signifying" is a word that's had any number of definitions. Like Gates, I find helpful the account of it provided by anthropologist Claudia Mitchell-Kernan. Through studying an African American community, she saw that signifying takes various forms. At the same time, she discerned commonalities among them. A recurring feature of signifying, she reports, is the "encoding [of] messages or meanings": that is, "an element of indirection" (311). The speaker engages in verbal play whereby "[t]he apparent significance of the message differs from its real significance" (325). Basically, Gates points out, Douglass's autobiographies call attention to this duplicity when they comment on slaves' singing. Douglass observes that despite the seeming joyousness of slaves' songs, these actually express despair at bondage (Gates 67).

Similar "indirection" might be going on in his 1876 speech. Though it ends by apparently commending Lincoln, Douglass may have intended that some of his audience would interpret him differently. Perhaps he hoped they'd give greater credence to his earlier dismay over Lincoln, regarding this as his text's real drift. Perhaps he was implicitly signaling this message to his black listeners in particular, even as white ones bought his pro-Lincoln conclusion.

On the surface, this ending returns Douglass to epideictic norms that his criticisms of Lincoln breached. Yet, I want to suggest that even the criticisms may not be as anti-epideictic as they seem. They can be taken to demonstrate that epideictic rhetoric has more flexibility than usually assumed. That is, perhaps Douglass's rhetorical refusal reveals a *potential* of the epideictic tradition, one that is too often repressed.

"[T]he prevailing view of epideictic discourse," Cynthia Sheard reminds us, is that it's a form of "ritual celebration, invoking traditional values" (776). In this conception, epideictic rhetoric massages its audience's shared beliefs, often becoming little more than an artful display of consensus. It's a view that denies epideictic speeches room for Douglass's range of feeling: hence, the shock effect that his churlishness toward Lincoln can produce. Several theorists of epideictic, however, have drawn a more complex picture of it. Most notably, Perelman and Olbrechts-Tyteca grant epideictic a role in many kinds of arguments, which they see as attempts to strengthen the audience's adherence to certain ideals. Other theorists argue that an epideictic text can, after all, inject what *The New Rhetoric* calls "a discordant note." From an avowedly Derridean perspective, for example, Brooke Rollins sees the eulogy as an occasion on which the rhetor and the audience must struggle with the deceased's alterity or otherness. James Jasinski points out that "while ritual and epideictic discourse are commonly considered to be tools for promoting cultural continuity and social hegemony," several nineteenth-century activists used epideictic occasions to challenge prevailing dogmas, Douglass's Fourth of July speech being an example (78). Similarly, Sheard contends that an epideictic text, far from just ratifying doxa, may foster new attitudes and actions. Drawing epideictic closer to deliberative rhetoric, she argues that it can provoke "critical self-reflection," so that the audience is "envisioning and *actualizing* alternative realities, possible worlds" (787).

Sheard's model seems pertinent to Douglass's speech about Lincoln. True, he voiced common values of his listeners, especially when he criticized the South's rebellion, hailed slavery's end, and finally esteemed Lincoln's leadership. If much of his original audience wanted a unified country and saw Lincoln as its champion, Douglass did as well. Thus, his speech was largely epideictic in the familiar sense of the term. But, as I've noted, Douglass also pressed his listeners to admit their racial differences. The long inequality of whites and blacks, he suggested, had made the latter chafe at Lincoln's temporizing. Moreover, Douglass's speech was a warning against current complacency. He treated black citizenship as an unfinished project rather than an achieved feat. An integrated America, Douglass made clear, was still just a promise. It had to be realized, not simply presumed. Thus, though big stretches of his speech reinforced the crowd's worship of Lincoln, Douglass's rhetorical refusal did gesture toward "possible worlds." And in doing so, perhaps this gesture is best interpreted not as a rebuke to the epideictic tradition but as disclosure of its often-hidden possibilities.

Whether or not a rhetorical refusal is embedded in more conventional discourse, it can indeed have a heuristic value. Besides enlarging our own available set of rhetorical moves, it can lead us to refine our rhetorical theories. Among other things, we might wind up rethinking a tradition's scope, sensing that more can be done within it than we have supposed. After all, as Catherine Schryer observes, "[G]enres are evolving, dynamic entities that both shape and are shaped by their users" (77). If epideictic speeches are "acts of unveiling," then Douglass's refusal may unveil not only the essence of Lincoln but also capacities of epideictic itself.

Katrina and Kanye

Of course, epideictic isn't the only genre through which rhetors might raise racial issues that unsettle narratives of nationhood. Consider a rhetorical refusal that recently occurred within a modern-day American genre, the telethon. On September 2, 2005, NBC television devoted an hour to soliciting funds for victims of Hurricane Katrina. Throughout the disaster and its aftermath—both extensively covered by the media—the suffering of African Americans had been appallingly evident. So, too, had the federal government's failure to help them. Still, it's rare for telethons to hurl charges of racial bias. Usually, audiences for this kind of show expect it not to dwell on political conflicts. Following tradition, the NBC program's script didn't scold government officials. Nor did it acknowledge that racial inequality endured in the United States. While the script did make concrete references to the hurricane's victims, the overall framework was humanistic. The participating celebrities were supposed to appeal to the general public on behalf of the common good. After all, more of the public would contribute if addressed as "Americans" rather than as a certain partisan bloc. African American rapper Kanye West, however, didn't stick with the plan. Appearing with comedian Mike Myers—who kept reading from the cue cards—West made caustic ad-libs, engaging in what Bhabha might call "minority discourse." Whereas Myers by no means identified himself as white, West conspicuously spoke of himself as black and fumed at how members of his race were being treated. Protesting how the media had depicted black victims of Katrina, West said, "I hate the way they portray us." Angered by the presence in New Orleans of the National Guard, he declared that "they've given them permission to go down and shoot us!" Furious at the president, he contended that "George Bush doesn't care about black people!" (qtd. in de Moraes). These blunt assertions of racial oppression broke dramatically from telethon protocol. No surprise, then, that the show's producers didn't allow West to continue. Immediately after his remark about Bush, they cut off his segment, shifting the camera to conspicuously anxious emcee Chris Tucker. Nevertheless, for weeks afterward, debate raged over West's rhetorical refusal. People argued heatedly about his departure from script.

It may be simplistic to claim that West's refusal follows in the tradition of Douglass's. I have trouble imagining, for example, Douglass confessing as West did on the broadcast that he had "been shopping before even giving a donation" (qtd. in de Moraes). Nevertheless, West does resemble Douglass in criticizing injustice toward black Americans instead of engaging in the discourse of national unity expected of him. Moreover, West's acerbic remark about a current president seems to echo one that Douglass made about the president he was assigned to honor. When I hear "George Bush doesn't care about black people!," I hear "You are the children of Abraham Lincoln. We are at best only his step-children; children by adoption, children by forces of circumstance and necessity."

At the beginning of this chapter, I referred to America's memorializing of 9/11, noting that the commemorations stress national unity over social differences. From now on, however, Americans will have to figure out how they want to deal with the anniversary of another disaster: Katrina, a time in late August of 2005 when racial differences glared. Each year, will the country brood in late summer about the schisms revealed by Katrina, only to forget them when September 11 comes round? In the next chapter, I continue examining how rhetorical refusals can challenge national memory, moving now to America's remembrance of its wars.

The previous chapters have focused on texts usually labeled "nonfiction." It's a curious term, for it implies that "fictional" discourse is more common—a dubious claim, to say the least. Yet, typically, my home discipline of English privileges the imaginative writing found in novels, short stories, poems, and plays. In my book *Between the Lines: Relating Composition Theory and Literary Theory*, I criticize English studies' devotion to these few genres. I argue especially that such worship slights composition classes, which center on the study and production of expository or argumentative prose. Here, in this book, I'm still trying to change the priorities of English, by attending to various kinds of discourse it neglects.

Still, any study of rhetorical refusals needs to acknowledge that they can appear in works of fiction as well as in other forms of art. Indeed, this is something worth considering by rhetoricians in departments of communication who might otherwise attend only to rhetorical refusals performed in "real life" oral texts. As Derek Attridge reminds us, "[I]nnovation and unpredictability have been central to the practice and appreciation of Western art from its beginnings to the present day" (13). Attridge recognizes that Western art has also had its conventions, and he knows that innumerable examples of it have closely adhered to these norms. But he correctly notes that much art has challenged reigning aesthetic standards, becoming memorable for this very defiance. Within literary studies, a key word for this unconventionality is *defamiliarization*, a term coined by the Russian formalists. In part, it refers to how literature often tampers with mainstream writing styles, making readers critically self-conscious of them.

As a concept, defamiliarization has proven useful. Unfortunately, though, it's become a self-serving mantra for literary critics: a word they invoke, familiarly, to support a still-narrow canon. This thinking is too parochial.

All sorts of texts, not just so-called literature, have put protocols in question. Nevertheless, in this chapter I do want to examine a piece of fiction, considering how—and to what ends—a rhetorical refusal might function in an imaginary tale.

From literary history, any number of works might serve as my focus. I want to dwell, however, on one particular novel, Tim O'Brien's 1994 *In the Lake of the Woods*. I choose it for several reasons. First, it engages in an especially prominent rhetorical refusal, clearly breaking with expectations that its typical reader would bring. Second, it's a novel I've repeatedly taught, and so I've long wrestled with issues it poses. In analyzing it here, I'm influenced by my classes' discussions of it, when my students and I have pondered together O'Brien's strategies and aims. Finally, his book is useful for showing how a novel's rhetorical refusal might encourage people to remember more thoughtfully their country's past military campaigns, which the nation is otherwise apt to ignore or distort. In the case of O'Brien's novel, the country is the United States, and the main campaign is the Vietnam War. Thus, this chapter extends the previous one's concern with national memory by turning to how America now recalls what was, back then, one of its longest and most controversial periods of combat. After discussing how O'Brien's defiance of audience expectations promotes more critical remembering of that era, I will suggest how his novel provides a useful lens for analyzing a "nonfiction" book about that time: Bob Kerrey's 2002 memoir, *When I Was a Young Man*. In proposing that O'Brien's book can illuminate Kerrey's, I will also be arguing that "rhetorical" education should involve making connections between discourses that, on the surface, may seem worlds apart. But this notion of "rhetoric" hasn't always been common in English departments, and so first I want briefly to recall how they've defined the term.

Literary Rhetoric

To find and study a rhetorical refusal in O'Brien's text, we have to see his novel as rhetoric in the first place. But literary critics have defined rhetoric in various ways, which require sifting. For one venerable school of thought, still alive in quarters of English, the term signifies manipulative bombast. The same definition pervades vernacular discourse and the media, where rhetoric is often labeled "mere" rhetoric and seen as politicians' verbal ploys. Within literary studies, this negative sense of the word opposes rhetoric to true artistry. Basically, as William Butler Yeats defined the term, it's dismissed as "the will trying to do the work of the imagination" (215). This meaning of the word is, evidently, what Vernon Shetley has in mind when he laments that certain modes of contemporary poetry "rather quickly turned into rhetoric" (21). It's also what Adam Kirsch is thinking of when, citing Yeats's definition, he argues that Ezra Pound fell into "the snare of rhetoric" (143).

Some literature specialists perpetuate, too, another traditional notion of rhetoric, one that associates it with tropes and figures—that is, an author's linguistic tools. This was the concept that Cleanth Brooks put forth when he referred to a certain poem's "rhetorical organization" as its "levels of meanings, symbolizations, clashes of connotations, paradoxes, ironies, etc." (199). Similarly, Bernard Bergonzi defines rhetoric as "the formal, technical, and conventional aspects of poetry" (196). To be sure, there's nothing immediately wrong with conceiving rhetoric this way. But the critic may be easily tempted to stop with this idea of it, failing to consider audience and social context. Rhetorical analysis thereby becomes strictly formalist. This is what happens, for example, in Dennis Sobolev's essay on the rhetoric of Gerard Manley Hopkins's poems. There, the focus remains on Hopkins's use of metaphors, parallelisms, repetitions, and ellipses.[1]

The notion of rhetoric as human interaction has, however, grown somewhat more common in literary studies. Its popularity is partly due to Wayne Booth's 1961 book *The Rhetoric of Fiction*, which garnered renewed attention with a second edition in 1983. Over the last several years, Booth's concept of rhetoric has been advanced chiefly by his former student James Phelan. Phelan largely articulates a Booth-ian sense of rhetoric when, in his own 1996 book *Narrative as Rhetoric: Technique, Audiences, Ethics, Ideology*, he links the word with "the complex, multilayered processes of writing and reading, processes that call upon our cognition, emotions, desires, hopes, values, and beliefs" (19). This idea of rhetoric acknowledges that the writer of a literary work may have multiple aims. All the same, the concept encourages literature specialists to study texts as strategic instruments, as efforts to affect audiences in particular (if numerous) ways. Scholars who take this perspective may still have different emphases and premises. Not all of them share, for instance, Booth's interest in ethics. Moreover, advocates of this perspective may seek to correct one another. For instance, despite his admiration of Booth, Phelan questions his reliance on authorial intent

(19). Whatever the disagreements, though, today numerous literary critics see rhetoric as social aspects of discourse.

Consistent with this view, and yet valuably extending it, are notions of rhetoric that go beyond the lone reader's processing of the literary text to consider how diverse audiences react to it. These theories don't assume there's one right reading of the text. Rather, they consider how social and historical changes may spur different responses to it. This concern with the various contexts of a work's reception is evident, for example, in Steven Mailloux's vision of rhetoric. For him, rhetorical study of literature involves situating texts within shifting "cultural conversations," the larger social dialogues they enter. An English department taking this approach, then, wouldn't seal literature off from other discourse such as "nonfictional" prose. Rather, it would explore connections between literature and the rest of the textual universe. O'Brien's novel, I'll argue, is a good place to start.

To say that literature has rhetorical aspects doesn't mean it's the same as all other kinds of writing. Most novels differ significantly from op-ed columns. Although authors do use fiction, poetry, and drama to promote their ideas, many of these works aren't explicit arguments, packed with evidence and reasons that support one main claim. As I've noted, writers of literature can have multiple purposes. Moreover, when they seek to persuade their audiences of something, often their efforts are indirect. It's important for us to bear in mind, therefore, that genres have their own norms—which, through a rhetorical refusal, writers may flout. As we'll see, one such writer is O'Brien.

O'Brien's Refusal

In key respects, *In the Lake of the Woods* is hardly an eccentric novel. Much of its language is clear, even plain—far from the bewildering pyrotechnics of a *Finnegans Wake*. Moreover, few readers are apt to have difficulty tracing its main plot. In brief, the story focuses on John Wade, a Vietnam veteran who goes to Minnesota's Lake of the Woods with his wife, Kathy. The trip is their effort to find relief after Wade loses a senatorial primary. Eventually, we learn the cause of his political defeat: his participation in the My Lai massacre. Until the primary, he's managed to conceal his role in this atrocity from others, Kathy included. In part, his deception has stemmed from his anguish over the killings. Even during them, he was so stressed and disoriented that he shot a fellow soldier as well as an elderly farmer. Yet, clearly Wade's psychic pain has been lifelong. It reaches back to his boyhood, when his alcoholic father belittled him and eventually killed himself. Since then, Wade's insecurity has influenced much of his behavior. Indeed, when courting Kathy before and after the war, he was so anxious about their relationship that often he observed her secretly. At the lake, the couple labor to heal the tensions in their marriage. But one morning, John wakes up to find that Kathy has vanished from their cabin. Thus, much of the book is about the search for her, drawing this novel into the genre of mystery. At my public library, one copy of *Lake* even resides in the mystery section. This genre frame is reinforced by the narrator, who's probed Kathy's disappearance. Basically, he offers a retrospective report on it, with facts and guesses he's gleaned.

Notwithstanding this novel's accessibility, aspects of it are disconcerting. For one thing, the narrator's Vietnam service resembles O'Brien's, so readers may wonder exactly how much this figure is the author himself. The same question arises with O'Brien's more well-known 1990 book *The Things They Carried.* A collection of short stories about a platoon in Vietnam, it actually includes a character named Tim O'Brien. Though the narrator of *Lake* is anonymous, his life's closeness to O'Brien's is just as provocative. Unsettling, too, is the narrator's method of personal disclosure. Only sporadically does he make himself known as a particular person, with a particular background and particular views. Furthermore, when he turns autobiographical, he resorts to footnotes—common in scholarship, but not in fiction.

Still another offbeat element of *Lake* is its structure. Besides moving back and forth in time—which, granted, many novels do—the book weaves among four recurring types of chapters. One set, which does present a chronological series of events, focuses on the search for Kathy immediately following her disappearance. A second set recalls episodes from John Wade's prior life. With the third group of chapters, each labeled "Hypothesis," come scenes of Kathy's possible fate. The fourth category consists of chapters that are montages of quotations. Under the heading "Evidence," each of the chapters in this fourth group compiles statements by various people. Some of the latter are fictional, including friends, relatives, and acquaintances of the Wades. Also cited, however, are real figures: for example, collaborators in the My Lai massacre, including chief perpetrator William Calley; experts on trauma, especially the trauma of war; specialists in magic; biographers of Presidents Wilson, Johnson, and Nixon; chroniclers of the United States' nineteenth-century "Indian Wars"; British soldiers who retaliated severely against colonists in the American Revolution; and authors such as Fyodor Dostoyevsky, Nathaniel Hawthorne, and Edith Wharton. Eventually, I think, most readers of the novel can navigate its organization. Sooner or later, they recognize its four kinds of chapters, and they're able to construct a timeline for most of its events. Still, making sense of the structure requires interpretive labor. Especially challenging are the miscellaneous testimonies within each "Evidence" part. Putting these together in meaningful patterns takes work.

The novel's most unusual feature, though, is its omission of what happened to Kathy. We don't find out how she vanished or where she went. O'Brien sets up a mystery that he refuses to solve. He even compounds the frustration we may feel, in two ways related to John Wade. First, Wade himself seems hazy about what went on in the hours before Kathy vanished. Did he kill her in crazed despair over his political defeat? If so, it's a crime he's uncertain about. Furthermore, O'Brien ends the book by having Wade vanish, too. Piloting a boat into vast, fog-shrouded waters, Wade simply fades away, leaving unclear what role if any he played in his wife's exit. Again, did he kill Kathy? Or, had they planned a joint escape, aiming to start their lives over? Or, did she choose to flee from him? Or, did she accidentally get lost while boating alone on the lake? The "Hypothesis" chapters raise these possibilities, but the book doesn't verify any.

O'Brien's withholding of a solution amounts to a rhetorical refusal, as I've been defining the term. In "Secrecy and Disclosure as Rhetorical Forms," Edwin Black observes that a mystery is "an imposition of perplexity . . . an uncomfortable condition that agitates for alleviation" (137). Readers of a mystery novel may enjoy, even welcome, this discomfort up to a point, but typically they want and expect the author to relieve it at the end. O'Brien defies this expectation, however, by leaving his mystery open. When *Lake* was published, he told an interviewer that he was nervous about this move, fearing the lack of closure would drive readers off (Kahn). In effect, O'Brien engages in what *The New Rhetoric* calls an appearance/reality dissociation. Readers who make their way through *Lake* assuming it will follow all the conventions of mysteries find themselves derailed. At the same time, applicable here is Chaim Perelman and Lucie Olbrechts-Tyteca's notion of audiences judging audiences. O'Brien asks us to become the kind of readers who would view as parochial those who demand he adhere to mystery formulas.

On the several occasions when I've taught *Lake*, most of my students have actually liked it. Nevertheless, they brood about the ending's vagueness. Admittedly, the narrator previews this. Early on, he says that that "Kathy Wade is forever missing, and if you require solutions, you will have to look beyond these pages. Or read a different book" (30).[2] Many of my students report, though, that they disbelieved this passage when they read it. Of course, they're aware that people may disappear permanently in real life. But for my classes—and for most of us—fictional vanishing acts are another matter. We're used to seeing these cleared up.

When my students write about O'Brien's novel, many do choose one of the "Hypotheses," arguing that it's the best explanation for Kathy's disappearance. The big favorite is the next-to-last scenario, where John Wade turns downright mad and murders her. I can understand why students are drawn to this possibility. By holding it off so long, O'Brien leads us to suspect it's the ultimate truth. Moreover, the murder is described in painfully vivid detail, and this rawness seems authoritative. Having just destroyed plants in their cabin with boiled water from a teakettle, Wade pours it on his sleeping wife, and then dumps her body in the lake. Noting that such destruction echoes American atrocities in Vietnam, especially the massacre that Wade helped carry out, critic H. Bruce Franklin argues for accepting the homicide hypothesis. To him, Wade clearly did kill Kathy. If readers don't agree, he suggests, they're guilty of denial, just as America has forgotten its barbarism during the war (339).

Yet Franklin seems to deny the complexity of the novel. We have reasons not to privilege its murder scene. In an essay responding to Franklin, O'Brien is notably wary. Commenting on Franklin's overall interpretation of the book, O'Brien does say, "I dispute almost none of it," but the word "almost" seems crucial. Indeed, he seems to be making this statement with tongue planted firmly in cheek, for he then accuses literary criticism of slighting fiction's "ambiguities and uncertainties and unknowns of fact and motive." Such things, he says, end up "vanish[ing] in the great blinding clarity of abstraction" ("The Whole Story" 344). Within the novel itself, the person most convinced of Wade's guilt is, significantly, a dogmatic boor. A lake area local named Vinny Pearson, he's immediately and crassly suspicious of Wade, as if he doesn't need proof. Throughout the book, Vinny is sure of his forensic acumen, his last pronouncement being, "My guess? I don't need to guess. He did it. Wasted her. That stare of his, the way he didn't even feel nothing. I seen it a zillion times. . . . Who cares if we didn't never find no evidence? All it means is he sunk her good and deep" (296). Such coarse certainty itself arouses suspicion. It seems bullheadedness, not smarts. Just as important, the novel's narrator casts doubt on the murder scene soon after we read it. He's skeptical that Wade killed Kathy, given that in a romantic sense, Wade "was crazy about her" (300). Unsurprisingly, then, the narrator then brings up yet another hypothesis, the one in which the couple flee together to a new life. Not that the narrator himself feels certain of the facts. Recall his early confession that he hasn't solved the mystery, despite all of his research.

Thus, as readers, we're actually left with no definitive disclosure, even if a particular hypothesis attracts us. And such will remain our situation. We'll *never* see Kathy's vanishing explained. In this respect, we differ from characters in the book who want to know what happened. Within the world of the novel, perhaps they'll find out someday; within our realm of existence, we won't.

Relevant here are distinctions that Peter Rabinowitz makes in his classic article "Truth in Fiction: A Reexamination of Audiences." Rabinowitz argues that a fictional text evokes various kinds of audiences. For a given novel, we can identify what he calls its *narrative* audience by asking, "What sort of person would I have to pretend to be—what would I have to know and believe—if I wanted to take this work of fiction as real?" (128). The narrative audience of *Lake* consists of people who take Kathy as real, who want her found, and who hope that the truth will eventually emerge, if not in the near then in the distant future. When we ourselves study *Lake*, however, we're what Rabinowitz calls the *actual* audience: "the flesh-and-blood people who read the book" (126). Moreover, grasping O'Brien's aims and strategies—including what he's up to with his rhetorical refusal—involves determining the sort of readers he assumed as he wrote. This group, Rabinowitz refers to as the *authorial* audience (126). If the book is successful, its actual audience and its authorial one will essentially coincide. At any rate, both these groups are stuck with an unsolved case.

As, specifically, an unsolved "missing person" case, *Lake* does have precedents in art. Two of the most famous are cinematic. In Michelangelo Antonioni's 1960 film *L'Avventura*, a woman disappears from the small island that she and her friends have been exploring, and we never do find out where she's gone. Just as unclear is the fate of the schoolgirls in Peter

Weir's 1975 film *Picnic at Hanging Rock*.[3] On a field trip to the landscape of the title, they mysteriously vanish, their whereabouts still a puzzle at the end. Movies aside, this kind of narrative has shown up in prose fiction before *Lake*. For example, in 1985, Paul Auster produced *City of Glass*, a novel with a similarly inconclusive plot. After fruitlessly investigating a family's tortured relationships, the hero himself disappears, leaving just his notebook behind. Yet, the existence of such predecessors doesn't make *Lake*'s inconclusiveness less startling. Rhetorical refusals stand out even when the reader or viewer knows ancestors for them.

As we seek to understand the kind of novel that *Lake* actually is, we should keep in mind that fictional vanishing acts vary in rhetorical function. They can take on different kinds of significance within their respective works. I've grown quite aware of this possibility in teaching *Lake* together with Auster's book. While *Lake* won the Society of American Historians' James Fenimore Cooper Prize for Historical Fiction, it's hard for me to imagine that *City of Glass* ever could. Auster's novel isn't nearly as concerned with real, specific past events. He encourages us to see his book mainly as metafiction. With numerous devices, such as a character named Paul Auster, he spurs reflection on his very craft. Largely, his detective story is about how, in general, fiction relates to the world. This is the question raised by the hero's disappearance at the end. O'Brien, though, encourages another sort of inquiry. Mainly, I'd argue, he aims to extend Americans' reflection on the Vietnam War.

By failing to explain Kathy's disappearance, and by having her husband then vanish, O'Brien points to issues of history and politics that the novel also doesn't resolve. These include what the United States should make of its exploits in Vietnam. O'Brien implies that America hasn't accounted for its atrocities there, just as John Wade has resisted admitting his complicity in them. I use the verb "account for" in two senses: (1) to formulate an explanation for; (2) to acknowledge one's moral responsibility for. Both meanings seem pertinent here. I think O'Brien wants Americans to study their nation's conduct in Vietnam and to see it as signifying an immoral society they themselves have condoned. This agenda for his readers is his rationale for swerving from the mystery novel's usual satisfactions.

Vietnam

Though decades have passed since the United States military left Vietnam, Americans still debate its presence there. At times, this subject does seem about to fade from the national memory. Always, though, some event revives arguments about it. Such tension was evident in the month that *Lake* was published, October 1994. This was a time when U.S. firms were preparing to invest in Vietnam. Simultaneously, though, other groups criticized Vietnam's leaders, insisting they tell the fate of all missing U.S. soldiers. Recently, quarrels over the war resumed in the race for president, as Swift Boat veterans challenged John Kerry's Vietnam service record. In 2005, similar controversy brewed when Jane Fonda published *My Life So Far*. Recollecting her protests against the war, she reignited charges that she'd been a traitor. And now, America's presence in Iraq recalls its role in Vietnam, with people still wrangling over that intervention.

Because, apparently, the Vietnam War always haunts Americans, do they need *Lake* to remind them of it? Some may claim that they don't. But this is a position that O'Brien in essence disputes. As Franklin observes, O'Brien is concerned with an American habit of denial. Clearly he worries that his country still represses the war's most sordid aspects. "Wade's individual case of amnesia," Timothy Melley points out, "is inseparable from more serious collective memory failures" (112). The convenient erasing of memory is emphasized in one "Evidence" chapter, which quotes several My Lai killers' courtroom testimonies. Over and over, they claim they've forgotten details of what they did (137–38). Through his novel, O'Brien evidently prods the nation to resist the allure of obliviousness. With his rhetorical refusal, he pushes it to confront its misdeeds in Vietnam more.

Admittedly, the book's inconclusiveness can be viewed through other lenses. For example, it might inspire the philosophically minded to ponder fiction as a medium, reviewing what they seek from it. The narrator suggests, for instance, that part of us wants to see mystery sustained, even as another part wants answers: "The human desire for certainty collides with our love of enigma" (266). Also in a philosophical vein, the murky behavior of the Wades can signify a general human condition: people's opacity to one another. In the book's final pages, the narrator repeatedly brings up this theme. He asks, "Our own children, our fathers, our wives and husbands: Do we truly know them?" (295). He proclaims, "One way or another, it seems, we all perform vanishing tricks, effacing history, locking up our lives and slipping day by day into the groping shadows" (301).

Nevertheless, the uncertain ending seems most to solicit a psycho-political reading. On a psychological note, it echoes John Wade's self-division, his willful inability to admit what he's done and thought. To a great extent, the book is about his divorce from his own experiences. Throughout his life, Wade's had trouble learning from, let alone acknowledging, them. Central to this problem has been his chosen identity of magician. As a child, he takes up magic as a refuge from his father's abuse. "In the mirror," practicing his tricks, "John was no longer a lonely little kid. He had sovereignty over the world" (65). Eventually, he adopts a mental form of trickery, inwardly preferring illusion: "[H]e secretly kept the old stand-up mirror in his head" (65). This private pretense is exacerbated with his father's suicide, which he tries to persuade himself did not occur. From his boyhood on, then, he follows a program of covert self-deception: "He would repair what he could, he would endure, he would go from year to year without letting on that there were tricks" (46). Even during the search for Kathy at the lake, "Wade felt an estrangement from the actuality of the world, its basic now-ness, and in the end all he could conjure up was an image of illusion itself, pure reflection, a head full of mirrors" (278). Ironically, he senses that he's come to resemble his father, for both have subscribed to the idea that "you carry the burdens, entomb yourself in silence, conceal demon-history from all others and most times from yourself" (241).

The political dimension of the novel becomes quite apparent, of course, in the passages about Wade's experiences in Vietnam. There, he still practices his personal forms of magic. Significantly, his fellow soldiers know him only by the name "Sorcerer." But this military service increases his alienation from the world. Suffering from, even while collaborating in, the war's dissonant brutality, he comes back less prepared than ever to drop protective fantasy. Thus, the novel's rhetorical refusal seems linked not only to Wade's personal torment but also to his country's whole Vietnam intervention. We're encouraged to analyze and evaluate both.

This encouragement involves plunging *us* into a disequilibrium that resembles, if roughly, Wade's state of mind in the war. What Toby Herzog says about O'Brien's whole corpus of fiction applies a lot to *Lake*: "The resulting narrative confusion and contradiction heighten readers' sense of the chaotic nature of war in general and of America's experience in the Vietnam War in particular ("'True Lies'" 911). Presumably, we will be more motivated to examine this chapter in American history if we, too, feel dislocated. To be sure, we won't experience the angst of numerous Vietnam veterans. Whatever our sense of "confusion and contradiction," it will be less than theirs. I stress this point because in the growing academic field of trauma studies, there's a risk of supposing that traumas are ubiquitous and always comparable. This premise marks one of the field's founding texts, Shoshana Felman and Dori Laub's book *Testimony: Crises of Witnessing in Literature, Psychoanalysis, and History*. Describing her course on Holocaust testimonies, Felman claims that the class didn't just sympathize with the authors but actually experienced something like their sense of dislocation (47–56). She slights, however, obvious differences between the two groups. We shouldn't do the same with O'Brien's novel. *Lake's* open ending may disturb us, but it's unlikely to shatter us. Even so, the book's irresolution can prove catalytic, leading us to probe the war's horrors and its lingering pain.

Again, the book actually situates the war in larger historical context. In particular, the "Evidence" chapters conjure up other episodes in America's past, which O'Brien evidently thinks shed light on this one. An example is the set of statements about the "Indian Wars." They remind us that Americans long ago attacked supposedly uncivilized Others, just as they later did at My Lai. Though some quotations tell of Custer's own violent death, they still evoke him as vanquisher of tribes and thereby as forefather of Calley. The statements from the American Revolution invite similar links. True, they stress the British army's cruelty toward the colonists. They show that Americans themselves were victims of "brutal degeneracy" (260), to use one guilt-ridden British officer's term. All the same, the citations put mass killing within the American heritage. Of course, they also prove ironic. Though Americans were once slain as savages, they proceeded to slaughter My Lai's people, condemning *them* as less than human. O'Brien even implies that amnesia helped *cause* these murders. The soldiers ignored what Americans had suffered in an earlier war, their own country's fight for independence.

The violence alluded to in these vignettes is, O'Brien suggests, gender-related. Appropriately, Melley calls *Lake* a "psychodrama of masculinization" (116). As he notes, this view of the book further connects Wade's life to his country's past. In the "Evidence" parts, the harm inflicted by America's warriors and politicos has much to do with proving their manhood. As boy and adult, Wade feels this impulse. Throughout his life, he's ashamed that he's never been masculine enough for his father. Ironically, the latter's drinking and suicide reflect a similar sense of inadequacy. Wade's perpetual addiction to secrets reflects his own quest for manly authority, as does his surveillance of Kathy. Most spectacularly, at My Lai he cooperates with his unit's genocidal display of male power. Together, he and his fellow soldiers sustain the American tradition of violence, the bloody record that the "Evidence" sections evoke. On personal and social levels, then, in *Lake* patriarchal values become a lethal force.

But we need to remember two things. First, though Wade suffers from these values, nevertheless he upholds them. If, for most of the attack at My Lai, he's chiefly a pained bystander, he winds up committing two murders there. Then, he proceeds to cover them up. Literally, he alters army records, removing his name from Calley's roster. As far as My Lai is concerned, therefore, he was never present. Moreover, he conceals his role in the massacre from Kathy and his political allies, so that years go by before his involvement emerges. In general, Wade isn't just a victim of circumstance. He's also a shaper of it. As O'Brien said in an interview with Herzog, "There were numerous points in that man's life where choice was limited, for sure, but it wasn't excluded. . . . The man had clearly, despite everything, the capacity to choose otherwise in his life, to choose well in his life" (100–101). Because Wade does have agency, however finite it may be, we're free to consider how moral his actions are. Not that his ethical duties and failings are necessarily easy to pinpoint. But, by leaving the plot inconclusive, O'Brien invites continued deliberation about them.

Second, it's important for us to recall Kathy's prominence in the novel. Otherwise, as we focus on her husband, we may underestimate her role. Melley slights it when he asserts that the novel "is certainly not a tale about Kathy" (123). While he's right to call the book a "psychodrama of masculinization," he himself seems androcentric when he de-emphasizes her. He mimics Wade's habit of relegating her to the sidelines of Wade's own career. Kathy's disappearance is, in fact, the book's core mystery, the problem that comes to occupy her husband and other characters. In addition, several of the "Hypothesis" chapters grant her agency, too, by showing her escaping Wade's control. True, these scenarios are speculative and contradicted by others. Still, they underscore that she does have a will her husband has kept leashed. Moreover, even if they've gone off together—the scenario of their joint flight—Kathy remains a prime victim of Wade's solipsism and deceit. Thus, she would still be someone to whom he must explain and atone for his acts.

Indeed, the novel begins with their tentative, faltering efforts at conversation after the truth of his past has come out. Reeling from his disgrace and political loss, they come to the lake for peace, but at best it's only a temporary retreat. Quickly they find themselves groping for a language of moral encounter that might enable them to go on as a couple. These attempts are disrupted by Kathy's disappearance, and they're never renewed within the novel itself. Faced with the vagueness of the book's ending, we must imagine the further exchanges the pair would need to launch.

In this concern with conversation, *Lake* resembles the Hollywood "comedies of remarriage" studied by philosopher Stanley Cavell, most recently in his book *Cities of Words: Pedagogical Letters on a Register of the Moral Life*.[4] At first glance, O'Brien's dark novel may seem quite different from the farces that Cavell examines, such as *Adam's Rib, The Philadelphia Story, It Happened One Night, The Lady Eve, His Girl Friday*, and *The Awful Truth*. But there are commonalities beneath the tonal contrasts. True, the Wades are already wed, so the term "remarriage" doesn't apply to them literally. But, as with *Adam's Rib* and *The Lady Eve*, the term doesn't strictly fit several of the movies that Cavell discusses. As he notes, he focuses on stories about two people who may, officially, be "already together" but who have drifted apart. They must overcome "some inner obstacle between them" in order to be "*again, back* together" in a meaningful sense (10). More precisely, Cavell sees the pair as struggling toward what he calls Emersonian moral perfectionism, a key element of which is "the reassessment and reconstitution of one's life after a crisis in what appears its foundation or direction" (84). This "crisis" often is for both members of the pair "a moment of being humbled, or being humiliated" (17). The scandal that the Wades have suffered just before the novel begins is such a moment. Actually, their trip to the lake in its aftermath fits another motif that Cavell finds in his remarriage films: an eventual shift to "the country, a place of perspective Shakespeare calls the Green World" (10). But in this pastoral setting, the Wades don't clearly reform themselves. Nor do they seem to establish new closeness. If the films suggest that our morality depends upon "our ability to make ourselves intelligible to each other" (381), then ethically the Wades have far to go. As both disappear, they seem to have only begun the "mutual education" (234) that Cavell takes the remarriage genre to prize.

That both Kathy and John vanish is still another resemblance, if a rough one, between *Lake* and this genre. Cavell points out that typically, remarriage comedies "close with some indication that the principal pair, in reentering the state of matrimony, are crossing some border that leaves us out, behind, and with no visible secure embrace of their own, nothing to insure the risk that they will find, or refind, their happiness" (159). Though these films end gaily, Cavell observes, they don't guarantee their central union will last. Rather, they imply that the couple must continually attune themselves to each other. As we leave the two, we have to decide what dialogue they now require if they're to have an enduring and ethical bond. The Wades' mysterious exits present us the same task. Even if one or both of them are dead, their unfinished conversation is something we're implicitly asked to resume.

A Later "Cultural Conversation" and Another Text

As we imagine further dialogue between these characters, we can also apply the term *conversation* to the social contexts that *Lake* has moved through. Here I return to Mailloux's notion of relating texts to "cultural conversations" surrounding them. When I teach O'Brien's novel, I have students consider how Americans discussed the Vietnam War in the mid-1990s. This is, after all, the discourse that O'Brien aimed to affect. But I encourage them as well to consider what the book may contribute to later debates. In particular, how might O'Brien's rhetorical refusal help us weigh later texts about the war, including works that aren't clearly "literature"?

One text that his refusal helps us assess is Bob Kerrey's autobiography, *When I Was a Young Man*. In fact, when I teach O'Brien's novel, I bring in excerpts from Kerrey's memoir and have students compare the two texts. Like John Wade, Kerrey is a Vietnam veteran who entered politics, becoming governor of Nebraska and then senator from that state. A Democrat, he competed with Clinton for his party's presidential nomination, and he was thinking about reseeking it as Clinton's second term waned. Like Wade, however, Kerrey saw his ambitions endangered by his wartime past. In 1969, at the village of Thanh Phong, he had supervised the killing of several civilians, chiefly women and children. Though he'd never denied the incident, he'd never spoken of it publicly. But reporters were learning about it as he contemplated running for president once more. Their research may have been one reason he eventually abandoned that quest. In any case, when he left politics to become a college president, the inquiries didn't stop. In 2001, they led to a *New York Times Magazine* article and *Sixty Minutes II* broadcast on the Thanh Phong attack. Unfortunately for Kerrey, both raised an especially chilling hypothesis. While Kerrey claimed that his men had responded to gunfire directed at them, unit member Gerhard Klann told a ghastlier story. He recalled that Kerrey had ordered the villagers assembled and executed. In the days following the article and the newscast, Kerrey was harshly criticized. In the court of public opinion, he found himself charged with war crimes.

When this furor erupted, I thought immediately of *In the Lake of the Woods*. The scandal that plagued Kerrey isn't quite John Wade's, but the resemblances are striking. I'm not the only one who's sensed parallels. Melley, for instance, alludes to Kerrey in analyzing *Lake* (121), and a Web site devoted to O'Brien makes the same connection.[5] But I want to go further and compare *Lake* with the book that Kerrey has written. Unlike Wade, Kerrey went on to publish a memoir, which was partly an effort to clear his name.

Despite the storm aroused by news of the Thanh Phong killings, *When I Was a Young Man* recalls them just briefly. Kerrey spends only three paragraphs describing them. This brevity seems an attempt to limit their importance, suggesting they don't merit the fuss. Moreover, he sticks with the idea that the slaughter was defensive, the reaction of soldiers who'd been fired upon. He does say that, even so, "I felt a sickness in my heart for what we had done" (185). In addition, he concedes that his memory of the event is faulty: "In truth, I remember very little what happened in a clear and reliable way" (183). But he doesn't elaborate his implication that another version is possible. In particular, he doesn't admit that Klann's scenario is more shocking, for in it Kerrey and his men committed outright atrocity.

In a single-page coda to the book, Kerrey touches on the killings again, but once more his treatment is cursory. "One night of my life as a combatant in the Vietnam War," he notes, "has been previously examined in great detail by the press and the public" (270). While his statement recognizes that the attack on Thanh Phong has proven controversial, his reference to it is vague. Moreover, his tone is peevish, as if he scorns the media coverage. Next he suggests that he'd long planned to describe what had happened: "I agreed to talk publicly about that night in part because I was trying to write about it for this book" (271). His claim rings hollow, though, since the book he's produced spends meager time on the episode. Besides, once the media had reported it, the resulting uproar forced him to discuss it. Actually, by devoting so little of his book to the Thanh Phong attack, he seems to have aimed at *reducing* the clamor it had already caused. Clearly bothered by this noise, he then says that "I did not anticipate the intensity of the press interest and the public exposure that occurred to each of the six men I led that night" (271). This statement, too, however, seems disingenuous, for it sidesteps the fact that most of the angry scrutiny has been directed at *him*. Next, Kerrey reports that he and his unit met recently to review "that night" so that his version of it in the book reflects their achieved consensus. But he doesn't identify discrepancies and uncertainties among them that they had to work through. Gregory Vistica points out in his book *The Education of Lieutenant Kerrey* that, in fact, these men told him disparate stories before they convened. Indeed, he suspects that Kerrey pressured them to endorse Kerrey's own recollection. Whether or not this conjecture is fair, Kerrey is misleading in another respect. He doesn't reveal that absent from the meeting was Klann, who remembers them committing sheer massacre. Kerrey does end this brief epilogue by reiterating that his version of what occurred "is merely the best that I can remember today" (271). Yet, once more he fails to mention Klann's alternative story, which is worse than his.

Nor does Kerrey ponder the irony of his book's final words. What should we think of a memoir that ends by alluding to the *limits* of memory? Most of the book reflects confidence in its author's powers of recall. Even in the depiction of the Thanh Phong attack, the prose is matter-of-fact, despite Kerrey's admission that his memory here isn't altogether "reliable." What would his memoir have been like if he'd done more with such statements? If he'd used his text to examine other hypotheses about "that night"? If he'd elaborated how and why he may not be remembering it well? Of course, Klann's story may be defective as well. We should not assume it's the truth. Though Vistica's book is a valuable guide to the whole affair, he seems presumptuous when he asserts that Klann's tale is "more accurate" (273). As yet, there isn't enough evidence to support this bold a claim. Still, what took place "that night" is more debatable than Kerrey lets on.

Can Kerrey's reticence about unresolved issues be called a rhetorical refusal? I would say no. In his book, he's merely evasive about "that night" and the furor it's spawned, not even implying that some higher principle justifies his caginess. On the other hand, O'Brien does perform a rhetorical refusal when he resists telling the fate of the Wades. He withholds closure because, he implies, his readers may then head into something better: sustained and searching dialogue about the war.

Had *When I Was a Young Man* consistently explored the fallibility, partiality, and self-interestedness of memory—especially its author's memory of the slaughter at Thanh Phong—it might have been as enigmatic and experimental as *In the Lake of the Woods*. That Kerrey did not, after all, write such a book is hardly surprising. For one thing, it might have proved too daunting for the mass market he hoped to reach. More important, it might have prevented him from recovering the stature he'd lost. Though he no longer held public office, he still had the instincts of politicians—people who, as Wade's campaign manager observes, are "control freaks" (27).

As things have turned out, Kerrey has been pretty successful at rebuilding his reputation. Whatever scandal resulted from the revelations about him, the larger culture eventually lost interest, surely in part due to its own investment in avoiding issues of conscience. Frank Rich observes that "hardly did the Kerrey story emerge than boomer politicians and journalists rushed to lock it up again—by throwing up our hands and saying, 'Who are we to judge?' and "War is war"" (*Greatest* 11). Eventually, Kerrey was even appointed to the 9/11 Commission. Moreover, in this capacity he vigilantly investigated other people's memories, confronting military and government officials with questions of truth, knowledge, and responsibility that he preferred to evade in his book.

At any rate, O'Brien's novel is a good foil for *When I Was a Young Man*, foregrounding complexities that Kerrey's memoir slights. Literary study needs, I'd argue, to engage in such comparisons if it's to call itself "rhetorical" at all. That is, it needs to roam beyond classic literary genres, to connect apparently dissimilar discourses, and to probe cultural contexts. This project might very well include considering how rhetorical refusals like O'Brien's complicate America's memory of war.

CONCLUSION

I'm tempted to conclude this book by performing a rhetorical refusal myself. Doing so would be in the spirit of the preceding pages. I'd be signaling again that these acts appear in various works, including the book you hold. So, for example, if composition scholars tend to end their monographs by stressing classroom applications, I might end by protesting this emphasis on the practical.

Actually, I hope this book does have pedagogic value, giving teachers ideas they then share with their students. I believe, for example, the latter should know that rhetorical refusals have happened. They would also benefit from seeing these moves as possible for themselves. Of course, the recognition comes more readily if they try out these strategies. But practice needs to be joined by reflection. For a given composing task, students ought to discuss if, in fact, a rhetorical refusal is good—with "good" meaning ethical as well as effective. Probably, their inquiry would be aided if they examined this book's cases. When the people in these scenarios performed or evaluated a rhetorical refusal, they had to note and address any number of things.

The complexity of thinking that rhetorical refusals may require, both of their instigators and their audiences, is mainly why I refrain from performing one here. True, the gesture would fit my book's drift; it might prove entertaining to boot. But, as a final touch, it would be too neat. It would obscure the careful thought, the close attention to various elements, shown by many who've executed or assessed these acts. Besides, if I did end this way, I might be taken to imply that every rhetorical refusal is splendid. As I've stressed throughout, they need to be judged case by case.

Let me use this epilogue to pursue yet another option. I want to end by underscoring that potentially, at least, rhetorical refusals can help American political discourse become more inventive. Even veteran practitioners of such discourse might concede that it has come to rely too often upon pietistic commonplaces and familiar moves. Indeed, rare is the forum where a politician says something that the audience didn't expect. Again, not every rhetorical refusal would be a wonderful addition to civic dialogue; I hate to imagine officials like Ari Fleischer regularly using these strategies to stop probes of government. But what if citizens themselves had these strategies in their repertoires? *Their* civic speech might thereby spark better reflection in their audiences than does the usual language of politics. With this possibility in mind, I briefly review rhetorical refusals made by Sharon Olds, Stephen Colbert, and Cindy Sheehan. Each of these people was invited to interact with the Washington elite; each took the opportunity to protest America's war in Iraq.

In "The Rhetorical Situation," the classic article I referred to earlier, Lloyd Bitzer asserts that "a particular discourse comes into existence because of some condition or situation which invites utterance" (4). Many a subsequent theorist has criticized Bitzer, and fairly so, for suggesting that the "condition or situation" is an objective fact. They point out that inevitably, it must be interpreted: the rhetor must decide whether it exists, what its nature is, and how to address it. Even when the rhetor feels quite reasonably that an "invitation" is clearly at hand, he or she must decide what corresponding "utterance" is best, and this involves characterizing exactly what the invitation is *to*. Such considerations loom especially when the rhetor is invited to commingle with those whose policies the rhetor deplores.

Angered by the country's invasion and occupancy of Iraq, poet Olds declined the First Lady's invitation to participate in the 2005 National Book Festival and related White House events. Furthermore, Olds published her letter of refusal in the *Nation*. This behavior was by no means unprecedented for an American poet. As I noted earlier, in 1997 Adrienne Rich published a letter in which she rejected an arts award offered her by the Clinton administration. And back in 1965, Robert Lowell infuriated President Lyndon Johnson when, protesting American involvement in Vietnam, he rejected Johnson's invitation to participate in the White House Arts Festival. Lowell even went so far as to publish his letter declining the invitation on the very first page of the *New York Times*. Whatever her predecessors, though, Olds's act still amounts to a rhetorical refusal. It remains unusual for writers to spurn the White House as she did. Surely Laura Bush didn't expect to receive from this one a letter that ends this way: "So many Americans who had felt pride in our country now feel anguish and shame, for the current regime of blood, wounds and fire. I thought of the clean linens at your table, the shining knives and the flames of the candles, and I could not stomach it" (6). The image is that of a feast thrown by Lady Macbeth. Especially cutting, if I may use that word, is the writer's association of a dinner table's "knives" and "flames" with the carnage of war. Olds implies that whereas the White House should be nurturing, the current administration is deadly, to the point of her own physical revulsion.

Unlike Olds, Colbert did accept the invitation he was offered: to provide comedy at the 2006 White House Correspondents Association Dinner. This annual event gathers not only the capital's journalists but also government officials—including the president and First Lady, who sat just a few feet from Colbert as he spoke. Another ritualistic feature of the dinner is a monologue in which a comedian pokes fun at the nation's political circles. But Colbert's routine was exceptionally biting, especially toward President Bush. Repeatedly he portrayed Bush as a willfully ignorant leader who relies on "gut" feelings and photo-ops to keep the war going. Not that he exempted the White House press corps from scorn; repeatedly he depicted *them* as too cowardly to challenge Bush's Iraq policies. As a result, many saw Colbert as egregiously violating decorum. For days after, his performance was argued about on blogs and in other media. Though commentators didn't use the term rhetorical refusal, their debates indicated it could be applied to his speech.

Like Colbert, antiwar activist Sheehan accepted an invitation, which in her case came from congressional representative Lynn Woolsey. It wasn't to give a speech but to sit in the balcony for Bush's 2006 State of the Union address. In a widely reported and widely debated incident, however, Sheehan was ejected by Capitol police because she wore a black shirt that read "2,245 Dead. How Many More?" Though her "text" was just a number and a few words, clearly it was an antiwar statement, reflecting the fact that Sheehan had lost a son of her own in Iraq. Later in the evening, displaying evenhandedness, the police also ejected a congressman's wife for wearing the more explicit message "Support the Troops." But most likely the second woman wouldn't have been pulled from the balcony if Sheehan hadn't been; the latter was treated by the officers as more out of bounds. Many of the commentators who subsequently criticized Sheehan argued that the night was Bush's, not an opportunity for average citizens to express disagreement with him. In fact, it's unusual for someone at the State of the Union address to wear the words of protest that Sheehan did. When anyone in the balcony draws attention, it's almost always because the president has explicitly referred to that person as an example of how well America is functioning.[1] Hence, I would call Sheehan's message a rhetorical refusal. Had she worn a blank shirt, she might have been perceived as supporting the president, at least to the extent of tolerating his remarks. But this wasn't a perception she wished to encourage.

I am hardly urging Americans to rush out and treat invitations as each of these three people did. Still, I hope their refusals will get people thinking about how political discourse in the United States or elsewhere might take more risks. I realize that many Americans have never felt "invited" to participate in such discourse to begin with. Indeed, Sheehan first came to attention when Bush repeatedly refused to meet with her, and today, the nation poses all sorts of impediments to political engagement. As I write these concluding words, Americans have just gone to the polls for congressional elections, but many of them were turned away because they couldn't produce now-required photo IDs. Scholars of rhetoric must strive to create opportunities for people to have any civic role at all. All the same, rhetorical refusals are worth studying as possible performances when the opportunities exist.

But I don't want to end by sounding *unequivocally* positive about such refusals, or unequivocally negative either. Their variety is just too great for them to be simply praised or damned. Though I've put them in subcategories, we ought to note their sheer range. Learning how to perform or analyze calls for nuanced research. To investigate them is to examine different aims, forms, values, and conditions. Even the refusals I've just discussed here are merely three examples, meant to indicate a larger, more diverse group of acts. So, I end by affirming the *study* of rhetorical refusals, if only because it promises to expand many a rhetorician's scope. This is an offer we can't, or shouldn't, refuse.

NOTES

WORKS CITED

INDEX

NOTES

Introduction

1. See, e.g., McHugh and also Spelman 133–56.

2. Burke's most extensive discussion of the Negative is on pp. 419–69 of his book *Language as Symbolic Action*.

3. See my "Toward a Rhetoric of Visual Fragments."

4. For a detailed account of the whole affair at the University of Texas at Austin, see Brodkey.

5. Lyotard's main discussion of Holocaust survivors' testimonies occurs throughout his book *The Differend*.

1. Studying Rhetorical Refusals: Basic Principles

1. Consider, for example, the following remark by Wittgenstein: "When one says 'He gave a name to his sensation' one forgets that a great deal of stage-setting in the language is presupposed if the mere act of naming is to make sense. And when we speak of someone's having given a name to pain, what is presupposed is the existence of the grammar of the word 'pain'; it shews the post where the new word is stationed" (#257). Of Bakhtin's many statements on this subject, here is just one: "As a living, socio-ideological concrete thing, as heteroglot opinion, language, for the individual consciousness, lies on the borderline between oneself and the other. The word in language is half someone else's" ("Discourse" 293).

2. Actually, in the very first column by Agee reprinted in *Agee on Film*—a December 26, 1942, piece from the *Nation*—he recommends "that *Ravaged Earth*, which is made up of Japanese atrocities, be withdrawn until, if ever, careful enough minds, if any, shall have determined whether or not there is any morally responsible means of turning it loose on the public" (5). Also, in a March 24, 1945, column for the *Nation* reviewing violent, death-laden newsreels of the Iwo Jima battle, he wonders if "we have no business seeing this sort of experience except through our presence and participation" (140). He even compares such footage to pornography (140).

2. Evaluating Rhetorical Refusals: Categories and Criteria

1. See especially pp. 113–22 of Goodman's *Languages of Art*.

2. For an insightful account of Kael's war against pretension, especially in contrast to Susan Sontag's fondness for erudite art, see Seligman.

3. Croce's Refusal as a Test Case for Evaluation

1. In his book *Nobrow: The Culture of Marketing, the Marketing of Culture*, John Seabrook (a writer for the *New Yorker*) reports at length on Brown's editorial policies as a reflection of contemporary culture in general.

2. According to one reporter there, Jones denounced Croce's article as "not decent," even a "smear," saying it left him with "humiliation, deep anger and shame" (Salisbury).

4. Agents, "Truth," and Salience

1. Throughout this chapter, my references will be to the 1994 paperback edition of *Denying the Holocaust*, whose introduction includes thoughts about her subject that Lipstadt had since publication of the hardcover text.

2. For information about the libel trial in general, and about the revelations of Irving's malfeasance in particular, I have relied mainly on Lipstadt's *History on Trial*, Guttenplan's *The Holocaust on Trial*, and books by two members of Lipstadt's legal team, Richard Evans and Robert Jan van Pelt.

3. My colleague Alvin Rosenfelt, who was also present, corroborates Lang's account (personal conversation).

4. The title of Lipstadt's book about the trial, *History on Trial*, is similar to Guttenplan's, but my impression is that the media saw the proceedings as putting the Holocaust in question, not the entire documented past in general.

5. I think of a *New Yorker* cartoon in which one prisoner is saying to another, "Don't call yourself a murderer—you're just a person who happened to murder someone."

6. In *History on Trial*, Lipstadt associates Gibson with what she calls "'soft core' denial" (299).

7. Fish has elaborated his concept of "interpretive communities" in many of his books. A good starting point for examining his idea is *Is There a Text in This Class? The Authority of Interpretive Communities*.

8. McCloskey explains her distinction in "Big Rhetoric, Little Rhetoric."

9. I leave the reader to decide how Stephen Colbert's term *truthiness* might apply to this discussion.

5. When a Refusal's Context Changes

1. Said's most well known analysis of how theories travel remains his essay entitled, aptly enough, "Traveling Theory."

2. Most notably, Mailloux has elaborated this call in his books *Rhetorical Power* and *Reception Histories*.

3. See Fish's essay "No Bias, No Merit."

4. The terms *normal discourse* and *abnormal discourse* play key roles in Kuhn's book *The Structure of Scientific Revolutions*.

5. For much of my information about Clinton's grand jury hearing and surrounding events, I have relied on Peter Baker's *The Breach* and Jeffrey Toobin's *A Vast Conspiracy*.

6. The Embedding of a Rhetorical Refusal

1. As I refer to "these listeners," I'm mindful of the fact that plenty of Americans, especially in the South, loathed Lincoln when he was alive and continued to despise him after his death.

2. Sarah Vowell similarly praises the candor of Douglass's speech in her book *Assassination Vacation*, pointing out that "the problem with the fog of history, with the way the taboos against speaking ill of the dead tends to edit memorials down to saying nothing much more than the deceased's name, is that all the specifics get washed away, leaving behind some universal nobody" (118–19).

7. A Literary Rhetorical Refusal

1. I refer to the Yeats, Brooks, and Bergonzi examples in *Between the Lines* (114, 8, 16).

2. Here and later I quote from the 1995 paperback edition of the novel because it is more publicly accessible than the hardcover one. For whatever reason, the paperback drops a few of the original text's "Evidence" words, a deletion that seems insignificant.

3. Weir's film is far better known than its source, Joan Lindsay's novel of the same name.

4. Cavell focused on this genre exclusively in his earlier book *Pursuits of Happiness*.

5. The Web site, entitled *Tim O'Brien, Novelist*, is an excellent guide to his writings.

Conclusion

1. For an interesting discussion of the State of the Union addresses' use of people in the balcony, see Wells.

WORKS CITED

Agee, James. *Agee on Film: Criticism and Comment on the Movies.* New York: Modern Library, 2000.

———. "December 26, 1942." *Agee* 3–5.

———. "March 24, 1945." *Agee* 139–40.

———. "May 19, 1945." *Agee* 149–51.

———. "Pseudo-Folk." *Agee* 431–37.

Alcoff, Linda Martin. "The Problem of Speaking for Others." *Who Can Speak? Authority and Critical Identity.* Ed. Judith Roof and Robyn Wiegman. Urbana: U of Illinois P, 1995. 97–119.

Altieri, Charles. "What Is at Stake in Confessional Criticism." Veeser 55–67.

Andrukhovych, Yuri. "Europe—My Neurosis." *Sign and Sight* 21 Mar. 2006. 2 May 2007 <http://www.signandsight.com/features/670.html>.

Annesley, James. "Pure Shores: Travel, Consumption, and Alex Garland's *The Beach.*" *Modern Fiction Studies* 50 (2004): 551–69.

Aristotle. *On Rhetoric: A Theory of Civic Discourse.* Trans. and ed. George A. Kennedy. New York: Oxford UP, 1991.

Attridge, Derek. *The Singularity of Literature.* New York: Routledge, 2004.

"At What Price?" *Newsday* 9 July 1995: A33.

Auster, Paul. *City of Glass.* 1985. New York: Penguin, 1987.

Baker, Peter. *The Breach: Inside the Impeachment and Trial of William Jefferson Clinton.* New York: Scribner, 2000.

Bakhtin, M. M. "Discourse in the Novel." *The Dialogic Imagination: Four Essays by M. M. Bakhtin.* Trans. Caryl Emerson and Michael Holquist. Ed. Holquist. Austin: U of Texas P, 1981. 259–422.

———. "The Problem of Speech Genres." *Speech Genres and Other Late Essays.* Trans. Vern W. McGee. Ed. Caryl Emerson and Michael Holquist. Austin: U of Texas P, 1986. 60–102.

Bal, Mieke. "Visual Essentialism and the Object of Visual Culture." *Journal of Visual Culture* 2 (2003): 5–32.

Beck, Joan. "The Murder of Children." *St. Louis Post-Dispatch* 24 Oct. 1994: 19B.

Benjamin, Walter. "The Work of Art in the Age of Mechanical Reproduction." *Illuminations*. Trans. Harry Zohn. Ed. Hannah Arendt. New York: Schocken, 1969. 217–51.

Benson, Thomas W., ed. *Rhetoric and Political Culture in Nineteenth-Century America*. East Lansing: Michigan State UP, 1997.

Berger, Maurice, ed. *The Crisis of Criticism*. New York: New Press, 1998.

Bergonzi, Bernard. *Exploding English: Criticism, Theory, Culture*. New York: Oxford UP, 1990.

Bernard-Donals, Michael. "The Consequences of Holocaust Denial." Olson and Worsham 243–62.

Bhabha, Homi K. "Dance This Diss Around." Berger 41–50.

———. *The Location of Culture*. New York: Routledge, 1994.

Bill T. Jones—Still/Here with Bill Moyers. PBS. 14–19 Jan. 1997.

Bitzer, Lloyd. "The Rhetorical Situation." *Philosophy and Rhetoric* 1 (1968): 1–15.

Black, Edwin. *Rhetorical Criticism: A Study in Method*. New York: Macmillan, 1965.

———. "Secrecy and Disclosure as Rhetorical Forms." *Quarterly Journal of Speech* 74 (1988): 133–50.

Blackwelder, Scott. Letter. *San Francisco Chronicle* 11 Feb. 1997: E2.

Blight, David W. "'For Something beyond the Battlefield': Frederick Douglass and the Struggle for the Memory of the Civil War." *Journal of American History* 75 (1989): 1156–78.

Blom, Thomas. "Response to Maxine Hairston." *College Composition and Communication* 35 (1984): 489–93.

Booth, Wayne C. *The Rhetoric of Fiction*. 2nd ed. Chicago: U of Chicago P, 1983.

Brodkey, Linda. "Making a Federal Case Out of Difference: The Politics of Pedagogy, Publicity, and Postponement." *Writing Theory and Critical Theory*. Ed. John Clifford and John Schilb. New York: MLA, 1994. 236–61.

Brooks, Cleanth. *The Well-Wrought Urn: Studies in the Structure of Poetry*. New York: Harcourt, 1947.

Brustein, Robert. Letter. *New Yorker* 30 Jan. 1995: 10.

Burke, Kenneth. *Attitudes toward History*. 3rd ed. Berkeley: U of California P, 1984.

———. *A Grammar of Motives*. 1945. Berkeley: U of California P, 1969.

———. *Language as Symbolic Action: Essays on Life, Literature, and Method*. Berkeley: U of California P, 1966.

———. *Permanence and Change: An Anatomy of Purpose*. 3rd ed. Berkeley: U of California P, 1984.

———. "The Philosophy of Literary Form." *The Philosophy of Literary Form: Studies in Symbolic Edition*. 3rd ed. Berkeley: U of California P, 1973. 1–137.

———. "Revolutionary Symbolism in America." *American Writers' Congress*. Ed. Henry Hart. New York: International Publishers, 1937. 87–94.

————. "The Rhetoric of Hitler's 'Battle.'" *Philosophy* 191–220.

Buruma, Ian. "The Joys and Perils of Victimhood." *New York Review of Books* 8 Apr. 1999: 4–9.

Carnes, Mark C., ed. *Novel History: Historians and Novelists Confront America's Past (and Each Other)*. New York: Simon and Schuster, 2001.

Carroll, Noel. "The Ontology of Mass Art." *Journal of Aesthetics and Art Criticism* 55 (1997): 187–99.

Cavell, Stanley. *Cities of Words: Pedagogical Letters on a Register of the Moral Life.* Cambridge: Harvard UP, 2004.

————. *Pursuits of Happiness: The Hollywood Comedy of Remarriage.* Cambridge: Harvard UP, 1981.

Chait, Jonathan. "Defense Secretary." *New Republic* 10 June 2002: 20–23.

Charland, Maurice. "Rehabilitating Rhetoric: Confronting Blindspots in Discourse and Social Theory." *Communication* 11 (1990): 263–66. Rpt. in *Contemporary Rhetorical Theory: A Reader.* Ed. John Louis Lucaites, Celeste Michelle Condit, and Sally Caudill. New York: Guilford, 1999. 464–73.

Church, Timothy. "Actual Reviews Posted On Amazon.Com By Me, In Utter Slack-Jawed Ignorance Of The Books Involved, And With Grammatical Errors Intact." *McSweeney's.* 18 Apr. 2006 <http://www.mcsweeneys.net/2000/02/ 07amazon.html>.

Claiborne, William. "Dole Scores Entertainment Industry, Time Warner for 'Debasing' America." *Washington Post* 1 June 1995: A6.

Coe, Richard, Lorelei Lingard, and Tatiana Teslenko, eds. *The Rhetoric and Ideology of Genre: Strategies for Stability and Change.* Cresskill, NJ: Hampton, 2002.

Copeland, Roger. "Asides: Not/There: Manipulating the Myth of Victim Art." *American Theatre* Apr. 1995: 35–37.

Croce, Arlene. "Discussing the Undiscussable." *New Yorker* 26 Dec. 1994/1 Jan. 1995: 54–60. Rpt. in *Writing* 708–19. Also in Berger 15–29.

————. *Writing in the Dark, Dancing in* The New Yorker. New York: Farrar, Straus and Giroux, 2000.

Crowley, Sharon. *Toward a Civil Discourse: Rhetoric and Fundamentalism.* Pittsburgh: U of Pittsburgh P, 2006.

De Moraes, Lisa. "Kanye West's Torrent of Criticism, Live on NBC." *Washington Post* 3 Sept. 2005. Lexis-Nexis. Indiana U. Lib. 20 Oct. 2006 <http://www. lexis-nexis.com>.

Derrida, Jacques. "Limited Inc a b c . . ." Trans. Samuel Weber. Graff 29–110.

————. "Signature Event Context." Trans. Samuel Weber and Jeffrey Mehlman. Graff 1–23.

Diamond, Edwin. "Caught in the Buzz Machine?" *Nation* 2 Jan. 1995: 13–16.

Didion, Joan. Reply to Alfred Kazin. *New York Times Book Review* 10 Apr. 1977: 37.

————. Reply to John Romano. *New York Review of Books* 11 Oct. 1979: 51.

Douglass, Frederick. *Life and Times of Frederick Douglass*. In *Autobiographies*. Ed. Henry Louis Gates Jr. New York: Library of America, 1994. 453–1045.

———. "The Meaning of July Fourth for the Negro." *The Life and Writings of Frederick Douglass, Volume II: Pre-Civil War Decade, 1850–1860*. Ed. Philip S. Foner. New York: International Publishers, 1950. 181–204.

———. "Oration in Memory of Abraham Lincoln." Foner, *Life and Writings of Frederick Douglass, Volume IV*, 309–19.

Duffy, Martha. "Push Comes to Shove." *Time* 6 Feb. 1995: 68–70.

Eberly, Rosa. *Citizen Critics: Literary Public Spheres*. Urbana: U of Illinois P, 2000.

Ebert, Roger. *Ebert's Bigger Little Movie Glossary*. Kansas City, MO: Andrews McMeel, 1999.

———. "The Senator Plays Politics." *Chicago Sun-Times* 4 June 1995: 1.

Edbauer, Jenny. "Unframing Models of Public Distribution: From Rhetorical Situation to Rhetorical Ecologies." *Rhetoric Society Quarterly* 35.4 (2005): 5–24.

Ervin, Elizabeth. "Rhetorical Situations and the Straits of Inappropriateness: Teaching Feminist Activism." *Rhetoric Review* 25 (2006): 316–33.

Evans, Richard J. *Lying about Hitler: History, Holocaust, and the David Irving Trial*. New York: Basic Books, 2001.

Fahnestock, Jeanne. "Accommodating Science: The Rhetorical Life of Scientific Facts." *The Literature of Science: Perspectives on Popular Scientific Writings*. Ed. Murdo William McCrae. Athens: U of Georgia P, 1993. 17–36.

Farrell, Thomas. *Norms of Rhetorical Culture*. New Haven: Yale UP, 1993.

Felman, Shoshana, and Dori Laub. *Testimony: Crises of Witnessing in Literature, Psychoanalysis, and History*. New York: Routledge, 1992.

Felski, Rita. *Literature after Feminism*. Chicago: U of Chicago P, 2003.

Fish, Stanley. "Holocaust Denial and Academic Freedom." *Valparaiso University Law Review* 35 (2001): 499–524. Lexis-Nexis. Indiana U. Lib. 14 Aug. 2003 <http://www.lexis-nexis.com>.

———. *Is There a Text in This Class? The Authority of Interpretive Communities*. Cambridge: Harvard UP, 1980.

———. "No Bias, No Merit: The Case against Blind Submission." *Doing What Comes Naturally: Change, Rhetoric, and the Practice of Theory in Literary and Legal Studies*. Durham, NC: Duke UP, 1989. 163–79.

Fonda, Jane. *My Life So Far*. New York: Random House, 2005.

Foner, Philip S. "Frederick Douglass." Foner, *Life and Writings of Frederick Douglass, Volume IV*, 13–154.

———, ed. *The Life and Writings of Frederick Douglass, Volume IV: Reconstruction and After*. New York: International Publishers, 1955.

Foucault, Michel. "The Masked Philosopher." Trans. Alan Sheridan, amended. *Ethics, Subjectivity, and Truth: The Essential Works of Michael Foucault 1954–1984, Volume 1*. Ed. Paul Rabinow. New York: New Press, 1997. 321–28. Also in *The Essential Foucault*. Ed. Paul Rabinow and Nikolas S. Rose. New York: New Press, 2003. 174–79.

———. "What Is an Author?" *Language, Counter-Memory, Practice: Selected Essays and Interviews.* Trans. Donald F. Bouchard and Sherry Simon. Ed. Bouchard. Ithaca: Cornell UP, 1977. 113–38.

Franchot, Jenny. "The Punishment of Esther: Frederick Douglass and the Construction of the Feminine." Sundquist 141–65.

Franklin, H. Bruce. "Kicking the Denial Syndrome: Tim O'Brien's *In the Lake of the Woods.*" Carnes 332–43.

Freadman, Anne. "Uptake." Coe, Lingard, and Teslenko 39–53.

"The Freedmen's Monument to Lincoln." *Facing History and Ourselves.* 2004. 21 Apr. 2006 <http://www.facinghistorycampus.org/campus/memorials.nsf/home?OpenForm>.

Frey, Olivia. "Beyond Literary Darwinism: Women's Voices and Critical Discourse." *College English* 52 (1990): 507–26.

Gallop, Jane. Contribution to Forum on "The Inevitability of the Personal." *PMLA* 111 (1996): 1149–50.

Gans, Herbert J. *Popular Culture and High Culture: An Analysis and Evaluation of Taste.* Rev. ed. New York: Basic Books, 1999.

Garland, Alex. *The Beach.* London: Penguin, 1996.

Gates, Henry Louis, Jr. *The Signifying Monkey: A Theory of African-American Literary Criticism.* New York: Oxford UP, 1988.

Gebhardt, Richard C. "Editor's Column: Theme Issue Feedback and Fallout." *College Composition and Communication* 43 (1992): 295–96.

Goffman, Erving. *Frame Analysis: An Essay on the Organization of Experience.* Boston: Northeastern UP, 1986.

Goldstein, Richard. "The Croce Criterion." *Village Voice* 3 Jan. 1995: 8.

Goodman, Nelson. *Languages of Art: An Approach to a Theory of Symbols.* Indianapolis: Hackett, 1976.

Goodman, Susan. "She Lost It at the Movies." *Modern Maturity* Mar.– Apr. 1998. 18 July 1999 <http://www.aarp/org/mmaturity/march_april/kael.html>.

Gould, Stephen Jay, ed. *Best American Essays 2002.* Boston: Houghton Mifflin, 2002.

Graff, Gerald. *Beyond the Culture Wars: How Teaching the Conflicts Can Revitalize American Education.* New York: Norton, 1992.

———. "How I Learned to Stop Worrying and Love Stanley." Olson and Worsham 27–41.

———, ed. *Limited Inc.* Evanston: Northwestern UP, 1988.

Grannan, Caroline. Letter. *San Francisco Chronicle* 4 Feb. 1997: E3.

Grice, Paul. *Studies in the Way of Words.* Cambridge: Harvard UP, 1989.

Gross, Alan. "Rhetoric as a Technique and a Mode of Truth: Reflections on Chaim Perelman." *Philosophy and Rhetoric* 33 (2000): 319–35.

Guttenplan, D. D. *The Holocaust on Trial.* New York: Norton, 2001.

Habermas, Jurgen. *The Theory of Communicative Action, Volume One: Reason and the Rationalization of Society.* Trans. Thomas McCarthy. Boston: Beacon, 1984.

Hairston, Maxine. "Breaking Our Bonds and Reaffirming Our Connections." *College Composition and Communication* 36 (1985): 272–82. Also in *ADE Bulletin* 81 (Fall 1985): 1–5.

———. "Diversity, Ideology, and Teaching Writing." *College Composition and Communication* 43 (1992): 179–93.

———. "Reply by Maxine Hairston." *College Composition and Communication* 35 (1984): 493–94.

———. "Reply by Maxine Hairston." *College Composition and Communication* 44 (1993): 255–56.

———. "The Winds of Change: Thomas Kuhn and the Revolution in the Teaching of Writing." *College Composition and Communication* 33 (1982): 76–88.

Harden, Blaine. "Dole Raps Hollywood, Clinton over Drugs." *Chicago Sun-Times* 19 Sept. 1996: 20.

Hardt, Michael, and Antonio Negri. *Empire.* Cambridge: Harvard UP, 2000.

Hariman, Robert, and John Louis Lucaites. *No Caption Needed: Iconic Photographs, Public Culture, and Liberal Democracy.* Chicago: U of Chicago P, 2007.

Herzog, Toby C. "Tim O'Brien Interview." *South Carolina Review* 31.1 (1998): 78–109.

———. "Tim O'Brien's 'True Lies' (?)." *Modern Fiction Studies* 46 (2000): 893–916.

Hickey, Dave. *Air Guitar: Essays on Art and Democracy.* Los Angeles: Art issues. Press, 1997.

hooks, bell. Letter. *New Yorker* 30 Jan. 1995: 10–11.

Horn, Dave. "Hotline: When Will Third Street Be Wider?" *Herald-Times* [Bloomington, IN] 13 May 2005: A8.

Irving, David. *Lipstadt Trial Index.* 27 Feb. 2005. 20 Apr. 2006 <http://www.fpp.co.uk/Legal/Penguin/index.html>.

———. Opening statement. *Holocaust Denial on Trial.* 19 Apr. 2006 <http://www.holocaustdenialontrial.org/ieindex.html>.

"Irving Expands on Holocaust Views." *BBC News* 28 Feb. 2006. 18 Apr. 2006 <http://newvote.bbc.co.uk/mpapps/pagetools/print/news.bbc.co.uk/2/hi/europe/4757506.stm>.

Jann, Lisa. "Rant and Rave." *Seattle Times* 30 July 1999: H3.

Jasinski, James. "Rearticulating History in Epideictic Discourse: Frederick Douglass's 'The Meaning of the Fourth of July to the Negro.'" Benson 71–89.

Jowitt, Deborah. "Critic as Victim." *Village Voice* 10 Jan. 1995: 67–69.

Kael, Pauline. Rev. of *Betrayal. New Yorker* 11 July 1983: 95.

———. Rev. of *Fellini's Casanova. New Yorker* 28 Feb. 1977: 92.

Kahn, Joseph P. "The Things He Carries." *Boston Globe* 19 Oct. 1994: *Living* 6.

Kaufer, David S., and Brian S. Butler. *Rhetoric and the Arts of Design.* Mahwah, NJ: Erlbaum, 1996.

Kauffman, Linda, ed. *Gender and Theory: Dialogues on Feminist Criticism.* New York: Blackwell, 1989.

———. "The Long Goodbye: Against Personal Testimony, or An Infant Grifter

Grows Up." *Changing Subjects: The Making of Feminist Literary Criticism.* Ed. Gayle Greene and Coppelia Kahn. New York: Routledge, 1993. 129–46.

Kazin, Alfred. Letter. *New York Times Book Review* 10 Apr. 1977: 37.

Kennedy, Mark. "On the Outside, Natasha Lyonne Peers In." *Associated Press* 17 July 2000. Lexis-Nexis. Indiana U. Lib. 18 Apr. 2006 <http://www.lexis-nexis. com>.

Kerrey, Bob. *When I Was a Young Man: A Memoir.* New York: Harcourt, 2002.

Kirsch, Adam. "The Snare of Rhetoric." *American Scholar* 72.4 (2003): 140–43.

Kramer, Hilton. Letter. *New Yorker* 30 Jan. 1995: 11–12.

Kramer, Michael R., and Kathryn M. Olson. "The Strategic Potential of Sequencing Apologia Stases: President Clinton's Self-Defense in the Monica Lewinsky Scandal." *Western Journal of Communication* 66 (2002): 347–68.

Kuhn, Thomas S. *The Structure of Scientific Revolutions.* Chicago: U of Chicago P, 1962.

Kuntz, Phil, ed. *The Starr Report: The Starr Evidence: Complete Testimony from President Clinton and Monica Lewinsky, and Other Documents from the Independent Counsel's Investigation.* New York: Pocket Books, 1998.

Lang, Berel. "The Representation of Limits." *Probing the Limits of Representation: Nazism and the "Final Solution."* Ed. Saul Friedlander. Cambridge: Harvard UP, 1992. 300–17.

L'Avventura. Dir. Michelangelo Antonioni. Cino del Duca, 1960.

Lincoln's Eyes. Film. Abraham Lincoln Presidential Library and Museum, 2005.

Lind, Michael. *What Lincoln Believed: The Values and Convictions of America's Greatest President.* New York: Doubleday, 2005.

Lindsay, Joan Weigall. *Picnic at Hanging Rock.* 1967. New York: Penguin, 1977.

Lipstadt, Deborah. *Denying the Holocaust: The Growing Assault on Truth and Memory.* 1993. New York: Plume, 1994.

———. *History on Trial: My Day in Court with David Irving.* New York: Harper-Collins, 2005.

Lucaites, John Louis. "The Irony of 'Equality' in Black Abolitionist Discourse: The Case of Frederick Douglass's 'What to the Slave Is the Fourth of July?'" Benson 47–69.

Luhmann, Niklas. *The Reality of the Mass Media.* Trans. Kathleen Cross. Stanford: Stanford UP, 2000.

Lyon, Arabella. *Intentions: Negotiated, Contested, and Ignored.* University Park: Pennsylvania State UP, 1998.

Lyotard, Jean-Francois. *The Differend: Phrases in Dispute.* Trans. Georges Van Den Abbeele. Minneapolis: U of Minnesota P, 1988.

Macdonald, Dwight. "George Stevens: *The Greatest Story Ever Told." On Movies.* New York: Da Capo, 1981. 430–37.

———. "Masscult and Midcult." *Against the American Grain.* New York: Da Capo, 1983. 3–75.

MacVey, Carol. Letter. *New Yorker* 30 Jan. 1995: 13.

Mailloux, Steven. *Reception Histories: Rhetoric, Pragmatism, and American Cultural Politics*. Ithaca: Cornell UP, 1998.

———. *Rhetorical Power*. Ithaca: Cornell UP, 1989.

Maraniss, David. *The Clinton Enigma: A Four-and-a-Half Minute Speech Reveals This President's Entire Life*. New York: Simon and Schuster, 1998.

McCloskey, Deirdre. "Big Rhetoric, Little Rhetoric: Gaonkar on the Rhetoric of Science." *Rhetorical Hermeneutics: Invention and Interpretation in the Age of Science*. Ed. Alan G. Gross and William M. Keith. Albany: SUNY P, 1997. 101–12.

McHugh, Kathleen. "The Aesthetics of Wounding: Trauma, Self-Representation, and the Critical Voice." *Aesthetics in a Multicultural Age*. Ed. Emory Elliott, Louis Freitas Caton, and Jeffrey Rhyne. New York: Oxford UP, 2002. 241–53.

Melley, Timothy. "Postmodern Amnesia: Trauma and Forgetting in Tim O'Brien's *In the Lake of the Woods*." *Contemporary Literature* 44 (2003): 106–31.

Messer-Davidow, Ellen. "The Philosophical Bases of Feminist Literary Criticisms." *New Literary History* 19 (1987): 65–103.

Mill, John Stuart. *On Liberty*. Ed. Gertrude Himmelfarb. New York: Penguin, 1985.

Miller, Henry. *Tropic of Cancer*. 1934. New York: Modern Library, 1983.

Miller, James. *The Passion of Michael Foucault*. New York: Simon and Schuster, 1993.

Miller, Nancy K. *Getting Personal: Feminist Occasions and Other Autobiographical Acts*. New York: Routledge, 1991.

Minima, Gridley. "Thinly veiled philosophical tracts masquerading as: Reviews of Books I Haven't Read and Why I Haven't Read Them." *h2so4*. 18 Apr. 2006 <http://www.h2so4.net/politics/unread.html#limbaugh>.

Miskell, Jodi. "'Hitchhiker' Author Shares Perspective." *Indiana Daily Student* 13 Apr. 1999, sec. 1:1+.

Mitchell, W. J. T. "Offending Images." *Unsettling "Sensation": Arts-Policy Lessons from the Brooklyn Museum of Art Controversy*. Ed. Lawrence Rothfield. New Brunswick, NJ: Rutgers UP, 2001. 115–33.

Mitchell-Kernan, Claudia. "Signifying." *Mother Wit from the Laughing Barrel: Readings in the Interpretation of Afro-American Folklore*. Ed. Alan Dundes. 2nd ed. Jackson: U of Mississippi P, 1990. 310–28.

Moi, Toril. *What Is a Woman? And Other Essays*. New York: Oxford, 1999.

Morris, Zena. Letter. *Newsday* 20 July 1995: A41.

Nelson, Deborah. *Pursuing Privacy in Cold War America*. New York: Columbia UP, 2002.

Noonan, Peggy. "Mel Gibson: Keeping the Faith." *Reader's Digest* Mar. 2004: 88–95.

Novick, Peter. *The Holocaust in American Life*. Boston: Houghton Mifflin, 1999.

O'Brien, Tim. *In the Lake of the Woods*. 1994. New York: Penguin, 1995.

————. *The Things They Carried*. Boston: Houghton Mifflin, 1990.

————. "The Whole Story." Carnes 344–45.

Olds, Sharon. "No Thanks, Mrs. Bush." *Nation* 10 Oct. 2005: 5–6.

Olson, Gary A., and Lynn Worsham, eds. *Postmodern Sophistry: Stanley Fish and the Critical Enterprise*. Albany: SUNY P, 2004.

"Partial Transcript of the Steve Feuerstein Radio Interview with Hutton Gibson." *MCN Notepad*. 3 Mar. 2004. 19 Apr. 2006 <http://www.moviecitynews.com/notepad/2004/040303_npd.html>.

Patton, Cindy. *Fatal Advice: How Safe-Sex Education Went Wrong*. Durham, NC: Duke UP, 1996.

Perelman, Chaim. *The Realm of Rhetoric*. Trans. William Kluback. Notre Dame, IN: U of Notre Dame P, 1982.

Perelman, Chaim, and Lucie Olbrechts-Tyteca. *The New Rhetoric: A Treatise on Argumentation*. 1958. Trans. John Wilkinson and Purcell Weaver. Notre Dame, IN: U of Notre Dame P, 1969.

Pfeffinger, Eric. "*Last Samurai*? It Feels Like You've Seen It." *Herald-Times* [Bloomington, IN] 14 Dec. 2003: E5.

Phelan, James. *Narrative as Rhetoric: Technique, Audiences, Ethics, Ideology*. Columbus: Ohio State UP, 1996.

Picnic at Hanging Rock. Dir. Peter Weir. Australian Film Commission, 1975.

Porton, Richard. "The Politics of American Cinephilia: From the Popular Front to the Age of Video." *Cineaste* 27.4 (2002): 4–10.

Rabinowitz, Peter J. "Truth in Fiction: A Reexamination of Audiences." *Critical Inquiry* 4 (1977): 121–41.

Rampton, Richard. Opening statement. *Holocaust Denial on Trial*. 19 Apr. 2006 <http://www.holocaustdenialontrial.org/ieindex.html>.

Raymond, Janice. *Women as Wombs: Reproductive Technologies and the Battle over Women's Freedom*. New York: HarperCollins, 1993.

Reed, Ishmael. "Good Art, Bad Art and the Politicians." *Baltimore Sun* 11 June 1995: 1J.

Rich, Adrienne. "Why I Refused the National Medal for the Arts." *Arts of the Possible: Essays and Conversations*. New York: Norton, 2001. 98–105.

Rich, Frank. *The Greatest Story Ever Sold: The Decline and Fall of Truth from 9/11 to Katrina*. New York: Penguin, 2006.

————. "Mel Gibson Forgives Us for His Sins." *New York Times* 7 Mar. 2004: 2:1.

Rollins, Brooke. "The Ethics of Epideictic Rhetoric: Addressing the Problem of Presence through Derrida's Funeral Orations." *Rhetoric Society Quarterly* 35.1 (2005): 5–23.

Romano, John. Letter. *New York Review of Books* 11 Oct. 1979: 51.

Rushdie, Salman. *The Satanic Verses*. New York: Viking, 1989.

Sack, John. "Inside the Bunker." *Esquire* Feb. 2001: 98–104. Rpt. in *Best American Essays 2002*. Ed. Stephen Jay Gould. Boston: Houghton Mifflin, 2002. 280–94.

Safire, William, ed. *Lend Me Your Ears: Great Speeches in History*. New York: Norton, 1992.

Said, Edward. "Traveling Theory." *The World, the Text, and the Critic*. Cambridge: Harvard UP, 1983. 226–47.

Salisbury, Wilma. "Choreographer Criticizes the Critics." *Plain Dealer* [Cleveland, OH] 11 June 1995: 6J.

Schilb, John. *Between the Lines: Relating Composition Theory and Literary Theory*. Portsmouth, NH: Boynton, 1996.

———. "Scholarship in Composition and Literature: Some Comparisons." *Academic Advancement in Composition Studies*. Ed. Richard and Barbara Geselle Gebhardt. Thousand Oaks, CA: Sage, 1996. 21–31.

———. "Toward a Rhetoric of Visual Fragments: Analyzing Disjunctive Narratives." *JAC* 22 (2002): 743–64.

Schryer, Catherine F. "Genre and Power: A Chronotopic Analysis." Coe, Lingard, and Teslenko 73–102.

Seabrook, John. *Nobrow: The Culture of Marketing, the Marketing of Culture*. New York: Knopf, 2000.

Seligman, Craig. *Sontag and Kael: Opposites Attract Me*. New York: Counterpoint, 2004.

Sereny, Gitta. *Into That Darkness: An Examination of Conscience*. 1974. New York: Vintage, 1983.

Sheard, Cynthia Miecznikowski. "The Public Value of Epideictic Rhetoric." *College English* 58 (1996): 765–94.

Shermer, Michael, and Alex Grobman. *Denying History: Who Says the Holocaust Never Happened and Why Do They Say It?* Berkeley: U of California P, 2000.

Shetley, Vernon. *After the Death of Poetry: Poet and Audience in Contemporary America*. Durham, NC: Duke UP, 1993.

Shumway, David R. "Solidarity or Perspectivity?" Kauffman 107–17.

———. "The Star System in Literary Studies." *PMLA* 112 (1997): 85–100.

Simon, John. "My Beautiful Dinette." *New York* 7 June 1999: 90–91.

———. "Nothin' Doin'." *New York* 17 May 1999: 60–61.

———. "Royal Flush." *New York* 6 Sept. 1999: 57–58.

Simon, Roger. "Ebert and Siskel Review Dole's Criticism of Movies." *Baltimore Sun* 9 June 1995: 2A.

Simpson, David. *9/11: The Culture of Commemoration*. Chicago: U of Chicago P, 2006.

———. "Speaking Personally: The Culture of Autobiographical Criticism." Veeser 82–94.

Sobolev, Dennis. "Hopkins' Rhetoric: Between the Material and the Transcendent." *Language and Literature* 12 (2003): 99–115.

Spelman, Elizabeth. *Fruits of Sorrow*. Boston: Beacon, 1998.

Stauffer, John. "Across the Great Divide." *Time* 4 July 2005: 58–65.

Sturken, Marita, and Lisa Cartwright. *Practices of Looking: An Introduction to Visual Culture.* New York: Oxford UP, 2001.

Sullivan, Dale L. "The Epideictic Character of Rhetorical Criticism." *Rhetoric Review* 11 (1993): 339–49.

Sundquist, Eric J., ed. *Frederick Douglass: New Literary and Historical Essays.* New York: Cambridge UP, 1990.

———. "Introduction." Sundquist 1–22.

"Talk of the Town." *New Yorker* 5 Aug. 1944: 11–12.

Tanenhaus, Sam. "The NY Intellectuals' Shabby Legacy." *New York Press* 25 Jan. 2000. 18 Apr. 2006 <http://www.nypress.com/print.cfm?content_id=1122>.

Tannen, Deborah. *The Argument Culture: Moving from Debate to Dialogue.* New York: Random House, 1998.

Teachout, Terry. "Contentions: Victim Art." *Commentary* Mar. 1995: 58–61.

Tim O'Brien, Novelist. 21 Aug. 2005. 18 Apr. 2006 <http://www.illyria.com/tobhp. html>.

Tompkins, Jane. "Me and My Shadow." *New Literary History* 19 (1987): 169–78. Rpt. in Kauffman 121–39. Also in *The Intimate Critique: Autobiographical Literary Criticism.* Ed. Diane P. Freedman, Olivia Frey, and Frances Murphy Zauhar. Durham, NC: Duke UP, 1993. 23–40.

Toobin, Jeffrey. *A Vast Conspiracy: The Real Story of the Sex Scandal That Nearly Brought Down a President.* New York: Random House, 1999.

Trimbur, John. "Composition and the Circulation of Writing." *College Composition and Communication* 52 (2000): 188–219.

Van Pelt, Robert Jan. *The Case for Auschwitz: Evidence from the Irving Trial.* Bloomington: Indiana UP, 2002.

Veeser, H. Aram, ed. *Confessions of the Critics.* New York: Routledge, 1996.

Vidal-Naquet, Pierre. *Assassins of Memory: Essays on the Denial of the Holocaust.* Trans. Jeffrey Mehlman. New York: Columbia UP, 1992.

Vistica, Gregory L. *The Education of Lieutenant Kerrey.* New York: St. Martin's, 2003.

Vivian, Bradford. "Neoliberal Epideictic: Rhetorical Form and Commemorative Politics on September 11, 2002." *Quarterly Journal of Speech* 92 (2006): 1–26.

Vowell, Sarah. *Assassination Vacation.* New York: Simon and Schuster, 2005.

Wells, Susan. "Rogue Cops and Health Care: What Do We Want from Public Writing?" *College Composition and Communication* 47 (1996): 325–41.

White, Edmund. "Journals of the Plague Years." *Nation* 12 May 1997: 13–18.

Wiesel, Elie. "When Passion Is Dangerous." *Houston Chronicle* 19 Apr. 1992. *Parade* sec. Lexis-Nexis. Indiana U. Lib. 19 Apr. 2006 <http://www.lexis-nexis. com>.

Williams, Bernard. *Truth and Truthfulness: An Essay in Genealogy.* Princeton: Princeton UP, 2002.

Wittgenstein, Ludwig. *Philosophical Investigations*. Trans. G. E. M. Anscombe. 3rd ed. New York: Macmillan, 1968.

Woolf, Virginia. *A Room of One's Own*. New York: Harcourt, 1929.

Yeats, William Butler. *Essays and Introductions*. New York: Collier, 1961.

INDEX

Academy, 11, 96–98, 100, 121, 126
Adams, Douglas, 19
Adler, Renata, 47
African Americans, 143, 145–46, 148, 153–54,
    156. *See also* Douglass, Frederick
Agee, James, 40–42, 53–54, 71, 183n. 2
    (chap. 1)
agency, 17, 85, 90–91
Alcoff, Linda, 7, 19
Altieri, Charles, 124
Americans, culture and traditions of, 77,
    105–6, 143, 167, 169–70
Andrukhovych, Yuri, 3
Annesley, James, 130–31
anonymity, 118–19, 121
anti-art, 36–37
Antonioni, Michelangelo, 165
Apollo 13 (film), 54
appropriation of symbols or slogans, 79,
    88
argumentation, 12, 38, 70, 73
Aristotle, 149
associations, 32, 34, 67. *See also* dissocia-
    tions
Attridge, Derek, 158
"audience" as term, 9–10
audiences: attribution of authority to, 19;
    challenges to expectations of, 4–10;
    and dissociations, 34; in evaluation of
    rhetoric, 60; judging by, 30, 38–40, 163;
    and rhetorical refusals, 18; semi-blind
    reviews and requirements of, 48; types
    of, 165
Auster, Paul, 166

author function, 118–19
authorial identity, 118–21
authorial intent, 160

Bakhtin, Mikhail, 153, 183n. 1 (chap. 1)
Bal, Mieke, 73–74
Barbie, Klaus, 94
Baudrillard, Jean, 120
Bausch, Pina, 66
Beach, The (Garland), 130
Beck, Joan, 57
Benjamin, Walter, 52
Bennett, Robert, 138
Berger, Maurice, 2
Bergonzi, Bernard, 160
Betrayal (film), 46
Bhabha, Homi, 1, 146–47
"Big Rhetoric" vs. "little rhetoric," 101
Bill T. Jones—Still/Here with Bill Moyers
    (documentary), 61
Bitzer, Lloyd, 12–13, 15–16, 178
Black, Edwin, 114–15, 124, 139, 163
Blackwelder, Rob, 49
Blight, David, 146
blind reviews, 121
Blom, Thomas, 11–12
Booth, Wayne, 160
Bowers v. Hardwick, 117
Brando, Marlon, 6
"Breaking Our Bonds and Reaffirming Our
    Connections" (Hairston), 33–34
Brooklyn Museum, 54–55
Brooks, Cleanth, 160
Brown, Tina, 36, 61, 69

Brustein, Robert, 1
Buchanan, Patrick, 93–94
Burke, Kenneth, 5, 28, 31–32, 73, 84–85, 88, 90
Buruma, Ian, 66–68
Bush, George W., 179–80
Bush, Laura, 178–79
Butler, Brian, 9
Butz, Arthur, 83
"buzz," 69–71

Carmen Jones (film), 41
Carroll, Noel, 51
Cartwright, Lisa, 73
Cavell, Stanley, 171–72
censorship, 54–55
Chait, Jonathan, 8
Charland, Maurice, 17
Chomsky, Noam, 83
Chrupka, Marie, 56
Church, Timothy, 44
City of Glass (film), 166
Clinton, Bill: claim to privacy by, 134–35, 139–40; grand jury testimony of, 7–8, 132–33, 136–37; and Lewinsky affair, 7, 138; and perjury charge, 133, 137; Adrienne Rich's view of, 7
Colbert, Stephen, 23, 178–79
Conference on College Composition and Communication (CCCC), 13
context of rhetoric refusals, 81–84, 119, 151, 161
Cooperative Principle, 103–4
Copeland, Roger, 1–2
critics and criticism, 30, 47–49, 68, 73, 115, 130–31. See also individual critics
Croce, Arlene: audiences of, 39, 95–96, 116; on audiences of victim art, 40; as besieged critic, 64–65; dissociation from reviewing, 62–63; and humor, 45; prestige vs. self-depiction by, 20; Ishmael Reed on, 5; refusal to see Still/Here, 1–3, 30–31, 48–49, 69, 115
Crowley, Sharon, 17
C-SPAN, 107
cultural conversations, 172–75
cultural criticism, 73
culture wars, 51–52

debate, 11, 79–80, 95. See also argumentation; discourse; refusals to debate
deconstructionists, 99
defamiliarization, 158–59
"denier" as term, 90–96. See also Holocaust deniers
Denying the Holocaust (Lipstadt), 78, 96, 114
Derrida, Jacques, 114
Diamondback (newspaper), 111
Didion, Joan, 4–5
discourse: agent-centered, 90–91; disciplinary, 8; literary, 123–24, 126; minority, 146–47, 154, 156–57; political, 177–78
"Discussing the Undiscussable" (Croce): Tina Brown and, 70–71; evaluation of, 62–66; as non-review of Still/Here, 1–2, 4, 35–37, 50–51, 72–73; public response to, 115; as rhetorical refusal, 141
dissociations: appearance/reality, 32–33, 36–37, 44, 96, 98, 163; and argumentative high ground, 5, 32–33, 74; art/victim art, 65–66; audience and, 34; from censorship, 56–57; change in genre as, 35–36; definitional, 37–38, 50; inside/outside, 59; of procedure, 35–39, 44; from reviewing, 62–63; theories of, 30
Dole, Bob, 5, 57–58
Douglas, Stephen, 9
Douglass, Frederick, 82–83, 143–50, 154. See also Lincoln speech (Douglass)
Dreyfus, Hubert, 119–20
Duffy, Martha, 2

Eberly, Rosa, 56–57
Ebert, Roger, 50, 58–59
English Patient, The (film), 49–50, 62
epideictic rhetoric, 142–44, 149, 153–56
epistemic tests, of critics who refuse to see, 48–49, 61–62
epistemology, 48–50, 127
Ervin, Elizabeth, 17
Eyes Wide Shut (film), 55

face threats, 9
Fahnestock, Jeanne, 115
false puritan archetype, 59–60
Farrell, Thomas, 6, 17

Fatal Advice (Patton), 82
Faurisson, Robert, 83
Felman, Shoshana, 169
Felski, Rita, 129
feminism, 123–25
fiction, 22, 158
Fifth Amendment, 134
First Amendment, 55, 98, 110
Fish, Stanley, 97, 99–102, 120–21
Fleischer, Ari, 8
Fonda, Jane, 167
Foner, Philip, 151–52
Foucault, Michel, 118–22, 139–40
frame/framework, challenges to, 6
Franchot, Jenny, 152
Franklin, H. Bruce, 164, 167
Freadman, Anne, 136
Freedman, Diane P., 124
Frey, Olivia, 124
Friedlander, Saul, 83

Gadamer, Hans-George, 28
Gallop, Jane, 126
Gans, Herbert, 39
Garland, Alex, 130
Gates, Henry Louis, 120, 154
Gebhardt, Richard, 13–14
genres, changes in, 8, 35–36, 62–63, 156
Gettysburg Address, 143
Gibson, Hutton, 91–92
Gibson, Mel, 91–93, 108
Giuliani, Rudolph, 51–52, 54–56
Goffman, Erving, 6
Goldstein, Richard, 2
Goodman, Nelson, 51, 99
Goodman, Susan, 47
Gould, Stephen Jay, 108–9
Graff, Gerald, 110–11
Grannan, Caroline, 49–51, 62
Gray, Charles, 86, 90
Greatest Story Ever Told, The (film), 45–46
Grice, Paul, 103–5
Gross, Alan, 32–33, 97

Habermas, Jurgen, 103, 120
Hairston, Maxine: and audience, 39;
    "Breaking Our Bonds and Reaffirming
    Our Connections," 33–34; dissociations
in address by, 32–35; "Diversity, Ideol-
ogy, and Teaching Writing," 13; invo-
cation of Bitzer article, 15–16; prestige
and forum of, 20; and refusal to debate,
11–15, 18, 31–32; repackaging of text by,
116; "Winds of Change," 11–12
Hannity, Sean, 71
Hariman, Robert, 115
Herbert Gans, 39
Herzog, Toby, 168
Hickey, Dave, 55, 72, 106
Hillgruber, Andreas, 94
Holocaust denial, 85–86, 107
Holocaust deniers: college community and,
    94–95, 110–13; dangers of, 105–6; and
    illusion of reasoned inquiry, 98, 103–5;
    in Irving-Lipstadt trial, 89; Deborah
    Lipstadt on, 78, 80, 85; John Sack on,
    109. *See also* Irving, David
Holocaust relativization, 92–93
Holy Virgin Mary, The (Ofili collage), 51,
    54–55
hooks, bell, 2, 120
Hopkins, Gerard Manley, 160
Horn, Dave, 138
Horowitz, David, 97–98
Hurricane Katrina telethon, 156

identity politics, 125–26
ignorance, willful, 65
inappropriateness, principle of, 17
"Inside the Bunker" (Sack), 108
In the Lake of the Woods (O'Brien): com-
    pared to comedies of remarriage, 171–72;
    inconclusiveness of, 167–68; interpreta-
    tions of, 164–65; offbeat elements of,
    162–63; precedents for, in art, 165–66;
    prominence of Kathy in, 170–71; rhe-
    torical refusals in, 22–23, 159; story of,
    161–62; students' writing about, 164
irony, 149–50, 174
Irving, David: career phases of, 86–87;
    Stanley Fish's treatment of, 101; and
    "Holocaust denier" label, 87–88, 91;
    imprisonment of, 107–8; Deborah Lip-
    stadt and, 81, 90; misuse of documents
    by, 79–80; and John Sack, 108–9; and
    yellow star, 88

Irving-Lipstadt trial, 80–81, 89, 105, 107, 114

Jasinski, James, 155
Johnson, Lyndon, 178
Jones, Bill T.: in Bill Moyers documentary, 61; response of, to Croce's non-review, 64, 184n. 2 (chap. 3); *Still/Here*, 40, 50, 55, 63, 72
Jowitt, Deborah, 1, 63

Kael, Pauline, 46–48, 52–53
Kaufer, David, 9
Kauffman, Linda, 122, 125
Kazin, Alfred, 4
Kendall, David, 134
Kerrey, Bob, 23, 159, 172–75
Kerry, John, 167
Kirsch, Adam, 160
Klann, Gerhard, 173–74
Koons, Jeff, 55
Kramer, Hilton, 1
Kubrick, Stanley, 55–56
Kuhn, Thomas, 11–12

Lang, Berel, 83
Laskin, David, 53–54
Laub, Dori, 169
L'Aventura (film), 165
Leuchter, Fred, 87
libel cases, 89. *See also* Irving-Lipstadt trial
Limbaugh, Rush, 28–29
Lincoln, Abraham, 9, 143–46, 148
Lincoln's Eyes (film), 151
Lincoln speech (Douglass): audience, differences within, 145; audience's expectations of, 143–44, 150, 155; chief importance of, 146; compared to Fourth of July address, 147–48; complexity in, 143; criticism of Lincoln in, 144–45; dialogic aspect of, 153–56; as mixed text, 22; praise of Lincoln in, 148; responses to, 149–53; rhetorical refusal in, 141–42; social context of, 151
Lind, Michael, 152
Lipstadt, Deborah: on academy, 96–97; on American higher education, 77, 110;

critics of, 105–6; *Denying the Holocaust*, 78, 96, 114; historical context of refusal, 81–84; on Holocaust deniers, 9, 80, 85, 88–89, 104, 110; and David Irving, 81, 90; and issues of epistemology, 102; on pedagogy, 112–13; on postmodern thought, 98–99; and refusal to debate, 11, 78, 83–84, 93. *See also* Irving-Lipstadt trial
literary rhetoric, 159–61
literary scholarship, 123–24, 126, 129–31, 175
Lowell, Robert, 178
Lucaites, John, 115, 149
Luhmann, Niklas, 137–38
Lyon, Arabella, 27–29
Lyonne, Natasha, 27
Lyotard, Jean-Francois, 16

Macdonald, Dwight, 45–48, 52–53
MacVey, Carol, 65
Mailloux, Steven, 39, 114–15, 161, 172
Manhattan (film), 4
Mapplethorpe, Robert, 66
Maraniss, David, 136
"Masked Philosopher, The" (Foucault interview), 118
McCloskey, Deirdre, 101
McSweeney's (online magazine), 44–45
"Me and My Shadow" (Tompkins): critique of Messer-Davidow essay in, 126–27; impact of, 125–26; in literary studies, 122–24; possible faults in, 128–29
media, the, 109, 136, 138
Meese Commission on Pornography, 60
Melley, Timothy, 167, 169, 173
Messer-Davidow, Ellen, 123, 125–27
Mill, John Stuart, 77–78
Miller, Henry, 56–57
Miller, James, 119
Miller, Nancy, 124–25
Minghella, Anthony, 49–50
Minima, Gridley, 28–29
minority discourse, 146–47, 154, 156–57
Mitchell, W. J. T., 50–51, 73
Mitchell-Kernan, Claudia, 154
Moi, Toril, 124, 129

Morris, Zena, 54
Myers, Mike, 156–57

national memory, 142–43, 159, 166–67
Natural Born Killers (film), 58–59
Nelson, Deborah, 117
New Rhetoric, The (Perelman and Olbrechts-Tyteca): application of ideas in, to rhetorical refusals, 29–30; on audiences judging other audiences, 38, 95; on dissociation and association, 34; on dissociations, 32, 96; on epideictic, 144–45, 155; on person's essence and behavior, 90; on requisite for argumentation, 12
newsreels as pornography, 41–42, 183n. 2 (chap. 1)
New Yorker magazine, 36, 69–71
New York intellectuals, 53–54
New York Times, 47, 143
Nolte, Ernst, 94
Noonan, Peggy, 92–93
Novick, Peter, 105–6

objective/subjective opposition, 129
O'Brien, Tim, 22–23, 159, 161–66, 170. See also *In the Lake of the Woods* (O'Brien)
Ofili, Chris, 51, 54–55
Ohio State Lantern (student newspaper), 96
Oklahoma! (film), 41
Olbrechts-Tyteca, Lucie. See *New Rhetoric, The* (Perelman and Olbrechts-Tyteca)
Olds, Sharon, 23, 178–79
On Liberty (Mill), 77
ontology, 48, 50–52
O'Reilly, Bill, 71
Othello (film), 41

Parade magazine, 78–79
Partisan Review, 54
Partisans (Laskin), 53–54
Passion of the Christ, The (film), 92
Patton, Cindy, 82
Perelman, Chaim. See *New Rhetoric, The* (Perelman and Olbrechts-Tyteca)
Pfeffinger, Eric, 49
Phelan, James, 160

Picnic at Hanging Rock (film), 166
PMLA, 121
politics, 19–20, 166, 168, 177–78
pornography of atrocity, 2, 41–42, 183n. 2 (chap. 1)
"Portraits of Grief," 143
postmodernism, 16–17, 98–100
poststructuralism, 126
post-theory phase, in humanities, 122
Pound, Ezra, 160
private/public binary, 116–18, 123, 129, 134–35, 139–40
protocol violation, 4–5
publicity, effect of, 48–49, 70–71, 80, 106
public/private binary, 116–18, 123, 129, 134–35, 139–40

Rabinowitz, Peter, 165
Rampton, Richard, 89
Raymond, Janice, 81–82
reader-response theory, 126
reality TV, 126, 138
Reed, Ishmael, 5, 58
refusals to debate: dangers of, 28; Joan Didion and, 4–5; Frederick Douglass and, 82–83; Maxine Hairston and, 11–15, 18, 31–32; Deborah Lipstadt and, 11, 83–84, 93; Pierre Vidal-Naquet on, 84
refusals to see, 5, 42, 44, 48–50, 56–57
refusal to address announced topic, 7
refusal to be judged, 68
relativism, 99
renaming, 31–32
reviews, 44–49, 52–53, 57–58, 121. *See also individual reviewers and reviews*
revisionists, 86
rhetoric: author's notion of, 10–11; dangers of specificity in, 57–60; evaluation of, 60; as human interaction, 160; legitimate vs. meretricious, 73; literary critics on, 159–61; of partial attendance, 45–48, 52–53; of self-pity, 66–67
rhetorical agency, 17
rhetorical authority, 64
rhetorical critics, 115
rhetorical decorum, vs. higher principle, 5
rhetorical education, 159

rhetorical refusals: overview, 61–62; audiences for, 18; in the classroom, 111–12; comparisons of, 66–68; and complexity of thinking, 177; criteria of, 4–5; defined, briefly, 3; evaluation of, 61–62; in fiction, 22–23; hypothesizing, 28–29; implications for study of, 137; performers of, 20; study of, reasons for, 15–19; types of, 5–8
rhetorical situations, 12, 16
rhetorical theory, 70–71
rhetorical traditions, 153–54
Rhodes, Frank, 96
Rich, Adrienne, 6–7, 37–38, 178
Rich, Frank, 93, 174–75
Rollins, Brooke, 155
Romano, John, 4
Rorty, Richard, 99
rubric of Quality, 104
Rushdie, Salmon, 59

Sack, John, 108–9
Safire, William, 150, 152
Said, Edward, 114
salience, 80, 105–9
Savage, Michael, 71
Schryer, Catherine, 156
secrecy/disclosure, 139–40
Seligman, Craig, 69
semi-blind reviews, 45–48, 52–53
Sensation (museum show), 51, 55
September 11 memorial event (2002), 142–43
Sereny, Gitta, 90–91
Sheard, Cynthia, 154–55
Sheehan, Cindy, 23, 178–80
Shermer, Michael, 83
Shetley, Vernon, 160
Shoah. See Holocaust entries
Shumway, David, 121, 127
Siegel, Marcia, 1
Simon, John, 48
Simpson, David, 124, 126–27, 142–43
slaves and slavery, 82–83, 147, 154
Smith, Bradley, 95–96, 107
Sobolev, Dennis, 160
Sontag, Susan, 69
speech acts, theory of, 103–4

standards of judgment, 66
Stangl, Franz, 90–91
Starr, Kenneth, 59–60, 132–33, 136, 138
Stauffer, John, 151–53
Still/Here (Jones dance piece), 40, 50, 55, 63, 72. See also "Discussing the Undiscussable" (Croce)
student resistance, 111–12
Sturken, Marita, 73
Sullivan, Dale, 143–44
Sundquist, Eric, 152

Tanenhaus, Sam, 53–54
Tannen, Deborah, 120
"taste public," defined, 39
teaching moments, 111–12
Teachout, Terry, 2, 48–49, 69
Thanh Phong attack, 172–73
Things They Carried, The (O'Brien), 162
Time magazine, 151
Tompkins, Jane, 8, 122–29, 139–40
Toobin, Jeffrey, 133–34
trauma studies, 169
Trimbur, John, 115
Tropic of Cancer (Miller), 56–57
True Lies (film), 58
True Romance (film), 58
truth, 80, 96–97
truthfulness, 102–5
Tucker, Chris, 157
Turow, Scott, 44

vanishing acts, fictional, 166
Vanity Fair magazine, 69–70
Van Pelt, Robert Jan, 86, 106
victim art, 1–2, 30, 36, 40, 64, 68
victimhood, 66–68
Vidal-Naquet, Pierre, 84
Vietnam War, 83, 166–72
Vistica, Gregory, 174
visual culture, 73–74
Vivian, Bradford, 142

Warfield, Nelson, 58–59
Webster, Margaret, 41
Weir, Peter, 166
West, Cornel, 120

West, Kanye, 156–57
When I Was a Young Man (Kerrey), 23, 159, 172–75
White, Edmund, 68
Wiesel, Elie, 78–80
Williams, Bernard, 97, 103
Wisenberg, Sol, 134–35, 138
Women as Wombs (Raymond), 81–82
Woolf, Virginia, 120

Woolsey, Lynn, 179–80
World Trade Center attacks memorial event (2002), 142–43
Writing in the Dark (Croce), 2, 63, 115

Yeats, William Butler, 160

Zauhar, Frances M., 124
Zundel, Ernst, 87, 108–9

John Schilb, Culbertson Chair of Writing and professor of English at Indiana University, Bloomington, is the author of *Between the Lines: Relating Composition Theory and Literary Theory*. He has also coedited three books: *Contending with Words*, *Writing Theory and Critical Theory*, and the textbook *Making Literature Matter*. His work has appeared in such journals as *College Composition and Communication*, *College English*, *Rhetoric Review*, *JAC (Journal of Advanced Composition)*, *PRE/TEXT*, and *Pedagogy*. He is the current editor of *College English*.